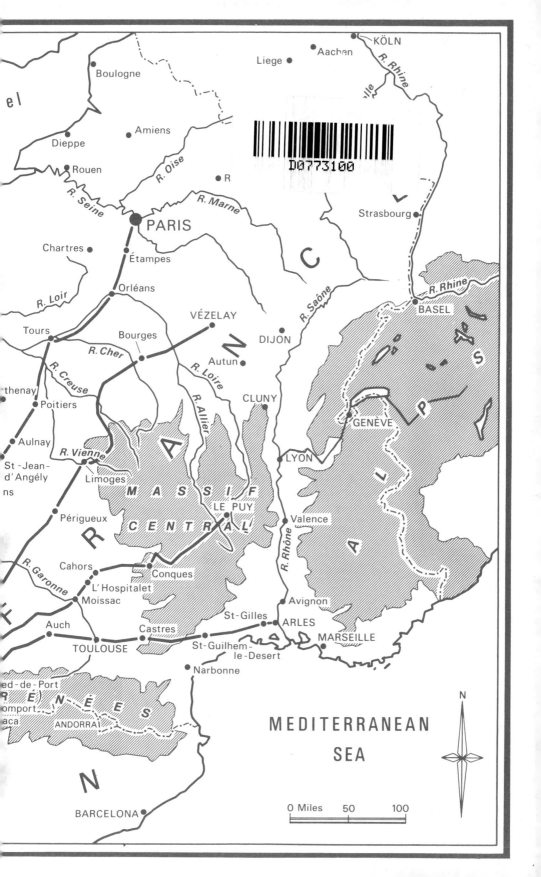

Boulogne

Liege

Aachen

KÖLN

R. Rhine

el

Amiens

Dieppe

Rouen

R. Oise

R

R. Seine

R. Marne

PARIS

Strasbourg

Chartres

Étampes

C

Orléans

R. Loir

VÉZELAY

R. Saône

R. Rhine

Tours

Bourges

DIJON

BASEL

R. Cher

N

Autun

thenay

R. Creuse

R. Loire

R. Allier

CLUNY

P

Poitiers

S

Aulnay

R. Vienne

A

GENÈVE

St-Jean-
d'Angély

Limoges

LYON

ns

M A S S I F

L

Périgueux

R

C E N T R A L

LE PUY

Valence

A

R. Garonne

Cahors

Conques

R. Rhône

L'Hospitalet
Moissac

Avignon

Auch

Castres

St-Gilles

ARLES

TOULOUSE

St-Guilhem-
le-Desert

MARSEILLE

Narbonne

ed-de-Port

P Y R É N É E S

omport

N

aca

ANDORRA

MEDITERRANEAN

N

SEA

BARCELONA

0 Miles   50   100

The Pilgrimage to Santiago

By the same author

SOUZA
ALFRED WALLIS
BRAQUE
JOSEF HERMAN
ELISABETH FRINK

The Pilgrimage to Santiago

———◆———

EDWIN MULLINS

SECKER & WARBURG
LONDON

First published in England 1974 by
Martin Secker & Warburg Limited
14 Carlisle Street, London W1V 6NN

Copyright © Edwin Mullins 1974

SBN: 436 29510 5

Printed in Great Britain by
Richard Clay (The Chaucer Press), Limited,
Bungay, Suffolk

For Frances, Jason and Selina,
my children

Contents

List of Illustrations

———◆———

Acknowledgments

I have many debts to acknowledge. For invaluable scholarly guidance I owe much to Sir Thomas Kendrick, former Director of the British Museum; to Professor Derek Lomax of the University of Birmingham; to Monsieur R. de la Coste-Messelière of the Archives Nationales in Paris; to Mademoiselle J. Warcollier of the Société des Amis de St-Jacques in Paris; to Los Amigos di Santiago in Estella; to Dr Clément Urrutibéhéty; to the Abbé G. Loubès; and to Mrs Constance Stors who allowed me to use material from her unpublished thesis written for London University. Others, too numerous to list, have given valuable assistance in providing local information at places along the pilgrim routes to Santiago de Compostela. And without the kindness of John Hopkins, Librarian of the Society of Antiquaries, and the rich resources of the London Library and the library of the Victoria and Albert Museum, I should have been hopelessly handicapped in obtaining historical and background material.

The many journeys in England, France and Spain which I have undertaken were in part made possible by the generosity and patience of John Anstey, Editor of the *Daily Telegraph Magazine*, and by the enthusiasm and cooperation shown by Christopher Martin, Robin Scott, Norman Swallow and John Drummond, all of BBC Television for whom I helped make a film on the subject. To Adam Woolfitt, who accompanied me on one of my journeys and took most of the photographs published in this book, I am likewise grateful, as I am to my wife who was my companion on part of another journey we did on foot, to Kit Barker who shared my enthusiasms during part of a third journey, and to close friends who, with good grace, undertook research, translating and typing for me. Finally, to Tom Rosenthal and David Farrer of Secker & Warburg, my publishers, I am indebted for their shrewd comments and advice, and indeed for bringing this book to the light of day at the end of the road.

CHAPTER I

---◆---

Tall Stories

The pilgrim in the Middle Ages shared with the modern tourist a conviction that certain places and certain objects possess unusual spiritual power, and that one was a better person for visiting them. Precisely how one came to be bettered may have been clearer to the mediaeval mind than it is to the traveller of the 20th century, since the benefits gained could then be attributed to the direct influence of God. Particular places and objects acted, in effect, as divine go-betweens in a quest for personal salvation. They held out a link with an authority superior to man's, and by extension they came to be invested with magic powers of their own. It was well known that the surest way of getting God to listen was to go to them and ask.

It has been a characteristic of pilgrimages and of the tourist industry that both have attached themselves to surviving remnants of an earlier era. The Middle Ages had a passion for religious relics; we have a passion for historical relics—ruined temples, preserved cities, objects laid out in museums, bits of yesterday to be collected. The Middle Ages themselves have become a part of our own store of relics. The 20th-century visitor to the Parthenon or Persepolis, through the kick he receives from being there, is attributing to these places a numinous and healing power which is not in essence different from the power that the mediaeval pilgrim attributed to the relics of the Roman martyrs or a fragment of the Holy Cross. We call that power Art, they called it God.

How far does the parallel usefully extend? In the mediaeval era this faith in relics was the product of a universal lack of faith in contemporary life, and of a consequent expectancy of destruction to come. This lack of confidence in today, with its accompanying vision of Hell tomorrow, led to the search for an ideal only to be found in the imagined perfection of the past. The only spiritual nourishment which made an absurd and nasty world bearable was to be obtained from these vestiges, these dry springs which proved that divine favour had once been received and was now withdrawn. So the pilgrim journeyed in order to pay the prescribed respects, out of duty, out of love, out of fear or out of a drive towards self-improvement or superiority, but always as a means of averting the daily grind and of going on a journey. Travel became synonymous with an abdication into the past. Is it still? Hopefully this is a book about relationships to the past.

When Baron Haussmann remoulded Paris at the bidding of Napoleon III in the mid-19th century he left out the Rue St-Jacques; that is, he left it precisely as it was and as it had been for more than a thousand years. But by carving the Boulevard St-Michel more or less alongside it, at a blow he cut away the rôle of the Rue St-Jacques as the main artery of the city since Roman times.

From then onwards the ever-increasing traffic crossing Paris from north to south sped at twice the speed and convenience down the Boulevard de Strasbourg and the Boulevard de Sebastopol, over the new bridges of the Seine, across the Île de la Cité, past the Palais de Justice and the Sainte-Chapelle; then swiftly out from the Place St-Michel to Montparnasse and the southern suburbs, the new broad highway exactly bisecting the old university city whose tangle of rickety tenements and grey alleys was pushed out of sight on either side behind ranks of Second Empire apartment blocks with military plane-trees stationed in front of them.

Suddenly a great many of the city's key buildings lined what was now a mere backstreet: the scattered buildings of the Sorbonne, the learned institutions, libraries, the great hospitals, the Hôtel-Dieu, the cathedral of Notre-Dame, the former Benedictine abbey of St-Martin-des-Champs to the north, and south of the river the churches of St-Sévérin and St-Julien-le-Pauvre; and farther south still, up the long slow hill past the university, through a district which today is still among the most decrepit and unloved in Paris, another church bearing the odd name of St-Jacques du Haut-Pas— St James of the High Step—and near it the high walls that hid a hospice of the same name.

Haut-Pas! From the Italian Altopasso, near Lucca, where a group of monks came from in the late Middle Ages to found here a place of charity to house and feed those plodding by on pilgrimage.

For this backstreet, the Rue St-Jacques and its northern extension the Rue St-Martin, which together cut a thin furrow through the old city from extremity to extremity, was not only the street of the Roman legions and of merchants and ambassadors, it was the route of pilgrims who for centuries gathered in Paris from all parts of northern Europe to take the way to the shrine of St James the Apostle in Santiago de Compostela, two months' trudge away in north-west Spain.

The journey began traditionally on the Right Bank. At the foot of the Rue St-Martin, where the Rue de Rivoli now cuts across, a few streets west of the Hôtel de Ville, is a public garden. This is the Place St-Jacques—the Square of St James—and here in the Middle Ages stood the Church of St-Jacques-de-la-Boucherie, so-called because it was erected near the Paris meat-market. The last thing pilgrims did before setting off was to attend mass in St-Jacques-de-la-Boucherie. Their staffs were blessed: they were going to be needed, against lameness and robbers, undergrowth and vicious dogs. Friends and well-wishers cheered them on their way and accompanied them a short distance across the river to the Île de la Cité, in front of Notre-Dame, then left them to make their way up the Rue St-Jacques out to the edge of the city where the twin towers and drawbridge of the Porte St-Jacques took them beyond the city gates and on to the open road south towards Étampes on the first stage of their trek to Orléans, Tours, Poitiers, Bordeaux, Roncesvalles and into Spain.

More than half a million travellers are said to have used the road to Compostela each year at the height of its popularity, in the 11th and 12th centuries: not all of them pilgrims, naturally, but there were enough of these to make it necessary soon to rebuild the church in the Place St-Jacques where they started from. The reconstructed St-Jacques-de-la-Boucherie was the last example of mediaeval church-building in Paris, not completed until the reign of François I in the early 16th century. The size of the site that is now a garden is the only witness to the scale of this rebuilt church, and to the number of people it must have held. It was razed to the ground in the Revolution, and all that remains is its monolithic bell-tower, the Tour St-Jacques, a solitary and hollow relic with its seven weathered gargoyles craning against the sky. Hilaire Belloc called it "this posthumous child of the mediaeval fancy". Michel de

Felins, architect of the tower, here embodied his appreciation of one of the great human enterprises of the Middle Ages, the pilgrimage to Santiago de Compostela, adding a laconic footnote in the shape of a milestone at the base of the tower inscribed "Zero".

Why did they do it?

Devotion, of course; but devotion to precisely what? Clearly the overwhelming majority of pilgrims to Santiago in the Middle Ages would never have undertaken so long and hazardous a journey far from home but for a spirit of genuine piety. Equally clearly, their piety was a form of after-life insurance against the promise of eternal damnation. This was preached relentlessly by a mediaeval church obsessed by the imminence of the Second Coming and the Day of Judgment, and it was preached no less eloquently by the sculptors and painters who decorated the churches in which those sermons were heard. The simple illiterate man in the Middle Ages had no choice. From the day he learned to use his eyes and ears to the day he died he was indoctrinated with the urgency of obtaining divine forgiveness and the purification of his soul, and the surest means by which such a thing could be obtained was by contact with the saints, who could intercede on his behalf. If the saints were martyrs, so much the better; if they were martyred apostles, then better still. Hence the morbid mediaeval cult of holy relics. Hence, too, the pre-eminence of three pilgrimages in the Middle Ages—the one to Jerusalem (the first in importance, but expensive and difficult to reach, and in any case under Moorish domination for much of the time), that to Rome (the second in importance, with the tombs of Peter and Paul, and of countless other Christians martyred by the Romans), and the one to Santiago de Compostela and the tomb of St James the Apostle. Though third in importance, Santiago became the most popular object of pilgrimage of the three in the later Middle Ages, and engendered an intensity of devotion that was maintained over the entire period of the entrenchment and growth of Christianity and Christian art in Europe, from the 11th to the 18th century. Throughout those centuries which saw the formation of Europe socially and culturally, it was the pilgrimage of Everyman; and because it enjoyed this rôle the route to Santiago became a principal high-road of Christian teaching, Christian institutions and Christian art.

Perhaps there was another reason for the hold it had on the popular imagination. Santiago, far away under the mists and Atlantic skies of Galicia, all woods and water in a Celtic landscape of menhirs and lost gods, exerted an appeal that was infinitely pre-Christian. The route to Santiago was a Roman trade-route. It was nicknamed by travellers *la voie lactée*, the Milky Way. It was the road under the stars. The pale arm of the Milky Way stretched out and pointed the way to the edge of the known world where the sun went down: to Cape Finisterre (from the Latin *finis terra*—the end of the earth). Historians who have studied the iconography of the pilgrim route have speculated on the meaning of the floral motif that recurs in mediaeval churches all along the way, as to whether it might in origin be, not a flower, but a sun image. We know that for pilgrims reaching Santiago in the Middle Ages it was as obligatory to venture on to the chapel of Nuestra Señora at Finisterre, the last finger of land crooked into the ocean, as it was to make the shorter and simpler journey to the Bay of Padrón where the body of St James himself is said to have arrived by sea. It is hard to find the explanation for such a balance of priorities, except by understanding that here may have been a journey to heaven more mystical and of a far earlier provenance than the Church can have been expected to acknowledge.

Be that as it may. The official tale is this, though there are minor variations. James the Apostle (James the Greater, that is, not to be confused with James the Lesser who was brother of Jesus) was the first Christian martyr after Stephen, and the first of the Twelve to be martyred. James was a fisherman. His father was Zebedee; his mother was Salome, thought to be the sister of the Virgin Mary. James therefore seems to have been Christ's first cousin. Responding to Christ's command that his apostles fan out across the earth and evangelise far and wide, James is supposed to have hastened to Spain where he spent a couple of years without making any conspicuous impact on the population until the appearance to him in Zaragoza of the Virgin Mary (still living at the time) upon a pillar between twin choirs of angels. Sustained and inspired by this miracle, James erected round the pillar the first church ever to be dedicated to the Virgin, and shortly afterwards returned to Jerusalem where he was beheaded by a Roman sword in about the year AD 44.

If the tale had ended at this point there would have been no pilgrimage to Santiago, indeed no Santiago at all. Everything rested upon the second part of the story, which is that immediately following the martyrdom of James, his body (with its head) was removed by disciples first to Jaffa on the coast, and then by stout ship down the length of the Mediterranean and up the Atlantic coast to the Bay of Padrón in north-west Spain, the voyage being accomplished in a week—proof of its miraculous nature. The party arrived thus far only to encounter once more Roman authorities who gaoled them, until in due course they were released by an angel. The Queen Lupa of the district, who was neither a Christian nor much interested in their tale, ordered the body of James to be buried on a hillside where lived a celebrated snake which would be sure to put an end to them all. But it was the snake that died—on seeing the sign of the cross—whereupon Queen Lupa was converted to the faith and at last the body of the martyr was allowed to be given decent burial, in a large stone coffin, where his disciples were themselves later buried.

The Romans left. The Visigoths came. Christianity eked its way into this lost corner of Europe. The Moors invaded from North Africa, and the Kingdom of the Asturias, as it was now known, became a weak outpost of Christendom hard besieged by the superior civilisation of Islam. The Asturians needed a religious leader comparable to the one whose spirit fired the Infidel—and they soon got one.

During more than 750 years since the burial of the corpse of St James, the site of his grave (it is not unreasonable to believe) was utterly forgotten. If, that is, it was ever known at all, or he was ever buried here at all. No records exist from these centuries which relate to the event. However, by the year AD 838 the grave of the apostle had certainly been revealed, and knowledge of it already widely spread, since an early 9th-century martyrology by one Florus de Lyon contains an addition made in that year noting the fact, and noting too the "extraordinary devotion paid by the inhabitants" to the bones of the apostle. The discovery of the tomb occurred in all probability in the earlier decades of the same century, within a few years of the coronation in Rome of Charlemagne as Emperor and chief defender of Christianity against the Infidel, and within living memory of Charlemagne's skirmishes against the

Moors in Spain. It was a time when Christian champions were beginning to be roused from their tents.

An 11th-century document fills in the story of the discovery of the tomb. A hermit by the name of Pelagius is said to have informed the local bishop of Iria Flavia, Theodomir, of a vision which had revealed to him the whereabouts of the tomb by means of a star accompanied by celestial music. In a deserted spot among hills some twelve miles from the seat of the bishop a stone tomb was duly discovered containing three bodies. These were immediately pronounced to be the remains of St James and of the disciples who had brought his body to Spain. The King of the Asturias, Alfonso II, visited the tomb, declared that St James was henceforth to be worshipped as the protector of Spain, and built a small church over the tomb in the saint's honour, and a monastery nearby. The town that grew round this monastery during the 9th century became known as Campo de la Estella, or Campus Stellae (the Field of the Star), later shortened to Compostela.

Alas, this legend of the discovery of the tomb by a hermit, and of the building of a small church over the site, can be traced back to no more authentic a source than a forged letter purporting to be by Pope Leo III. Nor is the etymology of the place any more accurate. The name Compostela does not in fact pre-date the 11th century, and it derives not from the Latin noun for a star but from the Latin verb *componere* meaning to bury. *Compositium* or *Compostum* simply means burial-ground, and recent excavations beneath the present cathedral at Santiago de Compostela have made it clear that here was the site of a Roman cemetery, or an early Christian necropolis, the existence of which must certainly have been known locally centuries before the holy fireworks and heavenly music revealed the site to the humble Pelagius. On the other hand, intimations that the entire story might be a fairytale were dispelled when these same excavations brought to light a tomb with, clearly inscribed upon it, the name of the bishop whom 11th-century documents claimed to have been the one led to the site by Pelagius. Theodomir at least was historical. The rest remains surmise.

A second misreading of texts seems to have played its part in shaping the tale. By the 9th century there were references to the body having been placed *in locum arcis marmoricis* (in a place of marble columns) or found *in arca marmorica* (in a marble tomb), and these descriptions claimed a historical authority from Greek texts dating from several centuries *before* the discovery of the tomb. These speak of St James having been buried at Anchaion in Marmarica, in other words in one of the Roman North African provinces not far from the Nile Delta—which indeed has a ring of feasibility about it. But in the translation from Greek to Latin Anchaion in Marmarica appears as *in arca marmorica*, and the entire sense is altered.

In this catalogue of confusions there is yet one further scribal error which promoted the view that St James was in Spain in his lifetime—in fact it is the only documentary evidence that exists to support such a claim. For almost six hundred years Church literature from the *Acts of the Apostles* onwards is entirely silent on the subject of St James's connection with Spain, alive or dead. Then from the early 7th century copies began to appear in western Europe of a Latin translation of a Greek list of apostles' mission-fields, known as the *Breviarium Apostolorum*. These Latin versions contain interpolations claiming that the apostle preached in Spain before returning to Jerusalem. The source of these interpolations seems to have been nothing more substantial than the mistaking of *Hispaniam* for the usual *Hierusalem* or *Hierosolyman*.

I am no church historian, but it would seem abundantly clear that this sequence of written errors arises from a psychological longing on the part of pious scribes to create the foundations of a useful Christian legend where those foundations were unfortunately lacking. In the Dark Ages the Christian faith survived in small cells, was consistently under siege by the forces of barbarism and needed desperately to maintain its lifelines with the early church of Christ and the apostles. At all events this was what happened. Errors and gentle distortions of fact came together to supply all that was needed to provide a base for what was soon to become one of the most powerful legends the Christian Church has ever embraced.

There is still one more confusion that may have contributed to rounding the character of the story. This is embodied in a theory advanced in recent times by a Spanish Benedictine monk, Fray Justo Pérez de Urbel, who is in the very sparse company of Spaniards capable of regarding the Santiago legend with something of a rational eye. Pérez de Urbel pointed out that at Iria Flavia (which was the seat of Bishop Theodomir at the time of the discovery of the tomb in the early 9th century) there existed a religious group who venerated the relics of various saints including those of a St James. The church in which they worshipped was dedicated to the Virgin Mary. Pérez went on to point out that an inscribed stone found at Merida, west of Madrid, clearly shows that similar relics were venerated there too, also in a church dedicated to the Virgin, as early as the beginning of the 7th century. The third link in Pérez de Urbel's argument is that the conquering Moors left on record how certain inhabitants of Merida fled to north-west Spain into Galicia. By attaching these three links together, and by making an assumption that this flight was by sea up the coast from what is now Portugal, it is possible to offer some sort of explanation for the legend of St James's body being transported by disciples in a ship to the Bay of Padrón (where Iria Flavia was). Sir Thomas Kendrick, whose own book *Saint James in Spain* is a masterly piece of detective work on the historical background of the Santiago legend, conjectures that this journey from Merida may have become associated with the later story of St James's mission to Spain after the death of Christ, so creating the legend of the saint's body returning to a land in which he had already preached in his lifetime.

So, bit by bit, the armature was pieced together upon which the Santiago legend could be modelled. It now required only the Moorish invasions of northern Spain, which began early in the 8th century during what Professor Trevor-Roper has described as the "darkest age of Europe", to add the necessary political urgency to the situation. And a man was at hand to promote this urgent cause— one of the key figures in shaping the Christian spirit of zeal and militancy during the early Middle Ages. This was St Beatus of Liébana, a learned Spanish monk and scholar who was born about the year 730.

The long-term importance of Beatus lay in the fact that he was responsible for a document which, once illustrated copies of it were widely distributed three hundred years later, became a primary source of much of the finest carving and mural painting of the Romanesque period. This coincided with the first great wave of church-building which was overtaking Europe in the 12th century. The document was Beatus's celebrated *Commentaries on the Apocalypse*. In the more immediate context of St James, Beatus himself was an impassioned advocate of the Santiago legend and of its significance in bolstering the forces of the Church against the Infidel. If a clutch of textual errors provided what passed for evidence that the body *might* be in Spain, it was Beatus who in the years immediately before the discovery prepared the atmosphere of excitement which overtook the Christian world when the news broke that the body really was in Spain.

After the discovery, embellishments to the tale not unnaturally abounded. Church literature of the Middle Ages is packed with them, the more so as accounts circulated of the miraculous influence of St James in every field, medical to military. *La Légende dorée*, composed in Italy during the 13th century by Jacques de Voragine, who later became Archbishop of Genoa, is among the most famous of these: a compilation of mediaeval legends relating to the lives of the saints, in which a confident account is given of St James's preaching mission to Spain, his return to the Holy Land, his martyrdom (by the Jews, de Voragine maintains) and the return of the body to Iria Flavia.

The most celebrated among all the propaganda literature surrounding the legend of Santiago is the *Codex Calixtinus*. Part of the *Codex* is actually a guidebook for pilgrims, composed in the 12th century and purporting to have the blessing of Pope Calixtus II, although it had nothing of the sort and is likely to have been the work of a French monk near Poitiers who had an interest (we don't know what interest) in popularising the pilgrimage, and who emerges as a character rich in unashamed and marvellous chauvinism. Two copies of the manuscript of the *Codex* survive, one at Santiago itself and the other at Ripoll Monastery in north-eastern Spain, and in the 1930s the guidebook section was translated into French (the original is naturally enough in Latin) by Jeanne Vielliard, since when many a modern pilgrim has picked his way across France and Spain forewarned that Basque boatmen are thieves and the Navarrais have amazing sexual habits, neither of which I have found to be particularly true, though it evidently was so in the 12th century.

Such was the fame of the Santiago pilgrimage throughout Europe in the Middle Ages, yet its promoters in the church were so vulnerable to sceptics (Erasmus among them) who suggested it all rested on a hysterical tale without foundation, that inevitably, sooner or later, archaeological evidence would be summoned in support. And so it was, though the movement to substantiate the legend with scientific facts got under way only once the Reformed Church had somewhat dented the popularity of the pilgrimage, and exploitation of one kind or another had considerably tarnished its image.

It was 16th-century Spain, the Spain of the Inquisition, which yielded a whole succession of finds and holy relics purporting to relate to St James and to lesser martyrs. A climate of fervent un-reason prevailed, and as little or no attempt was made by Church authorities to check or substantiate these astonishing discoveries they rapidly passed into popular lore and helped to raise the emo-tional pitch of popular faith.

The most remarkable of these cases of wish-fulfilment consisted of a series of finds in a cave in what is known as the Sacromonte (or Sacred Mountain), in the Granada district of southern Spain, towards the end of the 16th century. The finds began modestly enough with a sealed box in which was found a bone of St Stephen and half the cloth used by the Virgin Mary at the Crucifixion to dry her tears. More poignant discoveries followed: the cremated bodies of Christians martyred by Nero including—as if to prepare audiences for what was to come—one purporting to be a disciple of St James.

In retrospect it all seems an elaborately fashioned piece of decep-tion, made so very much simpler to carry out by the pious credulity of those on whom it was practised. To this day no one knows quite in what spirit the Sacromonte fakes were perpetrated; at any rate they were exceedingly carefully ordered, and by the time the *coup de grâce* was performed all Spain was on tenterhooks, and all eyes on the Sacromonte. They were not disappointed. The last and greatest finds consisted of eighteen books (the notorious lead-books of the Sacromonte, so-called because they were enclosed in lead) dating from the time of Christ and including a life of St James.

At last. This was what the Spanish Church had been waiting for since early in the 9th century. Now here it all was, the work—as it seemed—either of an Arab convert and martyr by the name of Tesiphon, or of his brother Cecilio who became the first Bishop of Granada. It scarcely mattered which it was since both had known Jesus, so the documents claimed, and after the Crucifixion both had travelled with St James to Spain acting as his secretaries, and had remained there. Relief and joy spread through Spain at the discovery of the lead-books, and pilgrims flocked to the Sacromonte. An official Council managed to authenticate them in 1600, scarcely troubling to look at the evidence, such was the eagerness to believe them true. The local archbishop, Pedro de Castro, who must be one of the suspects in this business, was a particularly fervent champion of the finds, closing his ears ever more indignantly to rumours that all was not well: for it was becoming increasingly clear to those with minds less clouded than the archbishop's that the lead-books were most unlikely to be what they claimed to be. In the face of an obstinate refusal on the part of Church and state authorities in Spain to reopen the case, an international row mounted around these amazing documents, dragging in King, Inquisition, Papal Nuncio and the Vatican, a situation which so embarrassed the Papacy that, under the threat of excommunication, Philip IV of Spain was finally prevailed upon to surrender the books to Rome, where they presumably remain to this day. In 1682 Pope Innocent XI officially pronounced the Sacromonte lead-books to be forgeries, and that was the final whimper of one of the most hysterical hue-and-cries in the history of the Spanish Church.

St James was, after all, the patron saint of Spain. And he was more than that: he was the country's rescuer; he was King Alfred, St George and Winston Churchill rolled into one. In the minds of many Spaniards St James had been personally responsible for driving the armies of Mohammed from their lands, and had proved himself to be so on countless occasions by appearing in the thick of the battle—usually when things were going badly—and personally routing and slaughtering the foe. It had been Beatus, author of the *Commentaries on the Apocalypse* in 776, who had first planted in the popular mind the idea of St James as the champion of Christianity in the fight against the Infidel, and it was not long after the discovery of the saint's tomb before he took his place on the battle-field as though he had ridden straight out of the pages of Beatus's *Commentaries*.

Santiago Matamoros! St James the Moor-slayer. No good Spaniard in the Middle Ages would have believed that his country could have been liberated from the Moors without the sword of his patron saint. And it is in this guise that he appears on so many of the churches along the pilgrim route to Compostela, on horseback, sword aloft, crushing the forces of Islam beneath his feet. First at Clavijo in the 9th century, then at Simancas in the 10th, at Coimbra by the side of El Cid in the 11th, at Las Navas de Tolosa in the breakthrough to Andalucia in the 13th century: altogether at least forty appearances in battle by the 17th century, according to a Spanish historian of the Santiago legend, Don Antonio Calderón. "The story of St James's military achievements soon grew longer and longer," writes Kendrick, "and by the end of the sixteenth century he had surpassed the performance of every other heavenly warrior." He even took his flashing sword to the New World, undeterred that the American Indians were not offering a powerful threat to Christendom but minding their own business.

The image of *Santiago Matamoros* immeasurably boosted the impact of the St James legend on Mediaeval and Renaissance Europe. It made him a tangible living hero, and what was more it offered proof of his active surveillance of the lives and fortunes of ordinary Christians. It also did wonders for the city of Santiago de Compostela, not least through one of the most audacious taxes any authority has ever managed to inflict on an innocent population. This was a corn and wine tax payable to the church of Santiago by the citizens of most, though not all, of the Spanish states that were free of Moorish rule, in thanksgiving to St James for his hand in bringing about their liberation.

Not surprisingly the Santiago authorities experienced some trouble collecting this tax, and the litigation that followed kept lawyers employed for centuries pinning down farmers who had never set eyes on the soldier apostle and who harboured the severest doubts whether such a figure had ever come to the rescue of their incompetent generals. Their worst suspicions were aroused by the fact that the tax was only enforced from the 12th century, though the authority for it rested in a document purporting to date from the 9th century and which no one, in any case, had ever set eyes on, except the Church authorities at Santiago, and they persistently refused to produce it in a court of law.

This hypothetical document was known as the Diploma of Ramiro I. Ramiro was ruler of the kingdom of the Asturias from 842 to 850 and is supposed to have led the Christian forces in the first battle against the Moors at which St James appeared to lend a helping hand—the Battle of Clavijo—and, in thanksgiving, to have issued his Diploma after the battle in the year 834, which he demonstrably could not have done since Ramiro was still eight years away from ascending the throne at the time. Even allowing for a scribal discrepancy of dates, there was still a suspicious ring to a tax enforced after so many years lying dormant, a tax, furthermore, whose sole beneficiary was a church that was also guardian of the one document which gave that tax any validity.

The Diploma, like the lead-books of the Sacromonte, was a forgery. All that could ultimately be produced by the Church authorities at Santiago was a 12th-century document which they claimed was a copy of the Diploma held in the cathedral archives, but no original in fact ever existed. The 12th-century copy *was* the original, the work of a cardinal canon of Santiago de Compostela, by the name of Don Pedro Marcio, apparently as a daring fraud to bring in funds to pay off debts incurred in the enlargement of Santiago Cathedral. As with the lead-books it proved exceedingly hard to pin anything on the Church authorities, and it was not until the very end of the 16th century that an objection—in this case from Castile—was actually allowed, and then the court's decision was reversed twenty years later, but only temporarily. Discredited though it was, in Galicia and in the south of Spain Ramiro's phoney Diploma remained an effective source of tax profit to the Church authorities in Santiago right up to Napoleonic times, receiving its final death-blow only in 1834.

It is a wry thought that one of the most magnificent cathedrals in the world, which Santiago unquestionably is, should have been paid for substantially out of a fraudulent tax perpetrated by the Church authorities themselves for the entire period of six hundred years over which the present building is spread, from Romanesque in the 12th century to High Baroque in the 18th.

A sordid history? Many have found it so, particularly the Reformed Church, as well as rational thinkers from Erasmus in the 16th century to Voltaire in the 18th. Sir Francis Drake, too, regarded Santiago de Compostela as a stronghold of "pernicious superstition", and, in the year following the Armada, Queen Elizabeth's official pirate sailed with an army of 14,000 to Galicia determined to destroy it, which mercifully he did not. The English attacked again repeatedly between the years 1700 and 1720, and it seems to have been during this period that the bones of St James were hidden away for protection, actually in the masonry behind the High Altar, although their precise whereabouts was forgotten for almost two hundred years until excavations in search of them were undertaken by Cardinal Payá y Rico in 1879, and the relics brought to light amid widespread jubilation. What was found was a small coffer containing the assorted bones of three men. When the skeletons were reassembled there followed one of those comedies that sometimes relieve pious occasions, when no one could satisfactorily decide which of the three was the body of the saint. The matter was only resolved to everyone's relief and satisfaction when a tiny fragment of St James's skull that had long been a revered possession of the cathedral at Pistoia in Tuscany was found to fit exactly one of the three ancient skulls. Spain breathed again.

The last chapters of the saga enshrine St James in respectability rather than further adventure or fraud. After the triumphant episode of the Pistoia skull-fragment, it was felt necessary by the Vatican to clear up any lingering doubts; and so, in 1884, Pope Leo XIII issued an Apostolic Letter in which he confirmed the identity of the three saints whose jumbled remains had been found in the coffer five years earlier. Whether the Vatican was seriously convinced by the new evidence, or whether the move was a largely political one, and why the Papacy had remained conspicuously silent on the Santiago relics for more than a thousand years, only to break that silence over a tiny morsel of skull, are questions which remain a mystery: certainly a great deal more mysterious than many of the 20th-century bids to sugar the Santiago legend with official recognition. A tale that, however suspect, was once emotive and urgent gradually became *kitsch*. Today it is folk-lore brushed up for the tourist industry. The Ministry of Information in Madrid displays a mural by a certain Rafael Pellicer representing St James as an allegory of tourism—which is at least candid. *Santiago Matamoros* with Green Shield stamps. Salvador Dali has had a go at it too: pilgrims to the Beaverbrook Museum in New Brunswick, Canada, can pay their respects to an airborne extravaganza with the saint radiantly entangled with celestial Gothic architecture. The Historical Military Archives in Madrid have gone one better, in the form of a portrait of General Franco and his army represented as modern warrior-pilgrims of the Church militant under the protection of the apostle himself who flies overhead on his white charger.

The Romantics turned to the Middle Ages to indulge their dreams. Do we still? To say that St James has been the stuff of dreams for more than a millennium is true enough: bad dreams, sentimental dreams, dreams of revenge, of salvation, of wealth, even dreams of truth. And yet how amazing and ironical it is that this legend, so improbable, so flawed, so disreputable, should have trodden a path through the history of western Europe that is flagged by some of the brightest achievements of our civilisation. The road to Santiago is a monument to the creative strength of crude blind faith.

CHAPTER II

Saints on the Loire

The long first stage out of Paris took the pilgrim thirty miles to Étampes. It is a dreary stretch, and must always have been; but at least it was flat—Oh so flat—and easy on tender feet. Étampes is a bleak strip of a town, with cobbled streets and a clutch of mediaeval churches of which the oldest is Notre-Dame-du-Fort—not that such a fortified chunk of masonry can have raised the spirits of many pilgrims as they knelt in one of the vast transepts opening on to the nave of this ogre's fortress. Nonetheless, the south portal is a reminder that Chartres is no farther off than Paris: slender pillar-figures on either side of the entrance, and carved arches above, together make up a shadow of the great west door at Chartres, though here at Étampes all the heads of the figures were lopped off during the French Revolution and the rest stand in the strongest need of a clean. An air of morose decay prevails.

Étampes is hardly a tonic to brace the soul for the countryside to follow, and anyone austere enough to cross it on foot would do well to slide into a prolonged daydream about the Loire and Poitou to come, or about salvation, or even about cheese, for this archetypal *morne plaine* is Brie country—which may account in some measure for the shape of the cheese.

A mean spring drizzle smeared the windscreen and numbed my mind. A thousand pylons, in every conceivable style known to the French electricity authorities, marched and countermarched across grey fields, wiring up the sky. It was like driving through the inside of a radio set. And in the midst of all this—Toury. The only welcoming sight between Paris to the Loire was this little passageway of a town set aside from the main road. Its single anonymous street suddenly opened on to a square with a mediaeval church and stone porch extending from end to end. Here was a touch of character in a characterless region. The squat arcade had the look of a stray from the south, a promise of the sun.

At Orléans pilgrims reached the Loire. Orléans was a major stopping-place because the town boasted two important relics. One was a chalice that belonged to an early bishop of the town, St Euverte (to whom an abbey was dedicated nearby). The second was an object of the greatest wonder and veneration, a fragment of the Holy Cross, one of several fragments that pilgrims might be meeting on their travels in the few months to follow, and one wonders how many of them puzzled over how so substantial an object should have splintered into so many and far-flung pieces. This fragment used to be displayed, along with the miraculous chalice, in the church of Sainte-Croix on the edge of the old town. Today a grandiose edifice, upgraded to the status of cathedral, has replaced it, erected in defiantly Gothic style during the 17th century when the rest of France had moved on to Classical. Its flamboyant tracery and unnecessary pinnacles push up amid an armoury of columns to a pair of crown-roast towers, which the swifts at least regard as heaven. Stones of an earlier church survive down in the crypt, but with no traces that I could see of the Holy Cross which gives the place its name, nor does the *Guide Michelin* even make mention of such a thing.

Orléans is a sour town, swollen a little too big for itself, and full of *clochards* and crumbled elegance. The mediaeval town was gathered round the northern end of a bridge, replaced in the 18th century by the present Pont George V a short distance downstream. This district retains some of its former warren-like character, even some of its character as a pilgrim town. A Renaissance mansion in a side-street close to the river stands empty and in disrepair, but its name, *La Maison de la Coquille*, tells of its association with the route to Santiago, the scallop-shell being the insignia worn by pilgrims to Compostela. How it came to be so is both complicated and unclear. Certainly the scallop-shell symbolised St James's miraculous powers, and the most popular of the many legends illustrating this power tells of a young nobleman whose bolting horse carried him into the sea near Padrón: he was saved from drowning by the apostle, who emerged from the waters with shells clinging to his garments. A variation on this legend is that the young widow of a drowned man prayed to St James, whereupon her bridegroom rose from the sea covered with white scallop-shells.

La Maison de la Coquille was possibly a hospice—most religious hospices were identified by a scallop-shell insignia—and if so it was one of many that would have stood in this part of the town. I noticed that the street nearby, which would have led to the old bridge, still bears the name Rue des Hôtelleries. Here, too, stood the 15th-century pilgrims' chapel, the Chapelle St-Jacques, where Joan of Arc prayed. What remains of it has been re-erected in the garden of the Renaissance town-hall, near the cathedral, where it has the appearance of an 18th-century folly, looking foolish among the ivy and the pigeon-droppings. It was removed here during the 19th century to make way for a splendid cast-iron market-place, which will itself no doubt be pulled down one day soon, like Les Halles in Paris, although Les Halles has found no permanent place in a mayor's back-garden. If Joan of Arc had shopped here things might have been different.

Originally the Chapelle St-Jacques in Orléans was attached to what was known as a *Confrérie* or Confraternity: a kind of pilgrims' guild which, in the case of the one at Orléans, can be traced back to the 13th century, though the majority of them are later in date. It is a witness to the popularity of the Santiago pilgrimage that the later Middle Ages saw the emergence of such guilds in most of the larger towns in western Europe. There were more than two hundred in France alone, the most celebrated of these being the one in Paris called the *Confrérie des Pèlerins de St-Jacques de l'Hôpital*. This was founded in 1315 by letters patent from the king. It was situated in the Rue St-Denis, and organised by a governor, a treasurer and several resident chaplains. Such guilds were secular organisations, run on charitable lines, and to a great extent they replaced the earlier organisations set up by the monastic orders and by the chivalric orders, which were the principal sources of charity available to pilgrims in the earlier Middle Ages. This shift of responsibility mirrors a subtle change in the nature of pilgrimages, and indeed in the nature of European society. By the 14th century towns had become secure enough, and organised enough, to promote and support charitable bodies without the umbrella of powerful monasteries; while pilgrims themselves were beginning to think of themselves as an esteemed group within their own society, like freemasons or, later still, vice-presidents of the local bank. Pilgrims were no longer solitary, perhaps no longer so strictly pious.

The funds that established these guilds were raised by members' subscriptions, and by donations from the well-to-do who also offered church ornaments and reliquaries for display in the confraternity chapels. The guild at Liège, so we are told, even claimed a relic of St James himself, brought from Santiago in the 11th century. Land also came the way of the guilds, which in turn produced further income, and with this wealth they financed their charitable functions. These consisted of medical treatment, where there was a hospital attached, and, above all, food and drink for passing pilgrims. In the case of the Paris confraternity, the fare was scarcely a gastronomic ordeal—two pieces of bread in the evenings, with wine, and on special days a little meat or vegetables. It is also on record that within a period of less than a year, between 1st August 1368 and 25th July (St James's Day) 1369, the same confraternity received no fewer than 16,690 pilgrims, though it is not stated where they were all going.

Anyone could join a confraternity—man, woman, priest—who could produce proof that he had actually been to Santiago de Compostela. To aid pilgrims in this respect (as well as to encourage future business) the canons of the cathedral in Santiago from the 14th century took to issuing a certificate to arrivals. This was called a *Compostela*. The trouble was, though it indeed proved that someone had been there, it did not prove who had been there nor how far he had travelled. Hence, in the later Middle Ages merchants on the make in northern Spain made a practice of visiting Santiago de Compostela and subsequently offering the certificates they obtained to weary pilgrims as they struggled over the Pyrenees with still another five hundred miles to go.

Having produced his *Compostela*, found a sponsor, and accepted the rules and regulations of the guild, the ex-pilgrim was a member for life. He had to obey the statutes which had been approved by the local bishop, and under pain of a fine he was commanded to attend the annual summer Mass sung in honour of St James, and to take part, if he were able, in the procession that followed. For this he would be expected to wear his confraternity costume—probably a smartened-up version of the established pilgrims' outfit of cloak, wallet, staff and broad hat with scallop-shell affixed.

The kind of invocation used at confraternity services may be judged from this one which we know was employed as late as the

18th century. It begins: *O Bienheureux Apôtre S. Jacques, Lumière et Flambeau du Monde, Trompette Divine, secrétaire de Jésus-Christ, témoin oculaire de ses plus grands miracles, dissipateur des vices et idolatries de ce monde, protomartyr entre les Apôtres, support des pèlerins, consolateur des affligés, conducteur des dévoyés, protecteur des Armées chrétiennes . . .*, and continues in a manner indicative of what the devout felt about the power of St James and of the journey to Santiago: *Nous vous supplions à mains jointes avoir pitié de nous, pauvres pécheurs, et prier Dieu pour nous, qu'il lui plaise nous garder de famine, peste, fièvres et d'épidémie, et de maladie dangereuse . . .*

Many confraternities subsided during the Reformation and the religious wars in France, though some remained powerful and prosperous long after their members had ceased to be genuine pilgrims. The French Revolution accounted for the majority of these. A very few lingered on through the 19th century, sustained by faithful ancients. One of the last on record was the confraternity of St-Génies-le-Bas in Languedoc, where the local church still owns the cross that was carried in procession on St James's Day every year. This ceremony continued well into the second quarter of the last century. By 1888, however, there remained but a single *confrère* by the name of Jacques Bertrand; and he, being treasurer, was able to report to his departed brethren that the account was now empty and, two years later, that the guild was formally dissolved.

Two conditions in Europe helped to make pilgrimages possible on the scale that existed in the Middle Ages. One was the vagueness of national boundaries, and the other a refreshing lack of any prevailing sense of nationalism. A Frenchman from the Midi, speaking Provençal, had less in common with a Parisian than he had with his neighbouring Genoese. The Catalans and Basques, then as now, lived on both sides of the Pyrenees, and spoke their own languages: the mountains were neither a political nor a cultural barrier. A large chunk of what is now France was owned by England. What is more, English kings were frequently French, or at least spoke French as their first language and preferred to pass more of their lives on the other side of the Channel than on this.

Imagine a state of affairs today in which citizens without any means of support, save their credentials and a scallop-shell, would be free to wander at their own pace between countries waging a war with one another. Yet this is exactly what took place during the Hundred Years' War. The route French pilgrims took from Paris and the north to Santiago led right through Aquitaine and Gascony which were held by England, and by the late 14th century English pilgrims travelling by land rather than disembarking near Bordeaux were obliged to cross the Channel and make their way through "hostile" territory for several hundred miles before reaching "friendly" lands. Wars in the Middle Ages were still for warriors and national possessions were divided by paper boundaries. The pilgrimage to Santiago was scarcely checked by the Hundred Years' War: pilgrims merely had to obtain permission to set off from their religious and secular authorities, and to swear an oath not to betray the loyalties they owed to their own monarch while on their journey.

There are a great many accounts of pilgrims in the later Middle Ages, which is no surprise since they were relatively as numerous as tourists today. The first record of a Santiago pilgrim comes from an Arab traveller called Ibd Dihya who noted that there were Normans visiting the tomb of St James in the year 844. Louis VII of France made the pilgrimage to Santiago in 1154, and St Francis of Assisi undertook the journey from Italy in the early 13th century. Later in the 13th century the poet Dante is thought to have been the first to define a pilgrim: in his *La Vita Nuova*, composed a century before Chaucer's *Canterbury Tales*, he writes (in William Anderson's translation for Penguin Classics) that "anyone is a pilgrim who is outside his fatherland", adding that the only true pilgrim "in the narrow sense" is "the man who travels to and from St James of Compostela", the others being either palmers who went to the Holy Land or *romei* who journeyed to Rome. It is Dante too who, in the *Convito*, writes of the Milky Way as the term used by the common people to describe "The Way of St James": due, he maintains, to the numbers of people who travelled there.

In the 11th and 12th centuries, when the pilgrimage to Santiago was at its zenith, far and away the largest number of pilgrims were still genuine penitents, and the costume which became identified with them came into existence largely to render them instantly recognisable and therefore inviolate. A pilgrim was everywhere a protected citizen, cloaked by a form of international law which guarded him from tolls and tariffs, entitled him to charity and safe-conduct, and condemned anyone robbing or killing him with the severest punishments—not least the punishments of God who was regarded as being the pilgrim's divine protector.

He was also protected by the credentials he carried with him, and not least by the code of mediaeval chivalry, which accounts for the various chivalric orders—Templars, Hospitallers and others—being as prominent as the Church itself in organising facilities for the pilgrim's safe-conduct and welfare. In Spain the pilgrim was made welcome, too, in those districts of towns along the route which had become populated by Frenchmen invited to settle there by the Spanish rulers after the devastations inflicted by the Moors. A Frankish quarter became synonymous with a pilgrim district in northern Spanish towns, and the name Villafranca still identifies places along the pilgrim way which were founded by French (or Frankish) settlers during those times. Doubtless a proportion of the settlers were themselves pilgrims, returning from Santiago and finding inducements enough to discard their staff and gourd in favour of a spade. It was a period of relative peace in western Europe, a period of considerable agricultural development, and of steady population movements. Whole sections of society were more or less permanently on the move: merchants, craftsmen, minstrels, scholars, students, as well as the outcasts—lepers, thieves, beggars and false priests. The roads, more even than today, were the veins along which the life of mediaeval society flowed, the lawless and the lawful.

Did pilgrims make detours? Probably not. At least the average penitent, or petty criminal sentenced by a canonical or civil court to trek to Santiago as a punishment, surely had only one objective in mind, which was to get there as quickly as possible and get back again safely, and adequately purified. A small percentage of pilgrims were wealthier men who did the journey in style on horseback, often with retainers. Such men would have stayed at inns rather than at charity hospices, and certainly would have lost no opportunity for a pleasing diversion that might take in a great monastery or a famous town to break the monotony of the journey. Günther, Bishop of Bamberg in Germany, made a veritable carnival of his pilgrimage in the year 1065, travelling with an entourage worthy of a monarch paying a state visit. Later, by the 14th century, pilgrimages became less pious affairs, undertaken as much for the pleasures of the journey as for the promise of salvation. The English poet William Langland, writing in the late 14th century, includes pilgrims to Santiago among a list of vagabonds and lay-abouts in *Piers Plowman*. And if Chaucer's Wife of Bath, who had also been there, was a typical pilgrim of the age then it is not surprising that the credibility of the journey as an undertaking of faith should have become widely questioned by the end of the Middle Ages.

All the same, if detours—at least detours in good faith—were rare, the accepted routes to Santiago can never have been quite as rigid as the 12th-century guidebook, the *Codex Calixtinus*, suggests. That there were numerous tributaries and alternative routes has become increasingly clear as historians have located widespread references to the Santiago cult both in France and Spain. The great Spanish monastery of Santo Domingo de Silos near Burgos, for example, is almost fifty miles south of the main pilgrim route, and yet a relief carving in the cloister representing the Journey to Emmaus depicts Christ plainly wearing the emblem of the scallop-shell.

From Orléans, then, the main body of pilgrims would have made their way west down the Loire to their next important halt, Tours. The few who were in a position to take their time and comfort on the way, together with those who were coming to join the Paris route from Burgundy, took in Sully-sur-Loire to the east of Orléans, where the Church of St-Ythier still has an early-16th-century window representing the pilgrimage to Compostela; and in particular they took in the abbey of St-Benoît-sur-Loire a few miles downriver.

The Loire is a river that never changes; or rather it changes once only. It is the longest river in France, 634 miles, rising in the Cévennes in the southern ranges of the Massif Central, and for its first long stretch it is a mountain river. But once it has broadened into the plain of Burgundy it assumes a new character, and it retains that character right across the central lowlands of France until it ends its course under the Atlantic clouds of Brittany in the far west and flows out between the oyster-beds and the naval dockyards of the Bay of Biscay: always silver and murky-green, scudding between sandbars, flooding regiments of tall poplars, and the mirror of the most opalescent skies in Europe.

Spring was the season for pilgrimages. This was not so much for the sake of Chaucer's "Aprille with his shoures soote" as for the lengthening days and the prospect of a whole summer ahead in which to make the journey and return before winter.

Now, on the Loire in the spring of my own journey, the "shoures" were very far from "soote". Looking down the nave of the abbey church of St-Benoît and out of the west door I saw rain cascading into the sunshine like snow. Evening service was finishing when I arrived. I parked the car in the puddles under the lime-trees and dashed for the porch just as the congregation of three or four hundred (out of a village population of 1500) was pressing out of the west door and fumbling for plastic hats and folding umbrellas. Soon the church had emptied itself into the porch, conveniently built on a Roman scale in a forest of honey-coloured columns round which children in ice-cream pink and stiff white dresses were playing hide-and-seek, their elders standing with blank expressions under the capitals carved with grimacing figures from the Apocalypse.

Above the long nave of bare Romanesque arches in smoky-white the rain went on drumming on the roof, even though the slanting sun was now warming the tracery of the apse at the far end. What began with imperial grandeur in the porch ended behind the High Altar as something delicate in form and intimate in scale. At its best Romanesque architecture seems to shrink, Gothic swells. This is a large church by any standards, yet it still closes around you, enfolds you in a cloak of stone. Up the steps from the crypt the aged and the bereaved were being aided from their prayers to the founder of the Benedictine Order, St Benedict, whose body was brought here when Monte Cassino, which he built in the 6th century, was sacked by the Barbarians. The rain continued. I walked back down the nave. A chunk of ceiling fell within three feet of trepanning me. "That happens," shrugged the priest to whom I presented the lump of masonry. He said it with exactly the same air as the somnolent gentleman in a café at Orléans whom I had asked, "How are you this morning?" and who had replied, "*Je suis en train d'y penser*" ("I'm just thinking about it").

I drove back through Orléans along the left bank of the Loire, and made a brief stop at Cléry. Here again was a reminder of the popularity of the Santiago pilgrimage. Cléry is not more than a village today, and it can never have been any larger; yet we know from a notary's document here that in 1616 the local confraternity had a membership of thirty-two men and one woman. Had they all been to Santiago? The Church of Notre-Dame is where Louis XI of France is buried and it has a 15th-century chapel to St James, built by the dean and his brother, both of whom were certainly pilgrims, as their tombs make clear. The walls are decorated around with scallop-shells and there are two 16th-century statues of the apostle, one a stone head and the other in dusty polychrome. At the west end of the nave is displayed a list of notable pilgrims who have called here, not all of them on their way to Compostela by any means since it includes Joan of Arc and her protector Dunois. Henry III apparently came in full pilgrim's costume in 1584. Catherine de' Medici and Cardinal Mazarin also paid their respects, and the list concludes with the Queen of Portugal in 1926. Whatever was she doing, I wondered.

Above the west door outside, a line of house-martins sat squeezed into the entrance of their nests in black and white outfits, looking like comfortable nuns in a row of pews.

In the Middle Ages the most important city on the Loire was Tours. The royal Loire did not exist in the heyday of the pilgrimage. There were few *châteaux*, no royal forests for hunting boar and stags. Tours was also the oldest and most revered place of pilgrimage in France, and a centre of worship five centuries before Frenchmen tacked it on to the route to Santiago. St-Martin de Tours rose from being a soldier in the Roman army in the 4th century to become the greatest of the French bishops of the Dark Ages. The sanctuary built over his tomb in the 5th century grew in fame until, following its destruction by the Normans, who devastated much of the Loire valley in the early Middle Ages, a new church of St-Martin was begun in the late 10th or early 11th century, to a scale and plan that had never been attempted for a Christian building in France. The 12th-century pilgrims' guide, the *Codex Calixtinus*, claims it was erected after the style of the cathedral at Santiago, though the author was swallowing his own propaganda here: St Martin's church certainly preceded St James's cathedral in the form we now know it and is much more likely to be its proto-type.

It was planned from the first to be a pilgrims' church: that is, it was designed specifically to accommodate huge congregations who participated in the elaborate liturgical functions held on the saint's day and at other special festivals; also to permit pilgrims to circulate freely round the area of the High Altar where the object of their veneration—the saint's relics—would be placed on display. Another feature of St Martin's church was a semicircle of five large chapels round the apse and projecting beyond the outer wall. Here pilgrims could pray privately and venerate other relics—relics perhaps of the second quality—which the church might acquire through grateful donors.

It is not known for certain when St Martin's great church was begun, but what is certain is that it must have been close in time to the Millennium. According to Émile Mâle, who was one of the most distinguished 20th-century writers on this period, the church may have been begun as early as AD 997. One of the less rewarding tasks in France in the year 997 would have been to find a church-man convinced that the world was not going to come to an end in three years' time. Is it possible to imagine that at such a time anyone would commission a church larger in size and more confident in its affirmation of the human spirit than any then known to the men building it? It would seem more reasonable to assume that St-Martin-de-Tours was in fact begun some decades later than Mâle suggested, when the fear of an imminent Big Bang had passed, to be replaced by a spirit of renewed optimism and a massive sense of relief and thanksgiving that the world was still intact.

Within a little more than a hundred years the pattern of St Martin's church had been followed in Santiago itself, some thousand miles away, as well as in pilgrim cities in at least three distinct areas of France—this at a time when France did not exist at all as a unified country, but was split up into separate states, frequently at war with one another, and possessing, in any case, their own distinct schools and styles of architecture. There exists, to my knowledge, no more eloquent testimony to the overriding cultural influence of the mediaeval pilgrimage to Santiago de Compostela than this.

Mâle considered St-Martin-de-Tours to be the mother-church of the great pilgrim routes. Not all scholars have agreed with him, but all have agreed that a small number of what are clearly the major pilgrim churches were built during the 11th and early 12th centuries, and that these owe their design (and indeed much of their decoration) to a common ideal or prototype. These churches, apart from Tours, were St-Martial at Limoges (now destroyed), St-Sernin at Toulouse (still intact), the abbey church of Ste-Foy at Conques (also intact), and the cathedral at Santiago de Compostela. To this short list can be pencilled in the great abbey church at Cluny (now virtually disappeared), which seems to have possessed many of the architectural elements pioneered at Tours and common to the other four pilgrim churches.

Laid out on a map of France and Spain these churches, six in all, take on an even greater significance in the history of the pilgrimage to Compostela. The 12th-century guidebook contained in the *Codex Calixtinus* is the primary source of our information on the principal routes pilgrims took, and the *Codex* enumerates four of these. One—the most important—extended from Paris south-west via Orléans, Tours, Poitiers, Bordeaux and the Pyrenees into Spain; the second was from Vézelay in Burgundy and took a similar direction south-west by way of Limoges and Périgueux, joining the Paris route just before the Pyrenees; the third began at Le Puy in the south-eastern Auvergne and travelled more or less westwards through Conques and Moissac, to join the Paris road at the same point as the route from Vézelay; while the last route came from Arles and St-Gilles in Provence and cut west across the south of France to Toulouse, then over the Pyrenees by a different pass, to link up with the other three routes not far from Pamplona: whereupon a single main route, known as the *camino francès*, continued westwards through Burgos and León to Santiago itself. So in effect the pilgrim churches that are of the type of St-Martin-de-Tours distribute themselves evenly among the routes described in the 12th-century guide: Tours was on the Paris road, Limoges on the one from Vézelay, Conques on the route from Le Puy, and Toulouse on the one from Provence—with Santiago itself at the end of the journey. As for Cluny, it was never strictly on any of the routes, but since the abbey of Cluny did more to cultivate and sponsor the pilgrimage in the 12th century than any other institution it is hardly a surprise to find its architecture reflecting some of the features of the pilgrim churches.

St-Martin-de-Tours is now mostly in the mind. The church was destroyed and rebuilt again late in the 12th century. Then it was vandalised by the Protestants during the religious wars in the 16th century, and finally demolished to make a market—yet another market—in the 19th. In the old part of the city you now walk down the Rue des Halles along what was formerly the nave, whose first arch is snapped off above. The Tour de l'Horloge on the right of the street was the south-west tower. Further down on the left is the Tour Charlemagne (so-called for no good reason) which once stood above the north transept. Today it vastly overshadows the little shops and market and dilapidated half-timbered houses. It even overshadows the grandiose hunk described as "in the Romano-Byzantine style" that has taken the place of the old church. This modern basilica is set at an angle of ninety degrees to its predecessor, swivelled round—so to speak—from a point in the crypt where St Martin lies in his tomb, turning forever and ever in it, I should imagine, at finding his sacred remains now enclosed within what closely resembles the lavatory of an early mainline station north of the Trent.

CHAPTER III

◆

Propaganda in the Sun

The pilgrimage gathered momentum as it went south. More tributaries joined it. Between Tours and Bordeaux the pilgrims from England travelling from the Channel ports joined the groups descending from Paris. Those from Normandy had crossed the Loire at Tours or at Angers. Or, if they had foregathered farther west at Mont St-Michel, then they had come down through Rennes and crossed the river at Nantes in the company of pilgrims from Brittany. Many other pilgrims reached Bordeaux direct from England by way of the River Gironde, having crossed the Bay of Biscay and landed in Soulac at the head of the estuary. It was a regular trade for ships' captains: they carried a cargo of wine from Bordeaux one way, and a cargo of pilgrims to Bordeaux the other. Good business.

Naturally, there were many factors other than private business interests that enabled pilgrimages to flourish in the later Middle Ages. The ravages of barbarian invasions had ceased. In the more stable society which followed there emerged a new social system and a new social order, which was feudalism. Feudalism, in turn, assisted an economic recovery in Europe, which naturally enough led to a population explosion and a movement of peoples into previously unused land. There was more money around—mostly for the feudal lords, it is true, but they could now afford to put a proportion of their new wealth into the land, which helped raise the serf's condition above subsistence level; and they were also pleased to subscribe to a strong Church which could be relied upon to back up their authority, as well as order the lives of their subjects. In consequence, money also went into the monasteries, which were the only sources of learning, and into a massive programme of church-building in every village, which was the only channel for spreading a modicum of that learning among the people. The period from the 11th to the 13th century was one of wide awareness of Christian teaching on a popular level, and of lavish Christian optimism on an educated level. It seems to me very doubtful whether the average peasant living in what is now France would, before the 11th century, have thought of himself as a committed Christian, but from the 11th century onwards he certainly would have done so. The Church, for so long a survivor in refuge, came down from its strongholds and saw to that.

Pilgrimages were a product of this teaching and of this social order. It is true that already in the 2nd century pilgrims had journeyed to Jerusalem, and later to Rome—the city of the martyrs. Yet, strange as it may seem, neither of these goals caught the popular imagination with the intensity that was aroused by Santiago de Compostela from the 11th century. One reason for this was the irresistible appeal of St James as symbol of the fight against the Infidel. This was a fight the more stirring and urgent because it was a war on the home front. It was a war in Europe, not the distant Middle East, and to most Christians the hub of Christianity was no longer Palestine but their own society, western Europe: Italy and France, Germany and England. Had not the terrifyingly well-organised forces of Islam pushed north almost as far as the Loire in the 8th century, and along the whole of the south of France to Arles, Avignon, and the Alps? Had not the city of St James itself been sacked in the 10th century, and the bells of the new cathedral carried off in triumph to Córdoba on the backs of Christian captives? The Holy War was first a war of survival, then a war of revenge, finally a war of triumph. St James was the standard-bearer of Christendom, and half Europe set out for his tomb to render him homage and thanks.

By the 11th century, when the pilgrimage was in full flood, the *Reconquista* was already sweeping Spain. Al-Mansur, scourge of Christians and conqueror of Santiago de Compostela, had died in 1002. By 1085 Burgundian soldiers had enabled the Spaniards to retake their capital, Toledo, and a Frenchman had been installed as its bishop. Ten years later the First Crusade set out for Jerusalem. Christendom was winning.

It had not always looked like that. Within a hundred years of the death of Mohammed in AD 632 those apparently disorganised Bedouin tribes, with no history of empire-building or of sustained warfare, had gathered themselves into a military nation capable of taking over all the former Roman colonies along the North African coast, sweeping aside the timid Visigothic rulers of the Iberian peninsula, harassing southern Italy, making easy inroads into Frankish territories in Gaul, and maintaining unchallenged control of the sea.

It was an extraordinary achievement in so short a time. In 636 Syria fell to them, in 638 Jerusalem, in 642 Egypt, in 650 parts of Sicily, and in 698 Carthage and much of the remainder of North Africa. Only thirteen years later they launched a massive invasion of Spain whose rulers crumbled at the first encounter, leaving only an isolated pocket in the north. In 720 the Moors overran their first important city north of the Pyrenees, Narbonne, and went on to besiege Toulouse. Within a further five years they had pushed up as far as Burgundy and ransacked Autun, and, to the west, were advancing past Bordeaux in the direction of Tours and Paris.

In the context of the great Christian pilgrimages which were to follow several centuries later, the key feature of this Islamic upsurge was not so much this new military prowess with which Christendom was confronted, or even the immeasurably superior civilisation that lay behind these triumphs on the battlefield, but the confidence and purpose bestowed on the Arab conquerors by burning religious faith. They believed. More strongly than the Christians, it seemed, they believed. They knew they were right. Christendom, it appeared, was made up of weak doubters to be swept aside—and swept aside they were. The Moslems were not just invaders, not at all like the Barbarians who had harassed the Romans and their successors in southern Europe. Theirs was a religious fight, and they carried in their hearts a courage and an inspiration which were drawn from their founder and prophet, Mohammed. The Christians had nothing like that. Theirs was not a Church militant—not yet—but it soon would be. When they did raise the blood temperature of their faith to the heat of battle the Christians had the example of the Infidel to thank for his example. It was Islam that taught European rulers the notion of a "holy war", and taught European churchmen the binding power of moral propaganda. Both were central to the spirit of pilgrimage.

It is food for thought what might have happened to Europe and to Christianity had the Arabs not been stopped, and stopped soon. London might be as Moorish as Baghdad, and the *Koran* be read in Canterbury. What is now merely an intriguing speculation was a real enough nightmare in the 8th century. From the imminence of that Islamic domination, as Gibbon wrote with a note of relief that was still undiminished a thousand years afterwards, "was Christendom delivered by the genius and fortune of one man". That individual was Charles Martel, who was founder of the Carolingian dynasty in France and was responsible as much as any single man for the establishment of a feudal system in western Europe, by the shrewd allocation of power and military responsibility to the landlords. By such means he was able to raise and maintain an army effective enough to hold his territories against the military machine of the Arabs. Martel it was who inflicted the first major reverse the Moorish armies suffered in Europe. This was north of Poitiers in the year 732, just twenty-one years after those armies had first crossed from North Africa into Spain.

The pilgrims did not make a hero of Martel, but they made a super-hero of his grandson. In the fabric of the Santiago legend it was the Emperor Charlemagne who became emblazoned as the first pilgrim to Compostela. History gives us a more sober account of the Emperor's exploits in Spain, and we know that the army he led south of the Pyrenees in 778 enjoyed only a moderate success against the Moors, and was actually defeated before Zaragoza, while the heroic rearguard action supposedly fought by Roland against the Infidel at Roncesvalles on the return northwards was actually a sly ambush by the local Basques or Navarrais in reprisal for Charlemagne's destruction of the city walls of their capital, Pamplona. Not the stuff of legend. Certainly not the stuff of the *Chanson de Roland* which was the favourite epic recited by pilgrims as they made their way into Spain in the later Middle Ages, and which, it has been suggested, may even have been composed for poets to sing along the pilgrim routes. This, the first classic of French literature, was written down in the middle of the 12th century, though nobody knows its true origin or author, if indeed it had a single author at all.

But the worst of the Moorish onslaughts were still to come. In the mid-9th century they were back in Barcelona, driving north of the Pyrenees as far as the Rhône Valley and Marseille. With the establishment of a separate caliphate—independent of Baghdad—at Córdoba in the early 10th century, the epicentre of Islamic culture and military organisation shifted west, and Córdoba became the last and most magnificent cultural capital of the Mohammedan empire. Pamplona was sacked in 924, and finally at the very end of the century Santiago de Compostela itself fell to the great warrior-lord Al-Mansur.

That was the worst that was to happen. After the death of Al-Mansur the caliphate of Córdoba crumbled. Then Toledo fell to the Christians. There followed a temporary reunion of Moslem Spain, but for the next hundred years the military field was relatively quiet, until in the 13th century the Christian armies pushed south even farther and seized Córdoba. This left only Granada in Moorish hands. And Granada, the last bastion of Moorish rule in Europe, finally succumbed to the Christian forces in 1492. It had been an Arab province for almost 800 years, nearly twice as long as it has been Spanish and Christian since.

From Tours southwards the Loire and its tributaries are the fingers of a hand splayed across the plain. By Saumur downstream they are joined into a single arm. But on the pilgrim road from Tours to Poitiers all five fingers had to be crossed: first the Loire itself, for those who had come down the right bank or approached Tours from the north; almost immediately afterwards, the Cher, in the Middle Ages not yet bridged upstream by a wealthy tax-collector to support the most magical of all the Loire *châteaux*, Chenonceaux; then the Indre flowing down from the castle of Loches, which Richard Cœur-de-Lion and King Philippe-Auguste of France wrested from one another at the turn of the 12th century and where 250 years later the ultimate enchantress among royal mistresses, Agnès Sorel, lived in some luxury. A longer trudge took pilgrims to the Creuse, index-finger on this hand of rivers; and finally to the broad Vienne, the thumb of an extended hand, flowing up from the south to turn westwards in a slow curve before Chinon, on its way to join the Loire.

Now, in late spring, the current of the Vienne was combing the water-crowfoot into lavish white tresses between bulrushes, where black reed-boats lay decaying in the ooze.

Towards Chinon, and some miles off the main route south, the tiny village of Tavant has a puzzling link with the pilgrimage, or with *a* pilgrimage—it is impossible to be precise about this. It consists of a figure of a man painted on a wall of the church crypt and dating from the early 12th century, in other words, at the height of the popularity of the Santiago pilgrimage. If this figure were a pilgrim of St James, then he would be among the very first of whom we have a picture, and it has often been claimed that he is. But though he wears the usual pouch for carrying food and carries the long pilgrim's staff, other features about him are more cryptic. The palm-branch in his hand, for instance, is a traditional emblem of pilgrims to Jerusalem, even though it was adopted, it is true, by Santiago pilgrims. And then there is the hat, which is an extraordinary hat bearing no resemblance to the wide-brimmed sun-hat, turned up at the brow, worn by the pilgrims of St James. It is clearly some sort of turban, and if it is a turban, the connection with the Middle East rather than with north-west Spain is re-inforced. Who, then, is this appealing figure and why should his portrait appear between the ninth and tenth columns of a village church crypt? Was he a palmer returned from the Holy Land in the wake of the First Crusade, maybe, wearing a tourist trophy on his head to impress his fellow-villagers? And did the artist who happened to be painting religious scenes in the church at the time perhaps decide to include so decorative a local celebrity? Or was he indeed a would-be Santiago pilgrim who was preparing to join the nearby route, in what he considered to be suitable costume? Or perhaps some sort of holy man well known in the district? Nobody knows.

From Tavant I went back to the main road at St-Maure-de-Touraine and headed for Poitiers along what was once the Roman road to the south-west. Later it became the pilgrim route, and now it is the main arterial road from Paris to Poitou and the Bordelais. South of Châtellerault curiosity led me on a diversion to Moussais-la-Bataille to see where Charles Martel had inflicted that first defeat on the advancing Moors in the year 732. I am not sure what one expects to see of a twelve-hundred-year-old battle site. All I got was white cows munching amid red poppies in the rain. I drove on to Poitiers.

The only visual impression of Poitiers I brought with me was of one of the most magical paintings in that Book of Hours, painted for the Duke of Berry in the early 14th century by the three Limbourg brothers, the *Très Riches Heures*, now preserved in the museum at Chantilly but so widely reproduced that it is the best known, I suppose, of all mediaeval illuminated manuscripts (painted, incidentally, about the time of the Battle of Agincourt and clearly an inspiration of Laurence Olivier's film *Henry V* with its fairytale castles apparently built of sugared cardboard). The castle of Poitiers appears as the illustration for the month of July in this manuscript: farmers are cutting ripe corn with sickles in the foreground; close by is the kneeling figure of a lady whose robe of *lapis lazuli* blue exactly matches the roof of the extraordinary triangular *château*, otherwise white as ivory, on the farther side of the River Clain and connected to the fields in the foreground by a slender wooden bridge supported on stone piers. Traces of those piers are supposed to be still visible in the water north of the modern town. But I could see nothing of them. The castle too had vanished, as had the jagged mountain wilderness in the background which the Limbourg brothers had introduced to relieve the even domesticity of the Poitevin landscape.

Modern Poitiers is a city of drab corridors that pass for streets and along which pass roughly four times as many cars as the city can contain, finding nowhere to park and nowhere to go. But to the pilgrim in the Middle Ages it was the city of St Hilary, or St-Hilaire, and after the remains of St Martin at Tours his were the next to venerate. He was in fact St Martin's mentor, a bishop and doctor in the 4th century: the 12th-century guidebook vouches for the fact that "among other miracles" Hilary helped defeat the Arian heresy and secure the unity of the faith, and that "his large and beautiful church has been favoured by frequent miracles".

This "large and beautiful" church of St-Hilaire-le-Grand had been built a century before the guide was compiled, apparently by an English architect by the name of Coorland, and it still stands, more or less in its original form, in a drab southern suburb of the city, on the site of smaller churches to the saint which were destroyed respectively by the Vandals in the 5th century and by the Normans in the 9th. Inside, it looks like a gigantic assembly-hall, and that is really what it was intended to be. Grand in concept, utilitarian in function, St-Hilaire-le-Grand is the first full-scale pilgrim church still standing on the route from Paris, and no church along the entire length of the pilgrim road gives a clearer impression of what the religious ceremonies held for pilgrims in their thousands must have been like. On either side of a broad nave run double aisles, relatively just as broad. Side chapels open out from the head of these aisles on a kind of mezzanine floor. On a higher level still are the High Altar, the huge north and south transepts, and the apse and ambulatory, with six further semi-circular chapels, each bulging out beyond the apsidal wall in precisely the manner of those archetypal pilgrim churches still standing at Conques and at Santiago itself. With such a design the vast congregation all round could keep a clear view of the High Altar, and pilgrims had space to circulate freely round the ambulatory and to inspect the relics of the saint; or they could pray in one of the many small chapels. It was built, as I say, like an assembly-hall.

Now, like Poitiers itself, the church of St Hilary looks a bit inflated for what it is. All that space will never again be filled with the fervent jamborees it played host to in the Middle Ages. The spirit has fled, leaving a barn. Stained glass of the modern French school—which Cubism has much to answer for—was staining the cool afternoon light the colour of strawberry and blackcurrant wine-gums, and meek pre-communicants in a row were, one by one, being given moral guidance in whispers by a grave elder. It was depressing and bleak.

Pilgrims who felt the need to venerate a further saint in Poitiers crossed over to the eastern edge of the city to a church built in honour of another figure in the early church history of Poitou, a lady called St-Radegonde, who founded a monastery here in the 6th century. This church was complete by the time of the 12th-century guidebook. Today it lies tucked among old houses in a quiet quarter of the town near the river, its handsome Romanesque façade and octagonal tower offering promise of far finer things than the pattern-book Gothic architecture contained within. Sunken under the altar is a lugubrious crypt where the grandiose tomb of the lady saint carries a metal lid, spiked for candles to resemble some instrument of torture; though much of the pervading atmosphere of mystery and fear is relieved by a soapy Madonna set up to guard it. A hundred yards away stands the earliest monument in Poitiers which is the early 4th-century baptistry: basically a plain Roman box, with a later church and narthex added, round which the main road into the city thoughtfully divides just as the Strand in London divides round St Clement Danes.

The glory of Poitiers is yet a third Romanesque church, one which has no specific link with the pilgrimage route to Compostela except that pilgrims crossing the city from the north on their way to the shrine of St-Hilaire would have passed right by its scaly old face. This is Notre-Dame-la-Grande, the west front of which I swear has no more than a few square centimetres of stone unadorned. Here is a façade to read like a book, a book without margins, one chapter flowing into the next, as arch above arch carries its weight of metamorphic beasts lashing and snapping and devouring their own tails between and around rows of gentle saints and apostles, all bound together by entwining foliage and writhing geometrical patterns that lead the eye a whirligig across the sombre stone. The Poitevin sculptors here carved a mediaeval mystery play, based, as it happens, on a sermon originally delivered by St Augustine, and in the Middle Ages used regularly in French churches as one of the lessons read at Matins on Christmas Day.

Sermons in stone. In the region south of Poitiers there will be scarcely a church in the smallest village between here and Bordeaux which does not carry some fragment of the same sermon carved on its façade or round the apse. The message seldom varies: what happens to you if you are good, and what happens to you if you are wicked; the rewards of Virtue and the punishments of Vice; eternal bliss balanced against eternal torture. The account of the Wise and Foolish Virgins provides one gentle illustration of this moral lesson; the Ascent of the Saved and the Fall of the Damned, a more vivid one. Gazing at these sculptures here in Poitiers, it was no surprise to me that people should have set off on pilgrimage in such numbers. High above the tussle for men's souls on the façade of Notre-Dame-la-Grande stands the figure of Christ in Majesty in his mandorla like a seal of office. Here was the promise of authority, the reassurance that it was all worth while. Whoever would have had the temerity to disbelieve it?

I had entered a region with the most concentrated church propaganda in the whole of France and perhaps in the whole of Europe. It is not a large area: Poitiers bounds it to the north, and it ends some way before Bordeaux to the south. The Atlantic is never more than seventy miles westwards, usually only thirty. And right through the middle of this region runs the main pilgrimage route to Santiago de Compostela, the long march for which these hundreds of magnificently decorated churches were, in effect, recruiting stations.

It is appropriate that the man who was one of the principal propagandists came from this region. He was Aymery Picaud, who is the most likely candidate for the authorship (or at least the editorship) of the *Codex Calixtinus*, that invaluable guidebook compiled in the interests of the church authorities at Santiago. Picaud was a monk from Parthenay-le-Vieux, thirty miles to the west of Poitiers, and he is known to have made the journey to Santiago himself in the company of a lady by the name of Ginberga Flandensis. We also know that this lady donated a manuscript of the *Codex*—very likely the original manuscript—to the cathedral there (where I have seen it preserved in the library), and that a few years later it was copied by Arnaldo da Monte, a monk from Ripoll Monastery in eastern Spain. The man for whom the *Codex* was compiled was most likely Don Pedro Elias, who was first the Dean of Santiago and then Archbishop from the year 1143.

The pilgrim's guide is only one of five books that together make up the *Codex Calixtinus* (also known as the *Liber Sancti Jacobi*). It starts with a letter, supposedly written by Pope Calixtus II, used here as a form of preface, or puff, but which is actually spurious. It is not known who did write it—maybe Picaud did. There follows, in Book One, an anthology of liturgical pieces composed in honour of St James. Book Two is an account of some twenty miracles which the saint is reckoned to have performed during the lifetime of the first and greatest archbishop of Santiago, Diego Gelmirez, who had succeeded in getting the see raised in status from that of a mere bishopric. Book Three recounts the legend (told as fact) of the evangelisation of Spain by the apostle, his martyrdom in Jerusalem, and the subsequent return of his body to Galicia. There follows another piece of fulsome romance in Book Four which deals with Charlemagne and Roland in their rôles as proto-pilgrims of St James: this section has become known as the *Pseudo-Turpin* since it purports to be an account written by Archbishop Turpin who accompanied the Emperor on his expedition to Spain. Needless to say it is not by him. Finally there is Book Five which is the guide itself.

The reader, says Picaud, who approaches the book without hesitation or scruple, will find truth in it. He might have added

"without discrimination", for the guide is so peppered with in-
genuous prejudices that the reader is kept in a state of wry amusement which may not have been the author's original intention.
One of the first clues to Picaud's identity is the unqualified praise
lavished on a single area of the pilgrim route—Poitou. Here, he
assures us, the land is fertile and the countryside laden with every
good thing; moreover the Poitevins themselves are an energetic
people, fine warriors, elegantly dressed, handsome of feature,
spiritual in mind, generous in outlook and the most excellent hosts.
Considering what Picaud has to say about almost every other area
between here and Santiago it is surprising that pilgrims reading
his guide did not decide they had travelled quite far enough already,
and stay put in Poitou.

The priory church of Picaud's home town, Parthenay-le-Vieux,
was built in the early years of the 12th century, very possibly in
Picaud's own lifetime, and it still stands. All that remains of the
priory itself are retaining walls that today enclose fruit-trees and
vegetable-plots, and a small area of the cloister that was discovered
in 1927, embedded into a farmhouse built out from the side of the
church. An octagonal tower tops the nave, its walls golden with
lichen, and a rounded apse fans out below it. The western end is
dominated by three sculpted portals of the kind one comes across
on church after church in the region immediately to the south.
Pairs of dogs (representing hell) and birds (representing paradise)
decorate the *voussoirs* which run in semi-circular bands above the
door, one above the other like eccentrically moulded car-tyres;
and in the centre of the left-hand portal is a superb piece of early
carving of a life-size mounted figure wearing a crown and tram-
pling an unfortunate foe. This again is a common figure on the
churches of Poitou and Saintonge to the south, and it represents
the first Christian Roman Emperor, Constantine, overcoming the
forces of paganism (though in fact the source of all these symbols
of the Church Triumphant was not a Christian statue at all but the
great bronze equestrian portrait of Marcus Aurelius in Rome,
now proudly in the middle of the Piazza Campidoglio on the
Capitol Hill, but actually preserved from earlier destruction in an
erroneous belief that it was Constantine himself).

I suppose Aymery Picaud may have been spurred on to prosely-
tise the cause of St James by the rousing sculpture on his local

church. He may equally well have been stirred by a more hot-blooded and urgent call than that; for it was in the year 1135 that one of the most forcefully persuasive preachers in the Middle Ages came to the district and gave a sermon only two miles from Parthenay-le-Vieux. This was a sermon of such powerful eloquence and conviction that the Duke of Aquitaine, William IX, who was in the congregation, is said to have been converted to the faith as he listened. The preacher was St Bernard, aristocrat and ascetic, founder of the Cistercian Order and guiding spirit of the crusading movement.

There are, in fact, two Parthenays, a couple of miles apart, and it was in the second Parthenay, in the Church of Notre-Dame-de-Couldre, that St Bernard is supposed to have conducted his dramatic conversion of the local ruler (who, incidentally, has also come down in history as reputedly the first of the troubadours). A bit of the church has survived—just. Only the portal remains, dating from the 12th century and smashed almost beyond recognition, but enough is there to pick out the familiar bands of carved figures—the Virtues and Vices again, and the twenty-four old men of the Apocalypse packed into the slender *voussoirs* like toy soldiers—and enough to appreciate the liveliness and quality the carving must once have possessed. What with St Bernard preaching inside, and the local stone-carvers outside, no wonder Parthenay was one of the major pilgrim towns in western France.

Though Parthenay is not strictly on one of the principal pilgrim routes, but on a minor route that by-passed Tours, in this area there is such a spider's web of pilgrim roads that it is impossible to be certain which carried the most traffic. Parthenay is today a kind of demonstration model of what a mediaeval town looked like: indeed, there is no town along any of the routes, even in Spain, which more clearly demonstrates how the pilgrimage made its mark on local life and architecture in the Middle Ages. To appreciate the impact of this I left my car well to the north of the town and approached it on foot the way pilgrims themselves had approached it for so many hundreds of years. And a strange feeling it was. Suddenly amid the stucco and the pebble-dash of an anonymous French suburb, flanked with Peugeots and plastic flower-pots, a decrepit chapel abutted on to the road. The east window had been blocked up with cheap brick and the entire east end botched together into a sort of house, with domestic windows punched here and there through the old walls. The rest was a barn, timbered over and laced with cobwebs, a few surviving stone arches hitching the roof high over a rotting Citroën and a chorus of white doves. This was the former Chapel of St James, situated in the heart of the Faubourg St-Jacques, across the river from the main area of the town.

Lodging facilities for pilgrims were generally provided outside the walls to enable travellers to come and go after the gates of the town were shut at night: here sprang up the principal hostels, with invariably a chapel of some kind attached, and it was round these amenities that the pilgrim district of a town grew up. Hundreds of French towns, from Paris down to places smaller even than Parthenay, retain at least the name of their Faubourg St-Jacques to this day.

Less than a hundred yards farther on, the road widened and opened up an aspect of the town itself on the far side of the river, with the remnants of a protective wall around it. Spanning the river was the 13th-century stone bridge, the main bridge into the town, and the road climbed narrowly up over this and entered the town through a massive twin-towered stone gate. So, from the Faubourg St-Jacques I crossed the Pont St-Jacques, passed under the Porte St-Jacques, and found myself in the street of St-Jacques. Here were half-timbered houses once occupied by merchants who had grown prosperous supplying provisions to the pilgrims passing through the town on their way south. They gave their houses fine stone lintels with the year engraved on them, and overhanging gables in wood, carved with corn motifs and human heads. The street of St-Jacques climbed the hill to the centre of the town and led under the walls of the citadel. From here pilgrims threaded their way through an entanglement of alleys and out of the town by a southern gate that no longer exists, soon to join the main Roman road that would shortly bring them to where a sermon longer, more chilling and more enchanting than any they had so far encountered was engraved round one of the greatest churches in all France—Aulnay.

Professor Pevsner has written that "a bicycle shed is a building; Lincoln Cathedral is a piece of architecture". I like that. But what, I wonder, would he say of a shoe-box, for that is much nearer what we have to consider at Aulnay and in the area generally. These buildings have been conceived as containers, with messages inscribed on the outside: not *written* messages, because they were intended for an illiterate congregation, but messages in pictures, symbols, designs and easily recognisable stories. There are very few churches in the Poitou and Saintonge region of western France in which the architectural principles are more sophisticated than those required to build a large-sized box; yet many of these churches are outstanding. This is due in some part to the weight of sculpture they bear, but in even greater part it is due to an understanding of the rôle of decoration in architecture which these church-builders and carvers possessed. Art is subservient to overall design. There are few pieces of sculpture on the three-hundred-odd carved churches in this area which stand out in the mind as works of individual brilliance, such as might make one pause in the neutral setting of a museum. It is only when they are in place, massed together as they are, alongside a wealth of geometrical patterning and extraordinarily intricate ribbons of tracery, that they come into their own and contribute to raising a stone box to the level of an architectural masterpiece. In the best of them it is the churches themselves that are sculptural works of art, not the individual images carved upon them. Aulnay is one of these.

The village of Aulnay is out of sight. The church is turned away from it: the congregation came from another direction, down the broad Roman road from Poitiers on the way south. Aulnay is set down right on that road, at the farthest point in Poitou before it becomes Saintonge, though the plain goes on and on without recognition of any change. With time, Aulnay has become only a monument. It is cared for by the Ministry of Public Works. It has long outlived its useful function: the west window bricked up like the Cyclops's blinded eye, the churchyard an antique stoneyard veined with white periwinkles that slink among the rubble.

But what a monument. Nowhere can you look at this church but a face looks back at you—a face to bring terror or hope: birds, horses, mermaids, four-legged creatures with wings and beaks, couples entwined by their tails, beasts bound by vine-shoots, elephants, giants, moustached owls; and then saints, apostles, angels, knights, maidens. In one mood, grotesquerie and black humour, in the other, solemnity and naïveté: the dark and the light. High above the great south portal at Aulnay, four knights crush the monsters of Evil beneath their shields. Below the knights are the familiar series of carved *voussoirs* bent above the entrance, their curved friezes sculpted in high-relief: each is recessed slightly from the one outside it and supported on columns, some of which are incised with formal patterns like the pillars in the nave of Durham Cathedral in miniature. The innermost band of carving, immediately above the door, is a frieze of beasts caught within the tendrils of a climbing plant; a Germanic- or Celtic-looking design. The next depicts the twelve apostles and the twelve prophets of the Apocalypse bearing crowns of gold and musical instruments, and vials filled with odours, after the account given in the fourth chapter of the *Book of Revelations*:

. . . and, behold, a throne.

And he that sat was to look upon like a jasper and a sardine stone: and there was a rainbow about the throne, in sight like unto an emerald.

And round about the throne were four and twenty seats: and upon the seats I saw four and twenty elders sitting, clothed in white raiment; and they had on their heads crowns of gold.

Only here the sculptors, having already carved twenty-four figures on the band below, took the liberty of raising the number of elders to thirty-one.

But it is the outer band of carving which contains the most extraordinary scene at Aulnay. Here is an evocation of chaos, of life without God: a world that is personified by a sequence of figures who can only have been let out of an asylum conceived in a nightmare, to howl and chatter and grimace in the ears of the mediaeval pilgrim as he made his way to Mass to hear—most likely—a sermon on a very similar theme. Even separated in time from us by the Renaissance, by the Reformation and the Age of Reason, by the mediaeval revival in the Romantic era, by centuries of comfortable agnosticism and now by the dispassion of tourism, the heart thumps at such a vision of an alternative world. And the reason these images evoke so powerful a reaction from the 20th-century spectator is that the mediaeval sculptors who made them managed to express Evil as if it were a kind of human insanity, a mental condition. They represented it not as a torment of the flesh, but of the mind: bedlam rather than the torture-chamber. And here we are very close indeed to an even bolder concept—one that intellectually might have been beyond the master-masons and carvers of Aulnay, but which their menagerie of fantasy cannot help suggesting—and that is the concept of Hell itself as a mental state, which seems an amazingly advanced idea to have found expression at that time.

Gazing at this south door of Aulnay, I found myself considering whether, ironically, it is not we who are illiterate now, faced with this language of allegory and symbol that must have been crystal-clear to those for whom it was carved; wondering, too, if we do not underestimate the mediaeval mind and its capacity to dwell inquiringly upon itself. Doctrinally, we know that beasts in mediaeval church art often represent pagan religions. Historically, we also know that bestiaries held a fascination for the 12th century, that illustrated versions of Beatus's *Commentaries on the Apocalypse* enjoyed widespread fame during this same period, and that one of the themes most frequently treated on these churches, the Battle of the Virtues and Vices, may be traced to the *Psychomachia* of the Roman author, Prudentius. We know all about *how* these beasts occur in mediaeval art, rather little about *why*. Yet it is unthinkable that the borderland between man and monster should be so consistently represented as fluid, were man himself not terrified that this was in fact so. These metamorphic creatures leering out of every cornice and capital must be impersonations of human fears and human temptations—fears that are exorcised by their being displayed openly on a church and by being subservient to so exquisite an architectural harmony; temptations that in life beckon a man towards disaster but are capable of being themselves finally ordered and rendered powerless. The magic of the church, and the unity of its form, prevail. Together they serve to rescue a man from himself, to organise and discipline his thoughts, his hopes, his journeys, and, in the case of Aulnay, to send him fortified upon his way.

The south door of Aulnay was carved about the year 1130—around the time St Bernard was drawing packed congregations to his sermons and converting the Duke of Aquitaine at Parthenay; perhaps, too, at about the time Aymery Picaud was gathering his

material for the *Liber Sancti Jacobi* at Parthenay-le-Vieux, in the
service of the church at Santiago de Compostela. By the end of that
century there was scarcely a village within an arc of fifty miles
west and south of Aulnay that would not have a new church
decorated, to a similar or lesser extent, by the same didactic school
of stone-carvers. Their styles vary: sometimes it seems possible
to pick out the same hand; at other times one is struck by the wide
differences in treatment of the same themes between villages only
a mile or so apart from one another. But they are all fundamentally
the same. They are all didactic, carved boxes.

Clearly, I was in for several days of detours, and the first of
these detours I picked off the map out of pure curiosity. This was
a village by the name of Puits-Jacquet, some fifteen miles from
Aulnay towards La Rochelle and the sea. *Puits* meaning a well, and
Jacquet meaning a follower of St James, it seemed reasonable to
expect some relic of the pilgrimage to be there. The village turned
out to be too small even to merit a nameboard, which is truly
remarkable in France where even a cluster of six houses is generally
identified before and afterwards, often with full credentials. At
Puits-Jacquet—nothing. But there was a well: whether it was of
any antiquity was hard to decide, since the owner, in whose back-
garden it rested, had garnished it with old tractor-seats from which
he was trailing nasturtiums. He had, though, arranged a row of
real scallop-shells to mark the edge of a nearby flower-bed, and
this encouraged me to inquire of the only living soul around
whether there might perhaps be some story attached to the place.
She was a friendly, moustached lady who told me a great deal about
her brother who had been mayor in 1951 and who, she said, had
lived there more than fifty years. But a pilgrimage? She had never
heard of such a thing. And the meaning behind the name of the
village? She pulled her shoulders up to her ears and made a face
like Fernandel.

I said good morning to the hairy lady and pressed on through
that most gentle of rolling country, the last cowslips thick and tall
in moist verges, and greenfinches flashing between hawthorn
bushes. A hoopoe swerved in front of the car and bounced away
on heavy black-and-white wings to alight on a dead tree across the
fields, its crest opened up like a Japanese fan. Crossing the River

Boutonne I rejoined the old pilgrim route which, after Aulnay, is no longer the modern road but follows the river valley for a few miles as far as St-Jean-d'Angély. (Another route by-passed St-Jean altogether and continued farther east.) I stopped at Nuaillé, my second sleepy village of the morning, in front of a church that was now used as farm-buildings but whose heaven-and-hell scenes on the sculpted portal identified this as being a poor cousin of Aulnay. The familiar twenty-four elders guarded the entrance, and a stone sarcophagus was set into the wall. I drove on.

St-Jean-d'Angély once boasted a prestigious relic. This was nothing less than the head of John the Baptist, said to have been brought from Alexandria and given to the Benedictines, who built a great abbey to receive it in the 9th century. Aymery Picaud does not even try to conceal his delight that such a three-star attraction should be in what he considered to be his own region. Day and night, he recounts, a choir of one hundred monks attended the priceless object with their devotion, and it was obligatory for all pilgrims to go and venerate the saint. There was nothing quite as holy as this again all the way to Santiago. But how things have changed in St-Jean-d'Angély. It became a Protestant town during the religious wars, and the Reformers duly burnt the abbey and abbey-church. Of the shrine of which Picaud was so proud nothing remains, though a later Gothic apse survives in ruin, part of its superstructure jutting into the sky like a broken tooth. Inside, when I was there, were rolled carpets, paint-pots, dead flowers, cobwebs and aspidistras—but no head of John the Baptist.

A few miles beyond St-Jean I made another detour to the village of Fenioux. A superb church surmounts a hill above a stream and a buttercup meadow. This is in origin one of the earliest churches in the region. Decorations and remains of columns in the tilting and topsy-turvy nave date from the Carolingian period in the 9th century. The façade is later in date and possesses, in an exaggerated form, a characteristic common to most of these "box" churches of the region: the predominance of its main portal. The west front of Fenioux is virtually all door. Opening out from the actual entrance on either side stand no fewer than nine vertical columns. These in turn are flanked by a pair of gigantic columns that rise to the very roof-line; and outside there are six more columns on each side, this time receding, but likewise extending to the full height of the church. There is simply no room for anything other than portal. At the east end the nave is surmounted by a scaly spire supported on more columns, and a richly carved smaller portal stands on the north side. But the real puzzle of Fenioux is to be found in the former graveyard across the road. It is a free-standing tower consisting of eleven smooth round pillars set above a funeral chamber, with the narrowest spiral stairway inside leading up to what is clearly a kind of watch-tower, which has narrow slits in the walls, opening outwards to command an excellent view all round. Whatever was this curious construction? That it had a funerary rôle is unquestionable, but why the watch-tower too, and where did the idea and the design originate? Did it watch over the dead, or guard the graveyard against desecration? Scholars have talked of comparisons with Seleucid minarets of the same period, and certainly it has a most Islamic appearance. Beyond that I do not know, and neither—as far as I can see—does anyone else.

The road across-country from Fenioux to Saintes brought me to the rich wooded valley of the Charente at the village of Taillebourg, which rang a bell as the name of a battle famous enough to have taken Delacroix a considerable acreage of canvas to describe (the painting now hangs in the Galérie des Batailles at Versailles). I was right: Taillebourg was the scene of a celebrated victory—though a short-lived one—by St Louis over the English, in the 13th century. One so easily forgets that this entire region of France was part of England for hundreds of years, and that to add to the historical confusion the English kings were themselves French, the Plantagenets being descendants of the counts of Anjou. A mile beyond Taillebourg was another reminder that historically I was in England. This was a village called St James—not St-Jacques. Whatever connection the place once had with the pilgrimage, it was thought natural to record it in the language of the country that owned it. It is likely that the community was actually founded by settlers from England, possibly vine-growers who had moved their business realising that here was a more favourable climate for wine-making than back home. It is not often appreciated that it was the English occupancy of the Bordeaux area during the Middle Ages which sent a hitherto considerable English wine industry into decline. And those ships, as we have seen, that sailed north to Bristol and London, laden with barrels of wine from England's newly-acquired territories in the sun, returned laden with pilgrims bound for Compostela.

The capital of the Saintonge region is Saintes, the saint in question being St-Eutrope, who was the town's first bishop in the 3rd century and subsequently a martyr; hence his relics were especially venerable and his shrine a popular attraction to pilgrims trudging south from Aulnay and St-Jean-d'Angély. Aymery Picaud was exorbitantly proud of the *beati Eutropii episcopi et martyris* (who he claims was from a noble Persian family), and he proceeds to supply an account of the saint's adventures and death at disproportionate length. Eutrope's tomb rests, to this day, in the crypt of the priory church which the monks of Cluny built in his honour during the 11th century. It must have been enormous, at least on the scale of St Hilary's church in Poitiers, and it was designed in the same fashion to accommodate huge congregations of pilgrims. But Napoleon pulled down everything save the crypt (which remains very fine indeed) and the raised choir. The church you see now from the exterior is mostly an unhappy Gothic-style replacement.

Saintes offered other attractions in the Middle Ages: in particular, there was the Abbaye aux Dames across the river from St-Eutrope. This was an immaculately blue-blooded institution, headed by an abbess who was always appointed from one of the noblest families in France, with an income to match, with a ladies' college that was likewise for the daughters of the rich. But the Abbaye des Dames also had attached to it among the earliest and most splendid churches in the region: the Église Ste-Marie, which was built, most probably, during the first quarter of the 12th century, and, even more than Aulnay, it is architecturally the mother-church from which all the marvellous little village churches of the area sprang. It offers one of the earliest examples of those sculpted *voussoirs*, or carved bands of stone, with the figures arranged in a series of closed ranks that curve round the top of the door, so the figures themselves radiate outwards—in this case from the hand of God in the centre. The dusty square in front of the church has more the air of a Spanish than a French town, which is appropriate since the design of this façade of Ste-Marie was carried by craftsmen during the 12th century towards Santiago and left its mark on a number of Spanish churches along the pilgrim route—not least on the cathedral of Santiago de Compostela itself. Today the façade of Ste-Marie is hideously scarred from its experiences as a clothing-shop attached to a military barracks in the 19th century; but it still remains one of the most impressive portals to be seen on the route to Santiago. Its carved decoration is positively knotted in complexity, and in its sinuousness it offers a hint that the Moors were here too, and the Celts besides. For all the solid, provincial Christian traditions of the abbey next door, the church of Ste-Marie retains a distinctly cosmopolitan and pagan look.

A storm was piling up from the Atlantic as I drove west from Saintes to look at as many as I could of those village churches of the Saintonge which I had still only read about. As it turned out, I could have spent a week doing this and still I would have missed some gems. Books have been written about these churches, and it speaks for the wealth of religious architecture in the region that each book includes a number which the others omit. The first I stopped at was Corme-Royal, which lies off to the right of the main road to Saintes from the oyster-beds of Marennes and the Île d'Oléron. Here, in the centre of the village, a rubble of walls enclosed the grounds of what must have been a small priory. Now tiny fields and vegetable gardens filled the area; chickens and brown spotted dogs strolled in the last blaze of sunlight before the rain. An expired 2-CV Citroën rusted in the nettles. From the garden, looking back, the south wall of a fortified church rose up behind chunky buttresses. The west door, protected from the eroding sea-winds by the high walls around it, was a scaled-down version of the portals at Aulnay and Saintes, except that the figures themselves were more elegant, more elongated. The usual messages were there, carved into the six arches of the façade: the parable of the Wise and Foolish Virgins, Virtue and Vice, a clutch of saints and apostles including what I took to be St James carrying a pilgrim's staff shaped as a tau-cross. It was the familiar sermon on the wall. Corme-Royal was slumbering, except for a mongol boy standing with loose arms in the church square, agog at the sight of a foreign car, a toy car in his own hand.

I drove on, through a landscape now purple with thunder-clouds, to Corme-Écluse to the south. The same sermon again, and superficially the same façade; yet in everything the decoration was different. Friezes, capitals, arches, bosses, all the carving looked soft, fibrous, and, as the storm finally broke over the village, the rain gave that delicately-worked surface the appearance of weathered coral.

Five minutes away, at Rioux, the rain had swept inland, and sunlight broke over one of the most perfect churches I am likely ever to set eyes on. This time there were no messages, except for grimacing gargoyles round the roof-line. The church was conceived as a hunk of abstract sculpture. Everything is geometrical decoration: diamond patterns, shell shapes, floral motifs, zig-zags, criss-crosses, foliage, scrolling, curlicues, chevrons, dogs'-teeth; these and many other motifs overlay much of the entire surface of the church and even bestow rhythmic patterns on the masonry of the church walls. Once again, the architecture itself is of the simplest: all this bravura decoration is controlled within the plainest formula of slab walls and rounded arches. The apse— which must be about the most perfect apse in all Romanesque art —consists of a sequence of vertical stone screens, each with a single window and four false arches above, separated from each other by columns rising to roof-level and shaped like extended telescopes pointed to the ground.

I said there were no messages at Rioux church except for the gargoyles. This is not, in fact, quite true. I may have found the portal unusually bare of figures, but there, set into the central false arch above the west door, was a solitary piece of sculpture of the Madonna and Child which as a work of art surpassed, as I thought, anything I had seen on the pilgrim route so far, and which was intended to offer the very simplest of messages—promise and reassurance. The promise of a better life to come, and the reassurance needed to cope with the present one. She smiles in the afternoon sun.

After Rioux—Marignac, its façade worn by the winds, and its three-lobed apse commanding a landscape of vines and crumbling stone barns; Chadenac, with its grave elegant figures of archangels whose robes ripple and billow like those of a Botticelli Venus, and which the great American scholar, Arthur Kingsley Porter, considered to be finer than the figures on the west door at Chartres; Echebrune, tucked into the woods, hiding another sumptuous façade of geometrical tracery, and whose lower columns display crude *graffiti* of a procession of pilgrims recognisable by their hats and staves; and finally Pérignac with its wonderful mandorla of Christ flanked by two archangels with flowing robes, and its curious band of horses' heads carved high above the west window.

I was beginning to have a surfeit of churches, and turned the car through the Cognac vineyards towards Saintes. In the last of the sunlight I sat on the balcony of my hotel room, with the end of my duty-free Scotch, and found myself puzzling over the relationship of what we have come to recognise and respect as fine art to all the simple carving I had seen. What was the difference between fine art and folk-art? Was it a question of universality, or of sophistication, or of intent? Much of what I had been looking at these last few days so plainly lacked any consciously artistic purpose, was even, in many cases, bluntly didactic; yet it was art all the same. Fine art? I found such a definition impossible to make. That evening I opened a book on Spain I had brought with me, written by one of the most erudite and entertaining snobs ever to put pen to paper—Richard Ford, whose *Handbook to Spain*, first published in 1845, was to be a constant delight to me in the weeks to come. Here, by chance, I came across a passage that seemed relevant to my thoughts:

> ... the idols of rude people preceded fine art, and in time obtained a conventional sanctity independent of form; nay, when beauty and grace were substituted, the stern deep religious sentiment was lost. Reverence was then merged in artistic admiration, and the altars, as at Rome, were visited as picture-galleries, and the siren beauty seduced the pilgrim and anchorite.

The imagination runs wild and free in the decoration of these little churches of the Saintonge, but the impression is deceptive. Flamboyance can be a form of exorcism: there is a moral sternness within. The implication is that life is hard, pleasure hard bought, a state of grace hard won. The mediaeval ethos favoured struggle —struggle against hardship, against the Devil, against the Infidel. One of the attractions of the journey to Compostela in the early days was that it was difficult, difficulty being intimately related to spirituality. The only path to salvation lay that way. The *Codex Calixtinus* guide never tries to make light of the hardships

St James represented as a pilgrim to his own shrine – dressed in familiar pilgrim's costume: from a 15th-century Book of Hours (*Oxford, Bodleian Library*)

(*Above*) Knights in armour from an illuminated manuscript in Burgos: emblems on shield and caparison indicate that the knight in the lower group belongs to the chivalric order of St James (*Photograph, J. Oronoz*)

(*Left*) A silver-gilt chalice or steeple-cup, with scallop-shell decorations suggesting that it probably belonged to a guild or confraternity of former pilgrims to Santiago: 16th century (*London, Victoria & Albert Museum*)

(*Left*) Pilgrims returning from Santiago playing games: from the Book of Hours of the Duchess of Burgundy (*Chantilly, Musée Condé*)

(*Below*) A panel from the 13th-century Reliquary of Charlemagne at Aix-la-Chapelle (now Aachen), depicting St James appearing to Charlemagne in a dream and directing him towards the still undiscovered site of his tomb in Galicia (*Aachen, Cathedral Treasury*)

Drawing of an elderly pilgrim to Santiago, by Antoine Watteau 1684–1721 (*Paris, Musée du Petit Palais*)

The traditional starting-point for the principal pilgrim road to Santiago, the Tour St-Jacques in Paris: all that remains of the large Gothic church of St-Jacques-de-la-Boucherie, destroyed in the French Revolution

The church of the former priory at Parthenay-le-Vieux, where Aymery Picaud, the author (or editor) of the 12th-century pilgrims' guidebook, was a monk

The mediaeval bridge and town-gate of St James at Parthenay, near the principal pilgrim route to the south, between the Loire and Bordeaux

The River Loire near Tours

Poitiers: the heavily sculptured 12th-century façade of the church of
Notre-Dame-la-Grande

involved in such a pilgrimage, in fact the reverse; and without understanding something of the mediaeval attitude to earthly comforts it would be easy to expect pilgrims to be put off by the guide, rather than reassured by it. Swamps, mosquitoes, robbers, hostile natives, taxing mountains, polluted water, bad wine, worse food, sickness—these are all to come in plenty. In the early centuries of the pilgrimage, at least, the journey was no pleasure trip, nor was it meant to be. Four hundred years later Montaigne could still point out with wry amusement that Italians liked to go to Santiago de Compostela while Galicians preferred to make their way to Our Lady of Loretto.

One of the cardinal sins in mediaeval Europe was avarice: there was not yet any sanctity in capitalism, and hoarding and investing money was not the practice of a wise and provident man but that of a miser. Poverty was not shameful, as it was later to become, but a virtue; and those who preached it recalled the teaching of Christ that "it is easier for a camel to go through the eye of a needle, than for a rich man to enter the kingdom of God".

This cult of poverty was seminal to the growth and popularity of pilgrimages. St Francis of Assisi, himself a pilgrim to Santiago de Compostela, practised it to the letter, and under his example a number of communities grew up in the later Middle Ages that were dedicated to poverty. It was this respect for poverty, and a disregard for personal gain, that most clearly set the pilgrimage to Santiago apart from the Crusades. For all the fine sentiments attending their inception, the Crusades were for the individual crusader an opportunity for employment, adventure and plunder.

A social condition which enhanced the popularity of the Santiago pilgrimage was the right accorded each Frenchman who was a free man—and the greatest number of early pilgrims were French—to leave his home, his family and his land for an unstated period of time, without forfeiting his property or his heritage. (Later, English pilgrims enjoyed the same protection.) In a period when the rural population of Europe was less settled in its territories than it is now, it was not at all unusual for a member of a family to drift across the continent seeking work wherever work could be had. Pilgrims were not alone in travelling great distances—the main roads of Europe in the later Middle Ages must at times have resembled a refugees' highway in Vietnam—but certainly he would only have felt able to do so provided he was reasonably sure that his family and possessions were secure.

Of course the climate of pilgrimages changed, and the credibility of the pilgrim himself deteriorated. This seems to have occurred gradually from the 13th century onwards, with the removal of many of those dangers and hazards which had helped make the Santiago journey so attractive in the first place. In particular, the decline of the Moorish threat cut away much of the action and romance from the pilgrimage. The easier it became, the more its appeal touched those who saw it as a means of trade and livelihood, or who wanted a good excuse to travel, to get away from the family, from debts, feuds, the law, perhaps just from boredom. The pilgrim, after all, was something of a privileged citizen of the world: the legal protection and exemption from dues accorded him was a bait for many who wanted to travel for quite other motives and who felt able to do so now that the worst dangers were past. In the year 1435 a gypsy taking his tribe across the Pyrenees into Spain had the wit to pose as a noble pilgrim accompanied, he explained, by a retinue appropriate to the status of the Count of Lesser Egypt, as he styled himself. Alas, his enterprising bluff was called at Jaca. It is not surprising that the cathedral authorities at Santiago found it useful to issue certificates to testify that pilgrims had really been there.

The most serious attacks on the pilgrimage did not come until the Reformation. These attacks were launched both at the corruption and exploitation that had to a large extent overtaken it by the early 16th century; but, even more seriously, they were launched upon the very notion of pilgrimages and the superstitious cult of relics in general. With the Reformation came the first concerted opposition to the acceptance of blind faith. Reform, humanism, rationalism, scepticism, each struck a deep wound at the Santiago cult. That an air of disillusionment even permeated Santiago itself in the 16th century is evident from the experience of an English doctor, Andrew Boorde, who visited the city as a pilgrim only to be told by the priest who gave him absolution that there were no relics of St James in the city at all, Charlemagne having removed them to Toulouse eight centuries earlier.

It is symptomatic, too, of this change of spirit that in the era of Dr Boorde's visit to Compostela there were already so many beggars posing as pilgrims there that the authorities forbade mendicant pilgrims to remain in the city longer than three days or they were punished with four hours in the pillory. A hundred years later Louis XIV of France banned the pilgrimage to Frenchmen altogether, although in this case the objection may have been as much political as moral—to check the flow of money and trade to Spain.

The financial issue was one that grew more contentious still in the 18th century, which was a period of an open opulence on the part of the Spanish Church in general, and of the cathedral authorities at Santiago de Compostela in particular. Their shameless manifestations of wealth, much of it derived from the faked tax levied on the Spanish people, was totally out of harmony with the new intellectual voices in Europe, Voltaire's above all. Santiago flourished in pomp, but was weakened in piety. By the mid-19th century Richard Ford observed that the pilgrimage habit in Spain was dying a death: "The carcass remains," he wrote, "but the spirit is fled." In 1867 fewer than fifty pilgrims attended the ceremonies in honour of the apostle who had once drawn hundreds of thousands to Santiago in the course of a year. In the present century there has been a powerful reversal of the trend—statistically at least. During the holy year of 1965 two-and-a-half million people are reckoned to have visited the city—though I wonder how Richard Ford would have defined them. Marshal Pétain and Pope John XXIII (before his elevation to the Papacy) were among the pilgrims of recent times; General de Gaulle also visited the city. Certainly the journey today presents few of the problems Aymery Picaud was at pains to point out eight hundred years ago: pilgrimages can be booked as package holidays, and organised trips have been made by car, train, aeroplane, car, horse, mule, bicycle, motorcycle, in fact by just about every means of transport known to man save—to my knowledge—stilts and a one-wheeled cycle.

Surviving monuments offer a distorted view of any past culture, though not perhaps so distorted a view as surviving documents. The great majority of written material on the Santiago pilgrimage that has come down to us dates from the 17th century or later, by which time the pilgrimage itself had long been in decline, its character altered, and its vitality as a cultural and spiritual force quite expired. Of early monuments there exist far more, though, once again, there is nothing that could be called a balance. Churches tend to survive, as do castles and bridges; but what would one not give for a few more early accounts of the journey itself, a few more songs and stories recited on the way, or one or two complete inns and hospices where the pilgrims stayed.

Pons is the next town south from Saintes. Apart from being proud to call itself *Cité des Biscuits*, Pons possesses one of the rarities to be found on the pilgrim route, which is the remains of a former hospital established in the late Middle Ages for the benefit of pilgrims, and kept by mediaeval knights as a charity. The word hospital is used here in the sense of hospitality: the way-farer was unlikely to find any skilled medical attention at such a place, and hospice is a more accurate description. But what he did get was a free bed, or more likely a palliasse or a pile of straw, plus food and wine. The hospice at Pons is unique in France, and there is only one other I know of in Spain which is as old; that at Puente la Reina in Navarre. The last registration of a pilgrim here at Pons was in 1729, since when the building has been converted to domestic and warehouse purposes, but what does survive intact is its handsome entrance on one side of the old Bordeaux road (as always just outside the town walls), plus the entrance to the chapel facing it across the road, and more than twenty yards in length of stone arch which links the two and which gave pilgrims protection from the weather.

Here pilgrims sat, on the broad stone benches provided, wait-ing to be let in at nightfall or waiting to find the energy to move on next day; and evidently one or two waited so long that they died, for behind the stone benches are graves cut into the rock base of the hospice wall. The healthier ones whiled away the time scratch-ing travellers' signs on the walls, and these are still there: mostly inverted horseshoes with a cross within, though there are a few curious stylised human figures, some different kinds of crosses, at least one mason's mallet and, in one case, a heraldic crest. How strangely moving these are, though quite why we should be moved by a pilgrim's defacement of a building and not by "Norman Blont was here" (which I also noticed), I am not entirely sure. There survives so little on the pilgrim route which has the touch of life about it, which is first-hand, that even these little scratchings are reminders that the pilgrimage was about people, not monuments. Here, where the *vélos* and the delivery vans buzz past, was a place where they sat, a place where they doodled, a place where they died.

I drove from Pons in the evening, westward to the estuary of the Gironde: to Talmont. Here by the dead and empty mud-flats was the last of my churches of the Saintonge, high on a cliff-edge. I found a fossilised shell among the stones below, where the west wall had once fallen into the sea. Pilgrims came to Talmont who wanted to take the route down the coast to Bayonne and the Spanish border. They crossed over from this promontory to tackle the wastes of the Landes. It was the end of the first part of their journey: a point of achievement, and a point of departure. Upon the apse and upon the doors of Talmont were carved the same sermons that had kept them company all the way. The same grotesques grinned after them across the water as they skinned their eyes for a sight of the farther shore, and for the little town of Soulac where—very likely—they would meet up with a shipload of other pilgrims to Santiago who were perhaps at that very moment gulping their first Bordeaux wine and thanking their lucky stars that they had survived the stormy voyage across the Bay of Biscay from England.

CHAPTER IV

Pilgrims from England

With the murder of Archbishop Thomas à Becket in 1170, England had her own martyr to venerate, and English pilgrims their own pilgrimage, one that was considerably nearer home than Santiago de Compostela. It may seem surprising, then, that the road to Canterbury should not have ousted in popularity the road to Santiago; but it did not, popular though it was. To many English pilgrims Canterbury was perhaps a bit easy. A gentle stroll through the Garden of England in the spirit of Chaucer's pilgrims was not necessarily a substitute for the rigours of a journey to north-west Spain where Moors, wolves, wars, bandits, disease and discomfort offered a more torrid test of faith and determination: in fact King Henry II of England, hearing of Thomas's murder in Canterbury Cathedral, first vowed that he would himself go to Santiago as a penitent and even requested safe conduct from King Ferdinand II of León (one of the kingdoms of northern Spain) for that purpose. Subsequently Henry changed his mind, no doubt for reasons of state, and substituted his celebrated penance in Canterbury before the tomb of his archbishop, friend and chancellor.

Until the Reformation there continued to be regular pilgrimages from England to the tomb of St James. Indeed, it is interesting that one of the few references to St James which connects him in any way with Spain, before the discovery of the apostle's body early in the 9th century, was actually made by an Englishman, Adhelm, Abbot of Malmesbury, in a Latin poem written about the year 709, in which he makes it clear that James was responsible for bringing the gospel to the Iberian peninsula. At a time when almost none of the leading religious writers of the age thought fit to record any such information, this assertion by a relatively obscure Englishman is somewhat surprising and indicates, at least, that the cult of St James was early and deeply rooted in this country.

A piece of tangible evidence that this was so lies in the number of

English churches dedicated to St James. According to the church scholar, Francis Bond, there are known to have been at least four hundred and fourteen of these, of which the majority can be shown to have had some connection with the pilgrimage to Santiago. Considering that St James the Great is an apostle so scantily mentioned in the Bible as to be a virtual nonentity, over four hundred church dedications to him in one country is an extraordinarily high count. According to Bond's list St James was placed eighth in popularity after the Virgin (2335 churches), All Saints (1255), St Peter (1140) and Saints Michael, Andrew, John the Baptist and Nicholas; but he was well ahead of St Thomas of Canterbury (80), and leaving as mere also-rans such lesser *luminari* as St Werburga (12), St Pancras of Taormine (10), St Kew, St Gluvius, St Ive, St Teggvyddy and St Woolos (one church each).

The church of St James at Stoke Orchard in Gloucestershire, what is more, contains one of the earliest cycles of paintings on the life and legend of St James known anywhere, dating from the early 13th century. The paintings are contemporary, in other words, with the St James windows at Chartres and Bourges, though scarcely of the same quality. They are no masterpieces, and are in an atrocious state of decay. But the fact that these paintings existed, and that many other churches in England also contain fragments of painting depicting St James as a pilgrim, from a period only a little later than those at Stoke Orchard, further emphasises the existence of a flourishing cult during the early Middle Ages.

The Stoke Orchard paintings, only uncovered during the 1950s, were probably the gift of a wealthy local patron who, very likely, had himself been a pilgrim to Santiago; and to judge by the votive crosses scratched in the stone by the south entrance door the church became one of the regular halts for pilgrims making their way south to Bristol, the principal port from which pilgrims set sail for the Continent.

An infinitely finer church, which seems to have had a connection with the Santiago pilgrimage, lies a little farther west, at Kilpeck in Herefordshire. The exterior decorations on this gem of a Norman church so strongly echo the carvings on the churches of Saintonge and Poitou—with interlaced patterns round the windows, and apocalyptic beasts entwined among the pillars and arches around the door, or grimacing obscenely from the roof-line—that it is no surprise to read how the steward to one Hugh de Mortimer went on pilgrimage to Santiago in 1139 and on his return founded a number of churches in this area. Presumably he took with him a sculptor or draughtsman who recorded architectural details on the churches with which the steward was impressed on his journey, for there is no native precedent which could account for the carvings at Kilpeck. Equally surprising is the fact that they survived the stern eye and savage hand of the Protestants.

Yet another Norman church, at Fordington in Dorset, has a pediment depicting St James seemingly engaged in routing the Moors at the Battle of Clavijo, which may well be the earliest representation of the apostle to survive in England. Later representations of him are too numerous to list. In the chapel of Merton College, Oxford, he appears in pilgrim regalia on a memorial brass; and in the great church at Fairford in Gloucestershire he takes his place among the other apostles, again dressed as a pilgrim, in one of the late-mediaeval windows. A window in York Minster, depicting St James and St Catherine, we know to have been donated in 1381 by a certain Ines de Holme, in lieu of the expense of two pilgrimages to Santiago which he never made—a not untypical case at the time of a rich man buying himself out of a moral responsibility to the lasting benefit of us all.

For English pilgrims to Santiago the golden age, as in other countries, was the 12th century. Numerous conditions made this possible: the social stability brought about by feudalism, the consequent growth of Church authority backed by the new feudal lords, the spreading influence of the church of Cluny. Many factors that I have described elsewhere contributed to a Europe where it was possible for these pilgrimages to flourish: a Europe that was more secure, but, at the same time, a Europe made more aware, through the teachings of the Church, of a sense of sin. The Europe that emerged from the Dark Ages did not immediately shed its cloak of doubt. The foundations of the new Europe were laid upon the sombre fears of the old. If this had not been so, there would have been no massive response to the call for penitence and no widespread urge to set off on pilgrimages to distant and uncomfortable places. Only when this sense of moral urgency weakened did the habit of pilgrimage grow superficial or decadent, a change exemplified by the gentleman who balanced the cost of two journeys to

Santiago against that of a window in York and found the latter to
be more convenient. Clearly, such a man was no longer in danger
of possessing too strong a sense of sin.

A further aid to the Santiago pilgrimage was the tradition of sea-
traffic between the British Isles and north-west Spain. Long before
the city of Santiago existed, the Bay of Biscay had been sailed by the
Phoenicians and Carthaginians voyaging north, and by the Vikings
voyaging south. In spite of its dangers the Bay proved more a link
than a gulf between the Mediterranean countries and those in the
north; and many English pilgrims preferred to take advantage of
established sea routes direct to Galicia rather than undertake long
and hazardous land journeys from the Channel ports of Normandy
or from Bordeaux.

Unfortunately very few records of individual English pilgrimages
survive. The first, and scanty, record of an Englishman having
travelled as a pilgrim to Santiago is of a certain Ansgot, from Bur-
well in Lincolnshire, who donated churches, chapels and land after
his return, which must have been some time between 1093 and 1123.
At much the same time, a Richard Mauleveverer returned from
Santiago and made a similar donation in Yorkshire; and in 1102 a
pedlar who turned sailor, then merchant, then became a professional pilgrim and finally a hermit, Saint Godric of Finchale,
visited Santiago on his return from Jerusalem where he had been
known—according to a chronicle of the Crusades—as Godric the
English pirate. Saint, pilgrim, pirate, pedlar: such a man deserves
to have joined Chaucer's motley band in the Tabard Inn. For all one
knows, his example may even have given Chaucer a few insights
into the character and motivation of pilgrims.

In the 12th century this motivation seems to have been penitential, and genuinely so. Later, penitential pilgrimages came to be
imposed as well as voluntary: for instance, there is the case of
the parish priest near Chichester who would regularly fornicate,
repent, then fornicate again, until in 1283 the Archbishop of
Canterbury felt obliged to send him to Santiago as a penitent the
first year, to Rome the second and to Cologne the third. What is
not on record is whether the cure was successful, or whether he
thereafter weighted his repentance with the names of three foreign
cities in which he had also fornicated. Half a century later it is a
woman's misbehaviour we read of, that of a certain Mabel de

Boclande who was convicted of adultery and ordered to go to Santiago as an alternative to being beaten with rods six times round various churches. In the same year another lady, the god-mother of one John Mayde, was found guilty of sinning with her godson and she too was sent to Santiago. The Wife of Bath was certainly no prototype.

Once the pilgrimage came to be an imposed as well as a volun-tary penance, its character—and the character of those who under-took it—inevitably changed. There were not only those who undertook it as a form of punishment. There were others in the 13th century who were now making the journey in a spirit of official piety: these included clerics of all ranks, from the Arch-bishop of York in 1222 and the Bishop of Worcester in 1271, down to bright clerks ambitious of high rank, and innumerable parish priests who, by this time, were permitted to draw their full salary provided their pilgrimage did not exceed three years—a remark-ably generous leave of absence to get to Santiago and back again even on foot.

Pilgrims had, in fact, begun to enjoy privileges for going to Santiago. Documents issued by the Royal Chancellery agree to protect the property of a pilgrim during his absence, and doubtless it was this new form of royal protection which accounts for the large number of English gentry who began to make the journey.

Towards the end of the 14th century the pilgrimage became systematised still further. In addition to letters guaranteeing the protection of a pilgrim's property, the Royal Chancellery now issued letters to be presented to foreign rulers requesting that they would favour the English pilgrims who bore them. These letters were in effect forerunners of the modern passport, and there emerged a regular pattern—virtually a tourist trade—of pilgrims voyaging to Bordeaux or direct to north-west Spain, especially in Holy Years or Jubilee Years when St James's Day (25th July) fell upon a Sunday.

Ships' captains were issued with royal permits to carry a boatload of pilgrims rather than the normal cargo of freight, the earliest recorded licence of this kind being 1394, during a lull in the Hun-dred Years' War which had temporarily lessened the dangers of sea-travel and freed merchant ships from warlike obligations. The majority of these ships set out from ports in the West Country or from London. In 1428, the year Joan of Arc emerged to rally the dispirited forces of the King of France against the English, licences show us that 280 pilgrims sailed from London, 200 from Bristol, 122 from Weymouth, 90 from Dartmouth and so on. The greatest number of recorded licences for ships' captains and merchants was in 1434, a Holy Year, when some fifty ships sailed for Spain carrying 2310 pilgrims. By then, how many of these were penitents, and how many sight-seers? We have no means of knowing, but it would be consistent with the general decline, during the later Middle Ages, of the pilgrimage as a spiritual undertaking if one imagined the major-ity of those 2310 travellers to have been enterprising proto-tourists who combined the novel pleasures of foreign travel with an appro-priate genuflexion when required.

It is from the mid-15th century, during and after the culminating skirmishes of the Hundred Years' War, that we have two of the rare personal accounts by English pilgrims of their own journeys. The first, by a man who was born in France and died in England in 1446, is the account of Nompar de Caumont of his *voiatge a saint Jacques en compostelle*, and it is little more than a disappointing cata-logue of the stages of his journey. But the second, by a priest and Fellow of Eton College called William Wey, who made the pil-grimage from Plymouth in 1456, is more illuminating. The guide-book he compiled, called *Informacon for Pylgrymes*, contains plentiful observations and details concerning the Spanish kingdoms through which he passed; and in Corunna, where he stayed for three days before sailing home, he records how he heard an English friar preaching in the local Franciscan church, and that he counted no fewer than eighty foreign ships in the harbour, thirty-two of which were English. Another priest who was in Santiago during the same year as Wey was John Goodyear, Vicar of Chale in the Isle of Wight. Goodyear took with him an English wooden retable decor-ated with alabaster panels depicting the journey of St James's body to the Galician coast, and this retable is still preserved in the cathedral treasury at Santiago.

So much for private pilgrims, and the trade in conveying them to Spain. Little of this trade, however, would have existed at all if the Church in England had not already established strong links with those monastic orders on the Continent which sponsored the pil-grimage to Santiago, and, in particular, links with the Benedictine monastery of Cluny, the most powerful establishment of Church authority in Europe during the 11th and early 12th centuries, as we shall see. Cluny supplied monks to new monasteries and popes to the Vatican. Lewes Priory, founded in 1077, was colonised by monks from Cluny. So was Faversham, founded by King Stephen; and so was the great royal abbey at Reading, founded by Henry I, whose daughter Matilda became a pilgrim to Santiago and a fervent devotee of St James.

These new monasteries and abbeys in England formed highly effective outposts for the spread of the Santiago cult. Other religious orders besides the Benedictines formed similar connections in this country for similar recruiting purposes. The Augustinian monastery of Roncesvalles, at the gateway of Spain, kept a hospice in London near Charing Cross. Doubtless, would-be pilgrims were supplied with information and encouragement here, and equipped with a suitable list of hospices in France and Spain where they might find shelter on their journey. Charing Cross acted, among other things, as a kind of travel agency. This hospice was not actually founded until early in the 13th century, though the fact that Saxon coins dating from as early as the 10th century have been discovered at Roncesvalles may suggest that connections with England were already established long before that. John of Gaunt, Duke of Lancaster, became a patron of Charing Cross during the 14th century, and since he was also Chaucer's patron, the poet could have been paying a quiet compliment when he describes one of his pilgrims as "of Rouncivale", albeit a somewhat backhanded compliment in view of the character of the pilgrim—the Pardoner.

Little about Charing Cross today speaks of a spiritual connection with one of the great monastic foundations of Europe; yet, not far away, the court of Her Britannic Majesty is still officially entitled the Court of St James on account of a leper hospital that was consecrated to St James and formerly occupied the site of St James's Palace—a piece of esoteric information which I doubt if many foreign ambassadors know when they are received in full pomp and regalia by the monarch of England. These and most other links with the pilgrimage tradition in England were long ago severed in the orgy of Protestant destruction which smashed the English monasteries and scattered the ashes of St Thomas à Becket at Canterbury.

The Santiago cult in England was weightily patronised by royalty, and finally destroyed by royalty. Henry I founded the principal abbey devoted to the veneration of St James, at Reading, and Henry VIII annihilated it. One has to bear in mind that in the 12th century successive kings of England, unlike Henry VIII, were more Continental than they were English. They were Continental in language, in upbringing and frequently in their place of residence. Henry I was Norman, son of William the Conqueror; Stephen, next in succession, was Count of Boulogne; and Henry II, who succeeded Stephen, came from Anjou. Henry spent little of his life in England, spoke French, and by his marriage to Eleanor of Aquitaine came to rule over territories of which only a minor portion lay north of the English Channel.

The Continental character of English royalty was matched by England's leading churchmen. During the mid-12th century the Bishop of Winchester (England's capital city) and Abbot of Glastonbury (her richest abbey), was Henry of Blois, who was the younger brother of King Stephen and a former Cluniac monk.

It is scarcely surprising, then, that strong ties with the Church in France should have been established in England during the century when the pilgrimage to Santiago was at its zenith. Henry of Blois actually made the pilgrimage himself, as did Henry I's daughter Matilda, who married first the Emperor Henry V of Germany, and, when he died, married Geoffrey of Anjou, one of her sons by him later becoming Henry II of England.

It was Matilda who was instrumental in making Reading Abbey the centre of the Santiago cult in England. As the widow of the Holy Roman Emperor, when she visited Santiago de Compostela with a sumptuous retinue in about the year 1125, she was honoured with a gift of one of St James's hands. This she presented to her father, Henry I of England, who had founded Reading Abbey in 1121 and who now appointed the monks there to be custodians of England's most venerable relic. The abbey's coat of arms came to incorporate, against a blue ground, three golden scallop shells, symbol of St James and of the pilgrimage to his city.

The fact that Reading was situated on one of the main roads along which many pilgrims already passed on their way to the various sea-ports in the west of England must have contributed to the association of the new abbey with the Santiago pilgrimage.

Its founder had already been one of the major benefactors of the splendid abbey at Cluny; and when he conceived a plan to found his own abbey at Reading (partly as a royal memorial) it was to Cluny that Henry sent his request for monks who could be spared to build and establish it on the right lines. The abbot allotted him seven of his monks, as well as Peter, Prior of Cluny; and to this nucleus Henry added other monks from Lewes Priory, which had itself been colonised by monks from Cluny on its foundation half a century earlier and was the headquarters of the Cluniac Church in England. These were the monks who set about clearing the ground Henry had provided for his royal abbey, drawing up building plans, and obtaining the services of the best masons capable of constructing a church of vast dimensions, by English standards in those days. The abbey church had lateral aisles, two transepts, apsidal chapels and a generous ambulatory for pilgrims to circulate freely and view the relics that were to be placed by the High Altar on special occasions—all in characteristic Cluniac fashion.

Henry himself laid the foundation stone in the presence of many barons—including the man who was to be his successor to the throne of England, Stephen—and four years later he signed the abbey's foundation charter, probably at Rouen, where in 1135 he was to die (and where, eighty-one years later, King John was also to die, of a feast of lampreys). A letter survives, from Henry to the new abbot of Reading in the year of the abbey's foundation, which makes clear one of the principal functions of the royal abbey:

> Henry, King of England and Duke of Normandy, to the Abbot and Convent of Reading, greeting.
> Know ye that the glorious hand of the blessed James the Apostle, which Empress Matilda, my daughter, gave me on her return from Germany, I, at her request, send to you and grant for ever to the Church of Reading . . .

Henry intended that Reading Abbey should maintain as many as two hundred monks (though in effect it rarely exceeded half that number); and for the benefit of pilgrims it was to be equipped with a hospice which offered free food and lodging on a scale matching that of some of the great monastic foundations on the Continent. The leading English historian of the 12th century, William of Malmesbury, records that so lavish was the hospitality at Reading that guests and pilgrims regularly consumed more than the monks themselves.

There were inducements in plenty for pilgrims to visit Reading—besides the promise of food and drink. The holy relics which passed into the hands of the abbey must have made a formidable display when they were laid out round the High Altar on feast days. The conscientious pilgrim could worship, besides the celebrated hand of St James and the cloth it was wrapped in, such unexpected delights as the foreskin of Our Lord, which the Emperor Constantine had once owned (presumably brought back from the Holy Land by his indomitable mother Helena), a piece of Christ's shoe, blood from His side, some hair and garments of the Virgin Mary, the robe of Doubting Thomas, a tooth of St Luke, bits of Aaron's rod, a fragment of the rock which Moses struck, a collection of fingers of minor martyrs and two pieces of the Holy Cross. A venerable catalogue.

King John added further to the abbey's collection with a donation of the reputed head of the apostle Philip. He also promised to present enough gold to cover the abbey's principal treasure, the hand of St James, though the gold was never in fact delivered. King Henry III later made partial amends with a gift of the same quantity of silver. Altogether it is not surprising that Reading flourished. Patronised by successive monarchs, it grew in international esteem: in 1173 its abbot became Archbishop of Bordeaux, and in 1199 another abbot of Reading was appointed to no less a post than that of abbot of Cluny itself.

A certain decline in the importance of Reading Abbey may have been initiated by the decline of Cluny. Even so, Reading remained a bastion of monastic power in England throughout the later Middle Ages, and her last abbot was one of those unsung martyrs who, in 1539, chose to be executed by Henry VIII rather than surrender his abbey to the king. Reading Abbey was promptly destroyed, more thoroughly so than many other great abbeys and monasteries of England. It had been a royal foundation and accordingly earned a royal revenge. Much of the site is now a public park. Late in the 18th century part of it provided the site of Reading Gaol; and in the course of excavations workmen came across a mummified human hand (a left hand) concealed in the base of a wall. This was believed to be the very hand of St James which

Matilda had brought from Santiago de Compostela six hundred and fifty years earlier. Perhaps one of the last acts performed by the abbot before he was executed by Henry VIII had been to hide his abbey's most precious relic. The hand found its way to the Roman Catholic church of St Peter at Marlow-on-Thames, where it was preserved in the Sacristy and in whose humble custody, as far as I know, it remains to this day.

Maybe the hand with which Matilda returned from Santiago was not the hand of St James at all. Maybe it did not even belong to the body preserved in the cathedral at Santiago which, as we know, is most unlikely to be that of St James, in any case. Aymery Picaud, compiling his pilgrims' guide only a few decades after Matilda's pilgrimage, states categorically of the cathedral at Santiago that "the body of the apostle is here in its entirety [*corpus totum*]", though his source of information may of course have preceded Matilda's visit. In any case enough doubt surrounded the authenticity of the relic preserved at Marlow for at least one Catholic worthy to take himself to Santiago in order to find out. This was Father John Morris, SJ, who in 1882 published a report of his pilgrimage in which he satisfied himself that the left hand of the apostle's body was indeed missing. Noting that in the *Acts of the Apostles* (Chapter 12, Verse 2) it is stated that Herod "killed James the brother of John with the sword", Father Morris concluded that the hand at Marlow must have been struck off as the apostle raised it to protect his head from the Roman sword.

From Ansgot in the 11th century to Father John Morris in the 19th, English pilgrims to Santiago made the journey out of a variety of motives and were accorded a variety of receptions. No chapter on English pilgrims would be complete without a note on one of the least penitential pilgrimages ever made: that of John of Gaunt, Duke of Lancaster, in 1386. On the death of his first wife (whom, incidentally, he married in the abbey church at Reading), the Duke had, in 1372, married Constance, the daughter of Pedro of Castile; subsequently he cultivated a claim to the throne of Castile, a claim for which he managed to obtain the support of the Pope. Accordingly, under the lightest pretence of being a pilgrim, he landed at Corunna with a fleet of one hundred ships, gathered from every port in England between Bristol and Newcastle-upon-Tyne, and descended upon Santiago with a motley army which stupefied itself on Galician wine and created pandemonium throughout the region. In pursuit of his bid for the throne of Castile, the Duke did succeed in marrying off one of his two daughters to the King of Portugal and the other to the son and heir of Castile's ruler, but he and his unruly army also succeeded in arousing so many suspicions over Anglo-Saxon motives in coming to Santiago that for a period of time the city and Church authorities refused to allow any English pilgrims to visit the place at all. It was as though they saw in the ambitious Duke a dreadful augury of that ultimate slight to the sanctity of their beloved apostle's relics, the Reformation of the Church.

CHAPTER V

◆

Stepping-stones

Approaching Bordeaux, so the pilgrim was informed by his 12th-century mentor Aymery Picaud, he was now entering a region "where the wine is excellent, fish abundant, but the language crude".

Those who had continued directly south from Saintes through Pons, rather than heading west for Talmont and making the crossing of the Gironde to Soulac, soon found themselves with a detour of under a mile to reach the abbey of La Tenaille where they could be fortified by a sight of one of the nails from the Cross as well as of the pincers that were employed to pull it out.

I did not inquire whether these relics were still there. Since the abbey is now in ruins and, according to the *Guide Michelin*, partly transformed into a farm, I assumed that a nail—however holy—might have become a mere nail once more; so I decided not to deviate from my journey south, and passed instead through Mirambeau and shortly afterwards reached the estuary of the Gironde, upstream from Talmont, at Blaye. Here pilgrims in the Middle Ages would book a boat to Bordeaux some thirty miles further upstream. This saved them two broad river crossings between here and the city, as well as an unhealthy trek through the swamplands (some of which still remain between the petrol refineries and the vineyards north of Bordeaux) close to the confluence of the rivers Garonne and Dordogne.

But first there was a due pause at Blaye itself, a town of Roman origin whose connections with Rome survived in the figure of a 4th-century saint called simply St-Romain, and about whom I know nothing except that Picaud insisted that at Blaye, "one must ask for the protection of Saint Romain, patron of travellers". It was in the Augustinian abbey church dedicated to this Roman saint that pilgrims, already thinking about the crossing of the Pyrenees now not so far ahead of them, paid their respects to the body of Roland, Count of Brittany and favourite of Charlemagne, who had been killed in the famous ambush above Roncesvalles which pilgrims had been singing about in taverns and hospices all along the route. Here was a pilgrim's first real contact with the Charlemagne legend, a legend that Aymery Picaud and his Church worked so hard to attach to the cause of the Santiago pilgrimage, and which supplied that pilgrimage with just the popular romance it needed to rouse the imagination.

Another saint waited for the pilgrims at Bordeaux. This was St-Seurin (sometimes latinised as Severinus) who had been bishop here during the 5th century and was firmly on Picaud's list of accredited worthies to be venerated. The church bearing the saint's name stands today on the western edge of the city centre. In the Middle Ages there was also an important pilgrim hospice at Bordeaux, founded shortly after Picaud had gathered his material—at any rate, he makes no mention of it. This became known as the Hôpital St-James, in the English version of the name; indeed one of the donors to this hospital was King Henry II of England who also held the title of Duke of Guyenne, and was, of course, ruler of this area.

The Hôpital St-James at Bordeaux must have been among the earliest established for the benefit of pilgrims along the route to Santiago. We know that it received its gift of funds from Henry II in the year 1181. The provision of such institutions by charity was one of the results of a decree of the Lateran Council in Rome earlier that century, in 1123, which laid down that anyone convicted of robbing a pilgrim would be punished by excommunication. The pope in whose authority this decree was issued was none other than the pontiff whose name appears (fraudulently) as the author of the preface to Picaud's famous guidebook, Pope Calixtus II. It is clear that this decree authorised by Calixtus, which did so much to aid the pilgrimage to Santiago, must have been the reason for his name being associated with a document whose aim was blatantly to "sell" the pilgrimage.

In consequence of the Lateran Council's decree, charity hospitals —or hospices—sprung up along the pilgrim routes (I have already described the one still partially surviving at Pons, north of Bordeaux). These institutions protected the traveller from the notorious dishonesty of innkeepers, and supplied hospitality to the vast majority of pilgrims who were, by definition, poor. It was a period in which the concept of pilgrimage seems to have touched the conscience of the rich. (It also, as we shall see later, touched baser thoughts.) The foundation of hospices was not the undertaking of any one section of the ruling classes. Some, like the Hôpital St-James in Bordeaux, were patronised by princes and feudal nobles; others, like Pons, by one or other of the military orders such as the Hospitallers or the Templars; others again, like the celebrated hospices at Roncesvalles and Somport commanding the principal routes across the Pyrenees into Spain, by religious orders. The great Benedictine abbey of Cluny, which rose to a position of enormous power during the 11th and early 12th centuries, was responsible for founding a number of other hospices along the pilgrim routes. Then, in Spain particularly, there grew up a tradition of charitable services being supplied through the efforts of dedicated hermits, of whom the most celebrated was Santo Domingo de la Calzada who built the pilgrim hospice (now a plush government-owned hotel) in the town to the east of Burgos that took his name.

Many of these hospices were primitive enough, offering little more than a roof and bread and water. But some, to whom affluence had come through legacies and donations made to the order responsible for them, won a reputation for considerable generosity. Roncesvalles was one of these. Here the pilgrim who had just negotiated the climb up from St-Jean-Pied-de-Port would be offered an actual bed in a dormitory—male or female; he would have his feet washed for him on arrival; full meals would be offered during the period he was resting there (usually a maximum of two days), provisions supplied for the next part of his journey into Spain, and while he was staying at the hospice he could attend religious services organised by the monastery, be baptised if need be, listen to sermons, say confession, take communion and, should he succumb to all this, receive a decent burial.

Later in the Middle Ages many hospices were no longer attached to the great monasteries. Those that were not under the care of *commandéries* run by the military orders tended to be *aumôneries* under the control of the local authorities or perhaps the local lord. These were placed at the disposal of all travellers, not exclusively pilgrims, and were situated at the approach to towns outside the walls. The motives for supporting these places were by no means entirely charitable. Any stopping-place on one of the main pilgrim routes, or trade routes, soon found itself prospering like any tourist town today. Parthenay, near Poitiers, still preserves its street of well-to-do merchants' houses as proof of this. Charity had its commercial lining, but at least commerce saw to it that the rules of charity continued to be observed. There is one medical hospital I know of in France, at Cadillac-sur-Garonne to the south-east of Bordeaux, which was developed from a pilgrim hospice early in the 17th century and still keeps up the practice of reserving six beds for travellers who may be in need of them. The whole system was a form of public health service centuries before that term was coined.

From Bordeaux there was no way pilgrims could avoid the Landes. Neither was there for those who had landed at Soulac— either from England or across the Gironde estuary from Talmont— and were heading south along the coast towards Bayonne. Aymery Picaud is more than usually depressing about the Landes, as he does tend to be when describing places not in his native region, unless they happen to remind him of it. The Landes, he avows with some relish, is a desolate landscape where a man can find no comforts whatever: no bread, no wine, no meat, no fish, no water. There is only honey, millet and pigs. What is more, "if you should chance across the Landes in summer, take good care to protect your face against the gigantic flies which swarm everywhere, known as ox-flies; and if you do not pay attention to your feet, you will quickly plunge right up to your knees in sand-dunes which are pervasive in that area".

The Landes is not quite like that any more, though it is open to question as to whether it is any more hospitable. I rather like it: the emptiness and sometimes the desolation of it. The Landes began to be turned from a wasteland and a swamp into a vast national forest towards the end of the 18th century, and by the 1860s it must have looked very much as it does now. For two hours I drove through nothing but pine and oak forest made the denser by an undergrowth of tree-heather which in places rose as high as a bungalow. Every kilometre or so, the forest was broken by clearings in which stood painted wooden farms whose broad wings extended on either side to fuss over enormous broods of livestock. Here were the pigs that Picaud wrote of; geese too, hundreds of them fattened for their livers, geese reduced to swollen white sacks shuffling about on inadequate legs in cramped spaces and looking, I thought, rather like a congress of three-star chefs called by the editors of the *Guide Michelin*.

The main pilgrim route cut down the middle of the Landes: through Gradignan where the remains of the 13th-century priory of Gaillac flank the road out of Bordeaux, and a 15th-century statue of St James as a pilgrim decorates the church of St-Pierre. Then on through the forest, along what is now the main road to Bayonne and Biarritz, to Le Barp and Belin (where a tomb is said to have contained the bodies of many of Charlemagne's warriors slain at Roncesvalles, including Oliver); in mid-forest the modern highway breaks away from the pilgrim route which cut a little west to pass through Escource and then directly south to Lesperon, crossing back over the Bayonne road on its way to the River Adour, the southern boundary of the Landes, which it reached at the town of Dax.

Once across the Adour, the landscape changes abruptly: gentle hills and open farmland replace the forest plain. Suddenly the Pyrenees seem within reach. This is Gascony. Gritty names on the signposts read like a roll-call of detergents—Amou, Doazit, Momuy, Hinx, Vicq, Goos. We are in a curious borderland hard to label, historically English, agriculturally backward, politically non-conformist, linguistically half Basque and half Low Latin. The very word Gascony is an anglicisation of a French version of the Latin for Basque. No wonder Gascons find it hard to know who they are, harder still to cooperate with anyone who is not a Gascon and quite impossible with anyone who is. This is exemplified by their noblest product, Armagnac, at the ordinary three-star level as superior to average Cognac, in my view, as wholewheat bread is to white-sliced; but since cooperation is a word of no currency in Gascony the production of Armagnac tends to remain on a village level. One old still on wheels (or *alembic ambulant*, as it is charmingly called) made by the local boilermaker does a tour of duty round the district, and it is the manufacturer's wife who sticks the labels on the bottles. I hold the Gascons in the greatest affection for all the reasons above, though Aymery Picaud, needless to say, did not. He conceded that the bread was excellent and the red wine likewise, but he found the Gascons to be, at best, light-tongued gossips given to mockery, and, at worst, destitute and debauched gluttons who drank a great deal too much, all out of the same goblet, and who then dossed down on the floor, servants, master and mistress of the house all together. Not what he was accustomed to in Poitou.

From Dax to the Spanish border the pilgrim route ceases to follow any of the modern main roads for more than short distances; and for this reason it seemed an ideal stretch of the route to do on foot. Nothing is more tiring on the nerves and the feet, or more jading to the spirit, than to plod hour after hour along arterial highways with Citroëns brushing your elbow at eighty miles an hour and diesel fumes squirting in your nostrils; but there are few kindlier days I know than those spent strolling from village to village along country lanes and farm-tracks with the promise of a French menu and a litre of wine at the end of the day. I feel Picaud and I might at least have shaken hands on that.

At Peyrehorade on a tributary of the River Adour south of Dax I happily abandoned my car for a week, took out a rucksack and sandals and waited for Gillian who had parked the children in London and was to join me here for the next stretch of the journey. At dusk she duly got off the local bus in the town square and we spread out our maps like Churchill, and considered our strategy.

We rose and left the hotel even before the *croissants* were baked the next morning, and took the by-road which followed the river upstream along the north bank. Across the river the landscape grew lumpier and roads dipped out of sight between the hills so that the eye could no longer connect them up, as if a puzzle had been muddled up deliberately to lose the traveller his way. Behind rose a wall of white mountains. Spain! How many days away? Meanwhile this all seemed a deceptively easy practice, and a gentle hour along the river-bank brought us to the village of Sorde and to an inn facing the square where by now the *croissants* were baked and the morning sun had dispersed the goose-pimples. We sat outside and congratulated ourselves over bowls of coffee on having completed all of three miles. In a dark interior to our left smoked hams hung from the ceiling along with umbrellas.

Across the square was the huge chunk of abbey church which had made Sorde a key halt on the pilgrim route in the Middle Ages. The Benedictines had long since departed. Nobody was here now. The wind slapped a broken door to and fro, casting flakes of light into a cool nave. A few wicker chairs with dumpy legs. A stone font. Powdered masonry on the floor.

Out into the sun once again, we walked round the massive buttresses to the rear of the church where the sound of a weir led us down to an old paved ford across a side-stream, where yellow wagtails bobbed nervously among the tree-roots. Looking back, there was the old abbey pilgrims had once made for. A mere shell: one upper wall perforated to the sky, windows on the lower level a line of eye-sockets blind on to the river, weeping ivy.

Picaud reserves for Sorde one of his bitterest complaints of roguery by the native population towards the long-suffering pilgrim. Here, he says, the traveller is compelled to cross two rivers in quick succession—which is true. But though, as he points out, both rivers are narrow enough for a straightforward boat-crossing even with a horse—which Picaud clearly had—such is the wickedness of the local boatmen that (he implies) the crossing of the Red Sea by the tribes of Israel was child's play by comparison. There follows a careful account of how the boatmen insist on payment first; the pilgrim then being led to a vessel so narrow—carved out of a single tree-trunk—that it can scarcely support the horse, with its rider hopefully clutching the bridle alongside and trying not to tumble in. Should this happen, however—as is frequently the case since the boats are invariably overloaded deliberately in order to capsize them—the pilgrim may, if he is fortunate, escape death by drowning, though, should he drown, he is then gleefully robbed by the boatman, and the object of the whole exercise is achieved.

Perhaps, travellers still intent on persevering to Santiago, after Picaud's account of the horrors of the Landes and the debaucheries of the Gascons, might by this stage have grown hardened to this Cassandra, even to the point of taking some delight in his dark prophecies during their long trudge through the day. If so, they must by now have been looking forward eagerly to what was to come: for, having survived their river-crossing at Sorde, they were now about to enter "a country whose language is barbarous, land wooded, hilly, poor in its bread, wine and all kinds of foodstuffs". This was the Basque Country. Gillian and I had also brought our own reading, Richard Ford, that early-Victorian savant who gave away nothing to Picaud in his opinion of the people whom we were about to encounter for the first time.

"The Basques," writes Ford, and I pictured him adjusting his pince-nez as he prepared to quill this sentence, "have a language of their own, which few but themselves can understand; nor is it worth the trouble of learning, as it is without a written literature, while the conversation of the natives is scarcely of that high intellectual quality which repairs the study." (Exit the Basques doffing sweaty nightcaps) Ford swears, of their speech, that when they write Solomon they pronounce it Nebuchadnezzar; and that the Devil, in order to prepare for winning the Basques to his side, studied their language for seven long years and succeeded in learning three words. It seemed to Gillian and me that with such credentials the Basques must be well worth knowing.

From Sorde the pilgrim could take one of two routes south into the Basque Country: either back in a westerly direction to the abbey of Arthous and then by the Roman road to Bidache and on to Garris; alternatively, he could follow the river upstream and turn towards the hills through what is now Labastide-Villefranche, and continue by another road which brought him to Garris from the north-east. As there is no longer a way over the water at Sorde itself—not even one likely to sink you—we continued along the river and took the second route and, for all the forewarnings of Aymery Picaud and Richard Ford, walked into the Basque Country without knowing it, for breakfast.

This was our second day on foot. Feet and muscles had given out the previous afternoon, and we had sat and nursed blisters by a river greenish with snow-water, before hobbling into a plastic road-house in the village of Escos. Certain that the *croissants* would be as nasty as the dinner, we departed shortly after dawn, this time straight for those snow mountains which had been over our right shoulder all the previous day. There were too many aches for us to talk much, and we walked gingerly along dense verges for a couple of hours until roused from introspection by a cluster of white half-timbered farms whose wooden doors and shutters were brightly carved and painted a ubiquitous blood-red. In the midst of them stood a concrete quadrangle with a high wall at the end. I had never seen a pelota court before. It dawned on us that we had crossed some kind of frontier. There was a single café hidden behind a jungle of creeper, and inside, in the half-dark, six men in broad black berets talked at each other through the tobacco-smoke in a hard crackly language. The men dispersed as we came in and an old lady turned to greet us and bring over a tin pot of coffee that had been standing on an iron stove. This was Gabat.

It was Sunday. As we continued towards Garris, refreshed, rose-petals were being strewn across the road in readiness for a procession. People smiled and talked, which I do not think they would have done had we got out of a car to look. I became aware of how walking makes the world you pass through human in scale. In a car you are always a foreigner, on foot a visitor. There were wild strawberries by the roadside, and tiny sharp cherries. An iridescent beetle checked in the road before our feet. Blue columbines speckled the ripening hay. A kite flopped scraggily between the trees. Then a rash of new houses, with gardens inspired by Jacques Tati, appeared along one side of the road, their ironwork gates wrought with what looked like painted spaghetti; and Gillian remarked, a little sourly, I felt, considering the beauty of the morning, that the more twee the house the more Basque the name on the door. She was right: nothing could have been more Basque than the name of this village: Amendeuix-Oneix.

The next place was Garris, where the more westerly road up from the river valley joined the one we had taken. Garris is fairly typical of Basque villages, with large white houses scattered loosely up a single main street, their timbers all painted the same rather sickly red, and the spaces in between the timbers sometimes filled in with a zig-zag pattern of tiles laid flat. The older houses carry elegant stone buttresses rounded off at the base, and many of them have broad, rickety wooden balconies cut into fretwork patterns and painted the same blood-red as the other timbers. Houses in the Basque Country are rarely anonymous: most of the lintels, whether stone, or occasionally wood, bear carved inscriptions stating who built them and when, and sometimes why. We came across one particularly handsome house on the outskirts of the village which was built in 1654 by a man who, so the inscription suggested, was himself a pilgrim. It is now locally known as the Pellegrinia. The regional expert on pilgrim routes in the Basque Country, Dr Clément Urrutibéhéty of Saint-Palais, later suggested to me that it had almost certainly been a pilgrim hospice, pointing out that it was on the edge of the village, as you would expect, and stood opposite a rectangular walled area which, in his opinion, was the site of a small priory or convent associated with the hospice.

Saint-Palais was only a mile and a half farther on, and we stopped to buy a picnic lunch there and, as it turned out, to watch our first pelota match. This was a championship game between the local team and Pau which by the purest luck happened to be starting at midday, in about five minutes' time, on the town *fronton*, which is the name given to a pelota court. The flags were up, figures in cricket-whites and belt sashes were already practising against the concrete wall at either end of the *fronton*, while along the near side knots of spectators in Sunday suits and black pancake berets were puffing at yellow Gitanes and stretching their legs in the interval thoughtfully provided between Mass and the match.

There are numerous kinds of pelota (the word simply means ball) as I discovered later, the original version being the one played with the bare hand against an end-wall and side-walls, in exactly the manner of fives only without gloves. Anyone who has played fives, as I was once compelled to, will acknowledge that it is excruciatingly painful *with* gloves, which hardens my respect for Basque priests who are by repute the champions and patrons of the gloveless form of the game, in the French and Spanish villages where the local *fronton* is invariably right next to the church and often shares a wall with it. One painting in the Basque Museum at Bayonne shows the game being played actually inside the church.

Other forms of pelota are played with the aid of various styles of bat to make the game even faster, or of a long curved basket which is the extension of a glove worn on the hand and which enables a player to flick the hard ball at quite terrifying speeds, said to be as much as a hundred and fifty miles per hour. (In the United States I gather the game is called Jai-Alai which is supposed to be Basque for "merry festival" though it sounds more like the yell of an opponent struck by a pelota missile at a hundred and fifty miles an hour.)

The match we were watching in Saint-Palais was a version played between two teams and two facing walls a couple of hundred yards apart, and I do not believe I have ever been held so spell-bound by any ball-game, nor can I think of any game I have watched which is so elegant. The ball was served against the "home" wall, then scooped with the hand-held basket down to the far wall, either like a bullet at head-height, or in a lofty parabola high above the flanking plane-trees towards the circling buzzards, to drop into the

opposing court somewhere near the base of the rear wall, then to
be flicked back again to and fro in the same fashion, a rapid cross-
fire alternating with aerial mortar attacks, until one of the players in
mid-court would intercept the ball and make a kill. Gillian, whose
feet had given out, and who was now seated on one of the concrete
benches among the ranks of black berets, turned to her neighbour
and asked if he could please explain to her something of the rules of
the game. The bristly face turned slowly to her with the look of a
cricket fan asked by an American tourist to tell all, and ever so
gently he said *"Non!"* and turned back to the game. The rites
continued. From time to time one of the mortar-shells veered
towards the terraces, dispersing the berets, while all the time the
scorer over on the far side continued to chant the state of the game
in a high-pitched plain-song—in Basque.

In time we departed with our rucksacks and our picnic lunch, and
found the pilgrim path again, following it out of the afternoon sun
into a dank forest where we sat and ate our cheese and fruit and
listened to the woodwind chortle of a golden oriole among the
poplars.

Dr Urrutibéhéty—who could be nothing other than Basque
with a name like that—has a general medical practice in Saint-
Palais, but has devoted much of his spare time over many years to
scrupulous historical work on the old roads and boundaries of his
region, and today is as professional an archivist as he is a doctor.
Much of our present knowledge of the exact routes taken by
mediaeval travellers is the result of his researches. Saint-Palais is
only a few miles from where the route I had been taking from Paris
converges with two of the three other main pilgrim routes heading
for Santiago—those from Vézelay in Burgundy and Le Puy in the
Auvergne. Dr Urrutibéhéty has demonstrated that the cross-roads
where these three routes join lies on the southern side of a prominent hill immediately to the south of St-Palais, called Mont-St-
Sauveur. On his initiative there is now a modern *stèle* at this point,
surmounted by an ancient carved gravestone; and standing at this
point, behind a farm just off a by-road, Gillian and I could see
perfectly clearly the three old tracks pushing their way here between
deep hedges, joined by a lane which ran down from the top of the
hill itself (whose name St-Sauveur suggests there must have been
a chapel up there), and then becoming a single broad track striking

between the fields below and scrambling up the shale over the hill beyond in the direction of the Pyrenees. This cross-roads goes by the perplexing local name of—Gibraltar. There is in fact no connection with Britain's colonial rock, the name being the French version of a sequence of Basque corruptions of the word St-Sauveur, the etymology of which I have no intention of trying to explain further, though Dr Urrutibéhéty has spelt it out to me in scrupulous detail.

It was an inviting road up over the hill. We took it that hot early summer afternoon in peace of mind and innocent confidence that it would continue through the Middle Ages as far at least as the village of Ostabat, which was the first pilgrim halt after the joining of the ways, and which in mediaeval times boasted some twenty hospices to cope with all those travellers from England and northern France, Paris and Poitou, Burgundy and the Auvergne, besides all those who had come from even further afield—the Low Countries, Germany, Switzerland and eastern Europe. Poland alone has more than a hundred churches dedicated to the cult of St James, so all in all there must have been a vast motley of pilgrims seeking a roof and a bed of straw at Ostabat.

But what folly. Ostabat, once a place of rest for the greatest number of pilgrims in France, today offers nowhere to stay at all; and the road to it, after luring us too far along it to retreat anywhere else before nightfall, expires in a barbed-wire fence and a mountainside of deep gorse.

We had been walking on and off since six that morning. By four in the afternoon our legs looked as though they had stood in for St Sebastian. I was practising swearing in Basque. Gillian was ominously silent. My sense of direction had given out with my sense of humour.

Somewhere in this malevolent jungle appeared a man leading a pig—perhaps he was St Anthony—who gazed at us in some surprise. Ostabat, I inquired? He flapped a bronzed hand towards another venomous-looking hillside beyond, and grunted on with his pig. I would like to have kicked its arse and his. The sun got lower. We were rather beyond tiredness, but slithered up what could have been a path and came at length—at great length—to a bare, scabby hillside where the track no sooner proved that it was a track than it burst like some tracer-shell into a dozen other tracks heading in every possible direction, including the one we had come from. I selected one by the angle of the fast-disappearing sun, and by some overdue intervention of Providence we found ourselves shortly on the southern crest of the same scabby hill and in the distance a village that we insisted must be Ostabat since if it were not there was no other visible human habitation within the entire landscape now lying before us.

It *was* Ostabat, and a kindly café-owner, seeing our condition, requested his son to drive us to the nearest hotel a few kilometres on, at Larceveau. It was seven o'clock. We had done, I reckoned, forty-one kilometres since the morning, much of which might have been easier with wire-cutters. If mortification of the flesh is a passport to heaven, I muttered to Gillian over a double pastis, then we have just bought ourselves a first-class ticket in the front row.

Sunday evening. There was great singing in Larceveau that night: a first-communion party. I had never heard Basque singing before. It began casually with a group of men gathered at the bar while we were sitting down to dinner: the talk in Basque, full of Tchot-Chok-Choka noises, broke into folk-music—burst into would be a better way of describing those soaring, energetic songs that moved at terrific pace and volume, each man with his red wine taking up a well-practised part in the harmonies and trying to crack the roof with the crescendos before refuelling from the bottle in front of him. They had been singing all their lives—singing to drink and drinking to sing—and soon it became evident just how early in life it did all begin.

The women and children, in a froth of white, filed in and the singers at the bar joined them at a long dinner-table for thirty people, the men at one end, the children at the other, the women in the middle. The serious drinking then began among the men, the serious eating among the children, while the women prepared to take up their rôle as disapproving umpires. The singing broke out in even louder chorus as the landlord laid out a forest of wine-bottles on the table. Their contents poured out in perspiration all over them. Black Sunday jackets were peeled off, then ties, cuffs unbuttoned, belts loosened, tongues too. The women began to look uncomfortable; the children sniggered and nudged each other behind glasses of grenadine. The singing rose in volume, and clearly lowered in tone, song by song. Every so often the men would disappear for a fart and a pee, leaving the children flushed with delight and their mothers grey with sobriety, their heads lowered on to their Lancashire prints in attitudes of resigned horror, past even pretending they did not understand. We sadly did not.

The landlord went on serving as passively as he might in a Trappist refectory, while the children gobbled and giggled and threw bread for which they were desultorily smacked. Their evening which had begun with an introduction to the ways of God concluded with an introduction to the ways of the Basques.

The next morning we returned to Ostabat after a breakfast taken amid the rubble of the communion party. 18th- and 19th-century houses made up most of this village, handsome and four-square with the usual richly carved balconies and engraved stone lintels. A few older houses had the same curved buttresses we had noticed in Garris, and in several of the gardens between the houses the stumps of more ancient walls protruded among the potatoes and the lettuces. The pilgrim road approached the village from below, over a little ford. There were signs that this road must have been paved, though most of what paving may remain was buried, when we were there, under layers of chicken-muck and mire. A line of rickety farm-buildings was the site of many of the hospices kept for the pilgrims, and one of these was still standing in a semi-ruined state, its balcony frail as match-wood, its interior a home for hens and a battered tractor. The date on the lintel read 1829, but this must certainly be a later addition. White violets were peeping from cracks in the wall. A chorus of farm-dogs followed us up the street at snarling distance. Villages do not come any sleepier now than Ostabat.

Aymery Picaud points out that Ostabat had a reputation for harbouring fraudulent toll-gatherers, worthy—he insists—of being sent to the Devil. Taxes were sometimes doubled for the unknowing pilgrim although, as he makes clear, they were by law exempt from taxes and tolls of any kind. All this roguery only interrupts the passage of the good pilgrim, he goes on huffily, and if he had his way those who practised it would be punished by excommunication. But what else could you expect from the Basques? Now, a good Poitevin . . .

In the chestnut woods of the Bois d'Ostabat is a village of four

houses and a chapel. It is called Harambels, and it was built in the
10th and early 11th centuries as a *Communauté hôpitalière*. The men
who founded it were lay friars who brought with them their four
families to this wooded valley within a few miles of the junction of
three main pilgrim routes. Their Chapelle St-Nicolas is today among
the oldest pilgrim churches in western Europe: it is recorded in
documents as early as 1039, and, a century later, Picaud mentions
it in the *Codex Calixtinus*. The four original families had the names
Salla, Borda, Etcheto and Etcheverry. Gillian and I walked into
Harambels, past the chapel, and found four (admittedly rebuilt)
family houses and that was all: and those houses belonged to the
families Salla, Borda, Etcheto and Etcheverry. Here was a con-
tinuity of almost one thousand years.

The key to the chapel was kept by Mme Etcheverry who explained that she was not herself from Harambels but a foreigner
from Juxue, all of three miles away across the main road. It was her
husband who was the local, indeed the only one left, she explained,
now that the other three owners had moved elsewhere and let their
houses, or only used them occasionally.

The porch of the ancient chapel was built like a barn. A massive
semi-circular flight of steps led up to the west door. A carved
Chrism dominated the lintel, its Greek letters arranged in a circle
forming the word *Christos*. To one side of the door it was just
possible to pick out an engraving of two fishes arranged in the
shape of a cross. Mme Etcheverry worked the old iron key in the
door as if unlocking the combination of a safe, click by click, and
as the door at length swung open we seemed to be stepping into
some dusty jewel-chest. The walls and vaults were entirely panelled
and painted. There were streaky patterns, and coloured borders that
concealed secret doors and cupboards; and stiffly-painted figures of
saints who included the apostles and a pilgrim; while behind the altar
(used for services once a month) rose an amazing wooden retable
in old weathered shades of gilt, red and yellow that had been made
in the village at various times between the 14th and 16th centuries;
and to the right of the retable a 15th-century carving of St James,
also gilt.

We stayed in the cool of the chapel for a while, as Mme Etcheverry stood buttoned-up and silent at the rear; then she locked up
her jewel-box behind us as we stepped into the sunlight. The three-

Moissac: a detail of the carving of the prophet Jeremiah, one of the finest examples of mediaeval carving in Europe (12th century)

A roadside cross in the Basque Country

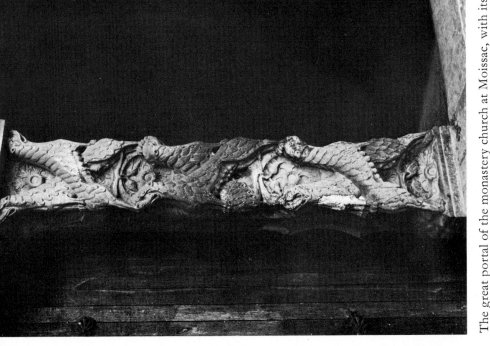

The great portal of the monastery church at Moissac, with its central column of 6 rampant lions supporting the tympanum

The great south door of the pilgrim church at Aulnay: the carvings represent scenes from the Revelation of St John the Divine

(*Above*) Aulnay, south door: detail from the frieze depicting hellish beasts

(*Left*) A masterpiece of carving on the village church at Chadenac in the Saintonge region: an allegory of Virtue and Vice

Aulnay, south door: details from a frieze of the old men of the Apocalypse, carrying vials and musical instruments

(*Above*) Detail from the exquisitely carved apse of the village church at Rioux: one of the numerous carved churches of the Saintonge region

(*Left*) Travellers' signs carved by pilgrims outside the pilgrim hospice at Pons

(*Above*) The tiny chapel of Harambels in the Basque Country—begun nearly a thousand years ago by four families of lay brothers whose successors still own and administer it, the chapel lies about a mile after three of the four main pilgrim roads meet

(*Right*) The fourth pilgrim road comes in to join the others in the Basque Country near St-Palais, crossing ancient stepping-stones, the Gué de Quinquil, over the River Bidouze

The Augustinian abbey of Roncesvalles, one of the most famous establishments along the road to Santiago, doubly appealing to pilgrims because of the associations with Charlemagne

The octagonal hermitage chapel of Eunate, just south of the Pyrenees, on the pilgrim road from Arles

pronged belfry, symbol of the Trinity, rose high above the plain tiled roof, casting streaks of shadow across a tiny graveyard where the four families of Harambels had been buried for a millennium. A pair of buzzards spiralled on the air currents above the chestnut trees, and we made our way back along a stream choked with undergrowth to the main road and the River Bidouze. Between here and Saint-Palais the road crosses and re-crosses the Bidouze, and a short distance beyond the second bridge, with Mont-St-Sauveur rising high on our left, we could see where the third pilgrim route—the one from Le Puy—came up from the river below us on its way round the flank of the mountain to join the other two at the Gibraltar cross-roads. Taking the old track into the dank undergrowth we could pick out the sheen of the river flowing fast between islands dense with alders, and suddenly before us lay a line of boulders that had been sawn into massive cubes and placed across the torrent with about a yard between each. Remnants of a stone wall were lodged among tree-roots where the boulders reached the near bank. The stepping-stones themselves had scarcely budged in a thousand years—two thousand years? Who knows how long ago this path was laid across the fast river? Here at any rate was the pilgrim way, intact. A dipper balanced on the edge of one of the stones, its white chest an inch or two above the current, before skimming up-river into the shadow of the overhanging trees.

It was an early afternoon for siestas, and mentally I took one as we doubled back past the turnings to Harambels and Ostabat on the road towards St-Jean-Pied-de-Port at the foot of the Pyrenees. The backdrop of white mountains had drawn closer until now it lowered behind the foothills out of sight. Steadily the mountains were closing around us, the woods too: white wild roses were draped in thin skeins over oak-trees. The summer quiet was warmed by bees and crickets in the hay-fields, by sheep-bells on the hills beyond. Every so often a belting Renault savaged the silence. On the right a stone cross marked the place where the pilgrim road from Ostabat came in from the west and crossed over the modern road. A primitive-looking crucifixion was carved in the stone, the face of Christ wearing an expression of mild surprise.

Whenever I am among mountains I have a longing to climb them: so, rather than continue straight to St-Jean, with a choice of either going on into Spain or of staying and kicking our heels for a day or two before it was time for Gillian to return home, we decided to cut left at St-Jean-le-Vieux and make for a village under the barrier of the high Pyrenees. Here, so our hotel proprietor at Larceveau had assured us, was an inn where you could get fresh river trout. The place was Estérençuby, which means village without a bridge, though it now has several. The road climbed imperceptibly, though what one notices on foot is that the hedgerows alter, and it is they that register the changes in altitude, in climate and in season. Here there were walnut-trees and pale pink mallows; the hayfields were greener; even the butterflies grew smaller and brighter. Huge honey-coloured cows with spreading horns chewed at us with aristocratic faces.

By evening the road duly brought us to the Hotel Etchegoyen, which was entirely empty like most French hotels except for two months a year, and where a diminutive Mme Etchegoyen welcomed us in French and then in Basque and showed us to a large balconied room overlooking green carpeted hills and rushing water. There below were the trout all right. She also showed us the bath which, to our delight, was stoppered with a wine-cork, though one stepped out from it on to a Turkish carpet.

We stayed three nights in Estérençuby, spending the days in the mountains, getting comprehensively lost now and again thanks to the mists which appeared with the suddenness of stage battle-smoke puffed in from the wings, and thanks equally to our military survey map which provided the illusion of accuracy by marking apparently every sheep-pen and goat-track but actually it only marked every other one, several of which had quite vanished from sight. The only living soul we met to ask the way one entire day turned out to be a Basque deaf-mute. The conspiracy seemed total. But the trout did not let us down, and the wine which fizzed lightly as Mme Etchegoyen banged it on the table with the paper table-cloth and the basket of bread completed a respite from what I was by now feeling had been too many consecutive days spent in the tracks of the Middle Ages.

The morning we left, Gillian said she awoke wondering why people were thumping dustbin lids. It was only the church bell. After breakfast I took a look at the village churchyard and in fascination scribbled down some of the family names on the grave-stones. The list read like this: Chuchpereneko, Kurutchetako,

Ahetzetcheverry, Intzaiko, Inchauspe, Ttipulainia, Erramunttoin-eko, Olloroteneko, Mendiburuko, Curutchet, Bidainberria . . . and so on. If I had seen Chimborazo, Cotopaxi and Popocatepetl there too I should not have felt surprised. Under the circumstances I concluded that the Devil, who had spent seven years studying Basque and learnt a mere three words, had done rather well.

St-Jean-Pied-de-Port means St John at the foot of the pass, and the pass is Roncesvalles. The main pilgrim route from here was not the present main road into Spain but a way over the higher mountains a little to the east, climbing up either from St-Jean or from St-Michel (for those who had by-passed St-Jean) to the Col de Cize, rejoining the valley road at Ibañeta, less than a mile before Roncesvalles itself. Charlemagne had used the valley road on his return from Spain in 778, and according to the *Chanson de Roland* it was at St-Jean-Pied-de-Port that he laid out the bodies of his warriors killed in the famous Basque ambush on his rearguard.

St-Jean is a town with a great deal of make-up and not much face. It is pretty. You can take good photographs of it, and it looks as though it might have been built for that purpose. There is, how-ever, a handsome pilgrims' street which descends from the old Porte St-Jacques where pilgrims entered the town walls from the north, and where they would have been welcomed by the prospect of two arrow-slits pointed directly at them, perhaps in precaution against another pilgrim calling himself the Count of Lesser Egypt. At the far end of the street a single-span mediaeval bridge took them over the same river that had provided us with trout up at Estérençuby, and out by the southern gate of the town. Tradition-ally they now bore palm-branches tied into the form of a cross, and these they would carry with them across the mountains, to plant in the ground at the top of the pass above Roncesvalles where legend had it that Charlemagne himself had planted a cross and knelt, not eastwards towards Jerusalem, but westwards towards the yet-undis-covered tomb of St James.

Gillian had to return to Bordeaux and London that afternoon. I was to return to collect my car where I had abandoned it at Peyre-horade the previous weekend. We had walked, searched and rested enough. Now we had a final French lunch that blurred into the afternoon; after which we climbed up to the Citadel and went to sleep under the lime-trees. I awoke to notice three vultures circling overhead. The three became five, then eleven and then twenty. I got up not unhastily, and within minutes all of them had moved away across the hills as silently as they had appeared. Having denied them their meat, I began to find it reassuring that there were still vultures at large in Europe.

CHAPTER VI

———◆———

The Politics of Salvation

The pilgrimage to Santiago was a vehicle for many interests. How many of those interests could be described as pious is a matter of interpretation. At least they were for the most part vested in the revival and strengthening of Christendom after the ravages of the Dark Ages, and in particular they were vested in the ambitions of the Church in France.

It was through France that the four main pilgrim routes passed on the way to Spain (though in origin these were not pilgrim routes at all but the four roads to the Pyrenees recommended to Roman travellers in at least two writings of the later Roman period, known as the *Antonine Itinerary* and the *Peutinger Tables*); and it was from France that political and military aid advanced into northern Spain to safeguard the route from the Pyrenees to Santiago de Compostela itself. Aid to the Santiago pilgrimage, and to the Spanish kingdoms harassed by the Moors, was synonymous. By protecting pilgrims along the length of their route the French Church automatically extended its influence across the Pyrenees; while the Frankish knights and feudal barons who went to fight there in the name of that Church established family links with the Spanish rulers which were to strengthen still further the voice of the French Church in Spain. And during the period when the Santiago pilgrimage was at its height, far and away the strongest arm of the Church in France was the Benedictine monastery of Cluny. It was the abbots of Cluny, supported by the Papacy, who made the decision to come to the aid of the Christian kingdoms in northern Spain fighting the Moors, and who promoted or at least approved the sending of no fewer than twenty military expeditions into the Iberian peninsula between the years 1017 and 1120.

Hence it was in the interests of the Spanish rulers to become patrons of Cluny. The first to do so was King Sancho III ("the Great") of Navarre, early in the 11th century. Navarre, with its capital Pamplona, was only just across the Pyrenees by the Pass of Roncesvalles, and easily accessible from France. The brilliant Saracen war-lord Al-Mansur had died in 1002, and with his death the grip of the Moors on Spain was weakened. Sancho III was concerned to take full advantage of this change in the balance of power. Cluniac monks were invited into Spain, and Cluny in return received and trained Spanish monks. Paternus was one who returned to Spain after a period at Cluny to become abbot of the important monastery of San Juan de la Peña, near Jaca.

Sancho's three sons, who became the kings of Navarre, Aragon and Castile respectively, each maintained these connections with the monastery of Cluny; and as the century progressed and the pilgrimage mounted in importance, so the Cluniac influence in northern Spain grew more pronounced. Under the powerful monarch, King Alfonso VI, Cluny was encouraged to build, or to assume authority over, a number of monasteries along the Spanish route in order to provide charity and protection for these pilgrims. An indication of what Alfonso felt about the value of this French participation in Spain's affairs was his very considerable gift of money to Cluny following the conquest of the Spanish capital of Toledo from the Moors in 1085.

Cluny, for its part, increased in wealth in proportion to its influence. Three years after Alfonso's gift of thanksgiving the monks at Cluny began the task of erecting a new abbey church on a scale befitting the seat of a vast political and spiritual empire. Pilgrims themselves may have been in general poor, but there was no lack of wealthy patrons of the pilgrimage movement. There was also a quantity of small donations which helped to swell the funds of the monasteries. These were far from negligible. The ambitious new buildings which Abbot Suger added to another famous abbey, St-Denis near Paris, in the middle of the 12th century were financed by pilgrims' offerings to the extent of two-thirds of the total cost.

As for Cluny, it received funds from numerous sources besides grateful Spanish monarchs; not least from the considerable areas of land it owned, as well as from those monasteries which became subservient to Cluny, and which were multiplying in number throughout the 11th century. There were private gifts too, made by French knights returning from the wars in Spain, who saw to it that they brought back adequate spoil for their pains. All these sources of donations added to Cluny's stock and power. Nine years after Alfonso's own lavish gift of funds, Santiago itself had a Cluniac bishop, Dalmatius, who held the position for sixteen years, to be succeeded by the most dynamic and ambitious of all Santiago's bishops, Diego Gelmirez, who held the see for a further thirty-nine years, during the latter years as the city's first archbishop.

It is a point of dispute just how far Cluny may be said to have organised the pilgrimage to Santiago de Compostela. That Cluny was enthusiastic about the pilgrim movement, and about the cult of St James, is well known. That a number of key monasteries along or near the route ultimately accepted the Cluniac reform and Cluniac authority is also beyond question. But it is easy to over-estimate the numbers of French monks from Cluny who actually worked in Spain in the 11th and 12th centuries. It may well be that Cluny's primary activity was to service the pilgrim route rather than actually organise it, by making monasteries and hospices available to pilgrims, and by using its political influence to see that tolls and other nuisances were removed from their path.

Today it is hard to appreciate just how central was the rôle of the great monasteries in European life during the later Middle Ages. St Hugh, who was abbot of Cluny for sixty years from the year 1049, exercised a power and influence in some ways comparable with that of a president of the United States in our own times; and the positions occupied in the 12th century by St Bernard, founder of the Cistercian Order, and Abbot Suger of St-Denis, were scarcely less important. Politically, spiritually and culturally, the great monasteries held a key to the shaping of Europe. They acted as universities, as patrons of art and architecture, founders of social services, centres of capital wealth as well as of vast political influence on an international scale.

The ideal of monastic life originated in the East, probably in Buddhist India and certainly before the time of Christ. In the early Christian period it was adopted in the Middle East by the Copts, and later in Europe during the decline of the Roman Empire and the lawlessness of the Dark Ages. The most important single figure in the establishment of monasticism in Europe was the Italian St Benedict who died in AD 543 and who was responsible for founding the monastery of Monte Cassino in Southern Italy. Other monasteries, following the Rule of St Benedict, began springing up in Italy soon after the saint's death, and within half a century the monastic movement had spread to other parts of Europe, supported by the initiative of Pope Gregory the Great who was himself a fervent admirer of St Benedict.

The monasteries became islands of stability and learning in the ocean of disorder and ignorance which engulfed Europe after the breakdown of Roman authority in western Europe. But from being retreats surviving in isolation they began to assume a unique rôle in the establishment of a new power structure in Europe under the Carolingian dynasty of the Franks in the 8th century. Charlemagne, himself brought up illiterate like other Carolingian rulers before him, saw the value of equipping his court with missionaries and learned men who had been trained in these monasteries. Alcuin, the greatest English scholar of his day, entered the future emperor's service in 782, and another outstanding churchman and scholar at the Frankish court was the Visigoth bishop, Theodulf. Charlemagne's own uncle, Carloman, son of Charles Martel who had inflicted the first decisive defeat on the Moors near Poitiers, himself gave up a half-share of the Frankish kingdom to become a monk at Monte Cassino.

Through being called in to support and enlighten the ruling courts of Europe, the monasteries became radically altered in character. They supplied what was, in effect, an intellectual élite, members of which could communicate with each other internationally by means of the Latin language. Unlike their rulers they enjoyed the gift of tongues. Hence they came to assume a vital rôle as ambassadors and ultimately as politicians and soldiers, arranging treaties, shaping policy, raising armies, even leading armies. Like the bishops, the powerful abbots of the 8th and 9th centuries were happy to cooperate with their illiterate and ignorant rulers and lend stability to their régimes, the rulers in return rewarding them and their institutions with gifts of land and property, with power, and with prestige.

Cluny was not itself one of the earliest monasteries to be founded under the Rule of St Benedict, which dates back only to the year 909. But, from the first, Cluny received privileges that identified it as specially favoured by the popes. In particular it was exempt from the usual authority of the local bishop, to which other monasteries were yoked. Cluny was autonomous, responsible only to the Pope. What was more, the monks of Cluny were given the right to elect their own abbot. Inevitably, this special relationship between Cluny and the Vatican led to the aggrandisement of both. Cluny received favours and privileges from the Papacy: the Vatican listened to the advice of its *protégé*, and later elected a number of abbots of Cluny to be Pope. Clearly the Vatican was anxious to secure a strong ally in France, particularly since, after the emergence of a strong Carolingian dynasty in the 8th century, the centre of Christian culture and influence had shifted from Rome northwards, to France, but also to England and to Germany. Without an ally in the north the Vatican could not hope to retain any measure of control over European affairs.

What remains quite clear is that when, in the late 11th century, a programme of radical ecclesiastical reform was put into effect by Pope Gregory VII and his successors in the Vatican, Cluny was the natural spearhead of the reforming movement. After all, Gregory himself had been a Cluniac monk, and so were his successors, Urban II (who proclaimed the First Crusade in 1095) and Pascal II. With St Hugh as Abbot of Cluny, and Gregory and Urban in the Vatican, Rome and Cluny were hand-in-glove. Cluny, which had already supported the Santiago pilgrimage as part of a campaign to strengthen the Spanish church against the Moors in Spain, now joined with the Vatican in raising support for a crusade against the Moors in the Holy Land. The Vatican, in return, placed numerous monasteries and subject priories in France under Cluniac authority, and following this example the French feudal dukes and barons did the same. Cluny became the capital of an ecclesiastical empire.

By the time Abbot Hugh died in 1109 there were no fewer than three hundred monks resident at Cluny, and the abbey itself spread over an area of twenty-five acres. The number of separate priories to accept its authority at one time was 1450, though some of them did so grudgingly. A great many of Cluny's possessions, what is more, were located on or near the main pilgrim routes to Santiago: Vézelay, Moissac, St-Gilles, St-Eutrope at Saintes, St-Jean d'Angély, Poitiers, St-Martial at Limoges, St-Julien-le-Pauvre in Paris, St-Étienne and St-Sernin in Toulouse; and in Spain: Leyre, Estella, Irache, Nájera, Burgos, Frómista, Carrión, Sahagún,

Astorga, Villafranca—these were all Cluniac priories on the road
to St James, where pilgrims in their thousands were made welcome
and sent refreshed on their way. In England the priory of St
Pancras, at Lewes in Sussex, was yet another Cluniac foundation;
and it is a mark of the immense prestige Cluny continued to enjoy
that (as I have already described in Chapter IV), when early in the
12th century King Henry I of England wished to found another
great institution at Reading, he sent a request to the abbot of Cluny
for some monks to come over in order to establish it.

However, during the period of the Cluniac reform of the monasteries in the 11th century criticism had inevitably begun to focus on
the growing wealth and opulence of Cluny. A monastic movement
which had started in Europe in the hands of a few ascetics living
apart from the affairs of the world, had within six hundred years
swollen into a gigantic instrument of power and riches.

The justification for Cluny's wealth lay in the charitable work it
financed and the holy wars it supported, not to speak of the noble
examples of church architecture and craftsmanship for which it was
responsible and which are today among the glories of mediaeval
art. But all too much of that wealth, it was plain to see, went into
undertakings that were at some distance from charity. Ornament,
as it appeared to the critics of Cluny, was being embraced for
ornament's sake, and the essential simplicity of the Christian faith
and of the place of Christian worship obscured and vulgarised. So
boomed the voice of the most eloquent of Cluny's critics, St Bernard of Clairvaux, in a famous sermon delivered in 1124 undis-
guisedly aimed at the great new abbey of Cluny which had been
completed at huge expense some dozen years before—the largest
church in all Europe.

Let me quote Professor Pevsner on Cluny. "Here was architecture," he writes, "so complex, so polyphonous, as earlier centuries
in the West could not have conceived, and the Greeks would have
detested, but the ideal expression no doubt of that proudest moment
in mediaeval Christianity, when the Reform had conquered the
throne of the popes, asserted the superiority of the papal tiara over
the imperial crown, and called up the knights of Europe to defend
the Holy Land in the first Crusade."

But a decline was to set in. Castigated by St Bernard, its authority
shrunken, its empire broken away, its purpose grown fatty on

complacency and wealth, Cluny became within a few hundred years an obese object within the Catholic church. The religious wars hit it severely. The monastery itself was badly damaged and its superb library largely destroyed. The Revolution was the *coup de grâce*: Cluny was finally closed down in 1790, and eight years later what remained of the buildings were sold off to a builders' merchant who used them as a stone quarry until 1823. Ironically, part of the abbey that survived became transformed into an art college. A second irony was that such a noble monument, established as a bastion of Christianity at a moment in history when Christianity was feeble and threatened on all its frontiers, should finally have crumbled from within.

Today Cluny is the smashed hub of a wheel whose spokes once stretched out through western Europe. All that remains is a few towers, a west portal, cloisters of a later date, fragments of the nave and numerous outbuildings which protrude like giants' bones among the man-sized shops and cafés of the modern town. One of these bones is now the Musée Ochier, where many of the surviving relics of the monastery are preserved, including what is left of the library. A further *musée lapidaire* within the present complex of buildings contains a few tantalising remnants of the carvings commissioned for the abbey church by Abbot Hugh in the 11th century. Here are graceful columns cut with fine geometrical patterns, and above all a stone colonnade which formerly half-circled the choir. Upon each of the pillars of this colonnade (though in plaster only, since the originals have been removed to Paris) stand capitals carved to represent musical figures—the various Tones of the Gregorian Chant—each figure quivering and fluttering with such vitality and grace that we are made to realise what has been irrevocably lost by the destruction of this place. They represent a true harmony of man's sense of pleasure, piety and craftsmanship. Here was the fountain of Romanesque sculpture in Burgundy, and all the masterpieces to be seen in this area flow from this source.

To the north and west of Cluny lies Autun, and about the same distance north and west again, Vézelay. The Cathédrale St-Lazare at Autun and the Basilique Ste-Madeleine at Vézelay incorporate the two finest monuments of Romanesque carving in Burgundy, and both owe what is best in them to Cluny.

In the 11th century Autun was endowed with the supposed relics of Lazarus, and a new church was accordingly built to accommodate the pilgrims who came here to revere them. The tomb of Lazarus no longer exists, but three of the carved figures forming part of it have been displayed in the Musée Rolin nearby. These date from the 12th century, a little later than the Cluny capitals, and the debt is obvious. The nature of the subject imposes a sternness on these figures of mourning which is alien to the airy, musical figures represented on the Cluny capitals; but a dramatic expressiveness is common to both, as well as a sense of movement conveyed by the rich folds in the clothing.

More important a link with Cluny is the famous tympanum on the west portal of Autun cathedral, carved, as we know from the name so confidently engraved below the feet of Christ, by one Gislebertus: *Gislebertus hoc fecit*, it reads. This masterpiece of Gislebertus is crudely done by comparison with the Cluny capitals; but, as at Cluny, it is not so much the skill in carving the human face and figure that is remarkable as the extraordinary sinewy folds given to the clothing of those elongated forms: here is that same fluttering, airborne quality we saw in those musical figures at Cluny.

There is another shared quality: the degree of sentiment with which these figures are imbued. All the best Burgundian sculpture of this period expresses a range of human passions with a directness and freshness present nowhere else in French Romanesque sculpture, and again it derives from Cluny, as those few rescued capitals from the choir of the abbey church bear witness. Gislebertus acquired from Cluny this same gift, demonstrated in his great tympanum at Autun, in the fifty-seven capitals he executed inside the cathedral itself, and most clearly of all in that intensely moving and subtle carving of Eve plucking the apple, which was once on the lintel of the north doorway above the figure of Lazarus himself, and is now superbly displayed in the Musée Rolin for us all to wonder at.

Autun was not strictly on one of the main pilgrim routes to Santiago de Compostela. Vézelay was. It was the starting-point of the Burgundian route, the *Via Lemovicensis* of the 12th-century pilgrims' guide. Here, besides Burgundians, gathered pilgrims from Belgium, Champagne and Lorraine; from England too: Richard Coeur-de-Lion came here as a pilgrim in 1190, along with

King Philippe-Auguste of France, though they were bound not for Santiago but for Jerusalem, as leaders of the Third Crusade. Forty-four years earlier St Bernard of Clairvaux had preached the Second Crusade here before a congregation that included Louis VII of France. Twenty-six years before that, over one thousand pilgrims had died when the church caught fire during a festival.

The origins of such fame and notoriety were none too reputable. Vézelay had been a Benedictine house since before the foundation of Cluny—indeed with some of the privileges that Cluny later came to enjoy—but it only grew to importance as a pilgrim centre during the 11th century, as the result of a claim made by the monks to possess the body of Mary Magdalen. Now this was a claim hard to substantiate even in an age which demanded little enough in the way of proof, and, in order to shore up the story, a legend of the Magdalen's sea voyage to the south of France was put about. Once this tale was established, it came within reach of possibility that her body might have ended up at Vézelay a mere five hundred miles distant. The invention had the desired effect: by the end of the 11th century a new and larger church was required to take all the worshippers.

Without the disreputable ambitions of a few Benedictine monks in the Middle Ages we would have been deprived of one of the glories of Burgundian architecture as well as some of the finest Romanesque carving in Europe: perhaps this is a moment to observe that the means employed to establish great institutions has not infrequently been base. Vézelay may have invented the body of Mary Magdalen, but Cluny could be accused of having to a large extent invented the pilgrimage to Santiago. The cathedral at Santiago, as we have seen, was heavily financed by a fraudulent tax. As for Conques, the greatest mediaeval treasury in France resides there today because some of its finest pieces were purely and simply stolen by one of the monks from another abbey at Agen.

The Basilique Ste-Madeleine at Vézelay proudly rides the spur of a hill. As pilgrims approached it from the east, the church must have looked like the high stern of a ship ready to sail westwards. It was their point of departure. Today, coming round to the west front is at first something of a disappointment. The whole façade was rebuilt, conscientiously it is true, in the mid-19th century by the young Viollet-le-Duc, after it had been damaged beyond recognition during the Revolution and before that during the religious wars. But Vézelay deceives in order to flatter. Once within the reconstructed narthex, the majesty of the place unfolds. I make no reservations about it, the tympanum of Vézelay, with its flanking portal, remains one of the loveliest examples of church art I have ever set eyes on, and the huge central figure of Christ among the most astonishing pieces of sculpture in the world.

The theme is Christ in Majesty offering his blessing to the apostles who surround him. His hands, disproportionately huge, are outstretched (though one is now broken off) and from his finger-tips extend rays of light to every one of them, like ribbons. He faces us but he is seated sideways, the twist of his body emphasised by the same patterns and folds in his raiment as we saw in Gislebertus's tympanum at Autun. These patterns do not only describe the form of the body beneath; they extend from two spiral-shapes, rather like conch-shells, one placed on his right thigh and the other inside his left knee. These spirals bear no relation to any movement of the body or drape of the clothing. They are a formal device designed to provide two focal points from which, as the eye fixes on them, a rippling motion is seen to spin off, one clockwise the other anti-clockwise, and radiate through the entire tympanum until all the attendant figures of the apostles and the line of smaller figures below are caught as if in the eddies of a current which is flowing in two directions simultaneously.

The blessing is offered to the apostles, yet it is not towards them that Christ is looking. He gazes straight at us. To pilgrims, as they crowded into the narthex to the sound of a Gregorian chant, it must have seemed that it was them he was blessing; and, as if to anticipate this reaction, the sculptor carved below the giant presence of Christ a frieze of smaller figures who represent the ordinary people of the earth, in line, filing in from the left and the right to be welcomed by St Peter and St Paul. They have been caught in the same swirling rhythm: the hems of their clothing are wind-blown, their limbs, their beasts and their weapons form agitated gestures of astonishment and delight.

Round the outer rim of the tympanum are twenty-nine lunettes, or circular carved panels, depicting the signs of the zodiac and the labours of the various months—tilling the ground, reaping corn, winnowing grain and so on—and between these lunettes and the main area of the tympanum are eight further panels, and here are represented the same images of a heathen world—the world without God—as confronted the pilgrim at Aulnay and those little churches of Poitou and Saintonge. Here are the ignorant people to be evangelised by the apostles, and from whom St James was in the process of delivering Spain—men depicted with wolves' heads, with gigantic noses, with strange and fearful weapons—a terrible grotesque parade of those who live in the dark.

From the narthex the pilgrim passed into the nave, flanked by columns with carved capitals, many of which employ the same stylistic devices as the great tympanum, and because the church was designed to admit light these are relatively easy to see, unlike those drowned in the gloom at Autun. The nave is of immense length and constructed of sandstone of many shades, from white through yellow to dark grey-green; and it leads at the far end to an early-Gothic choir and apse even more radiant and delicate in form, as if it had been intended as a kind of spiritual climax. To look back down the nave of Vézelay, from this choir as light as summer, is to enjoy one of the most successful blends of architectural styles ever conceived.

Vézelay was one starting-point for Santiago. Le Puy was another: from here ran the route across the southern Auvergne, the *Via Podensis*, and to Le Puy pilgrims gathered from the southern areas of Burgundy and the Rhône Valley as well as from Germany. The present Cathédrale Notre-Dame-du-Puy is 12th-century, but as with Vézelay it replaced a smaller church on the site when pilgrims became too numerous to be contained there. Vézelay had the body of the Magdalen to attract them; Le Puy became a pilgrim centre on the strength of a statue of the Virgin Mary said to have been brought from Egypt and donated by St Louis of France. The statue was an object of the deepest reverence, and inspired a cult all along the pilgrim route to Santiago where chapels devoted to the Virgin of Le Puy have sprung up in the most unlikely places, though the precious statue itself met its fate during the French Revolution and today Le Puy is a shrine without a holy relic to enshrine. But Le Puy has always been a sacred place: its pinnacles of rock jutting out of the plain marked it as a centre of worship from earliest times. The advent of Christianity merely rolled a purple carpet over the sacred stones; though it did not cover them completely, for the cathedral narthex encloses a dolmen, just as the cathedral at Le Mans in Normandy employs a dolmen as a cornerstone. The new church builders took care to propitiate the old gods.

Notre-Dame-du-Puy is a cathedral in the shadows. It rises to a grim elegance, the nave roofed by almost windowless domes that seem to press down and expunge the light, deepening the yellow-green stone. Long, jangling lanterns reinforce its oriental appearance, warming the Byzantine gloom with studs of orange and the flicker of flame on bronze. A small cloister of chequer-board patterns in stone huddles under the high walls, hiding in the twilight some graceful colonnades and three life-size statues of bishops who gaze towards the cathedral with expressions of careworn severity appropriate to the tone of the place. The west side of the cloisters offers a blinding view of the Rocher Corneille, rising above the roof-line, surmounted by its sixteen-metre statue of Notre-Dame-de-France apparently coated in tomato ketchup and donated by Napoleon III in evidence of what had happened to official artistic taste in France by the middle of the 19th century.

Even more theatrical than the Rocher Corneille is the Rocher St-Michel to the north and west of the cathedral. High upon that unlikely heap of grey rock on its launching-pad for heaven stands the Chapelle St-Michel-d'Aiguille, one of a group of pinnacle churches in Europe named after the Archangel Michael, of which St Michael's Mount in Cornwall and the Mont-St-Michel in Normandy are the best known. Such holy exhibitionism invites disappointment especially after a climb of 267 steps, but St-Michel-d'Aiguille is a gem: its façade is purely Moorish, with a three-lobed arch over the main door and, above that, geometrical patterns in coloured stone in the manner of the cathedral cloisters which, in fact, it precedes by a century. Inside, the chapel is shaped like a snail, its head being the entrance and the body coiled round a colonnade enclosing the altar in what looks like a shell of rock. Set into the wall by the altar is a little stick-like Christ, with popping eyes, that once belonged to a reliquary and reminds us that this chapel too was a place of pilgrimage.

After Paris, Vézelay and Le Puy, the fourth point of departure for Santiago was Arles, down near the mouth of the Rhône. From here began the *Via Tolosana*—so-named because the major city along the route was Toulouse—and along this the most southern way to Spain came pilgrims from Italy and from eastern Europe who crossed the Alps to Avignon or further south to Aix-en-Provence, or else followed the coast as far as Fréjus before cutting inland to Saint-Maximin and then westwards to Arles.

Arles, which had once been the third city of the Roman Empire after Rome and Constantinople, with a population of more than 100,000, enjoyed a renaissance in the Middle Ages as a centre of pilgrimage. Here the saint whom pilgrims venerated was a Greek evangelist called Trophime who may have been a disciple of St Paul and whose relics were kept in the cathedral that bears his name. The Carolingian church on the site had been rebuilt for the most part in the 12th century—again to accommodate pilgrims—and it remains the finest conglomeration of Romanesque carving in Provence. The west portal, displaying a Christ in Majesty above the door and figures of the saints on either side, has a statue of St James on the right, and the portal itself is decorated with scallop-shells.

But pilgrims did not only make for St-Trophime. The great formal necropolis known as Les Alyscamps, originally a Roman burial-ground until it was adopted as a Christian cemetery in the 4th century, offered an air of mystery and grandeur and a smell of death which the Middle Ages found almost as irresistible as did the 19th-century Romantics. It has been stripped of most of its splendour since Renaissance times, but in the days of the pilgrimage it contained no fewer than seventeen churches and chapels, along with carved sarcophagi, headstones and a great deal of sculpture. The church of St-Honorat, of which today only fragments remain amid the tree-lined rubble of Les Alyscamps, was a special attraction on account of the relics of early Christian martyrs kept there.

Pilgrims also went to the Benedictine abbey of Montmajour, to the west of the city in the swamp-lands which the monks there were dedicated to draining. And most of all they went to an even greater Benedictine abbey, one that was constructed under the authority of Cluny and whose sculptures inspired those on the west portal of St-Trophime: this was St-Gilles, today a terrible wreckage, thanks to the Protestants in the 16th century, but in the Middle Ages it was the first stop for pilgrims after leaving Arles. From there they proceeded by way of Lunel and Montpellier to St-Guilhem-le

Désert, where they could venerate a fragment of the True Cross presented to Charlemagne, as well as the body of St-Guilhem (or Guillaume) himself, who was Charlemagne's standard-bearer. If they arrived in time for Maundy Thursday then they took part in a procession through the streets of the village using snail-shells as oil-lamps, before attending a special service in the abbey church. They may even have taken a turn round the cloisters, a pleasure denied any modern pilgrim since these now reside in New York, the property of the Cloisters Museum, where they stand as a lasting monument to the French spirit of conservation.

The pilgrim route I chose to follow was from Paris, the one referred to in the 12th-century guide as the *Via Turonensis* since it passes through Tours. This was the *magnum iter Sancti Jacobi*. But many of the principal shrines, abbeys and monuments associated with the pilgrimage to Santiago lie off the *Via Turonensis*, on the three other routes nominated by the guide; and so, having taken this account as far as the Basque Country where two of the three other routes (the ones from Vézelay and Le Puy) join the road from Paris, it seemed an appropriate moment to halt the journey south-wards into Spain and take a look at some of the other major establishments in France whose very existence without the pilgrimage would have been unlikely.

Vézelay, Autun, Le Puy, Arles and St-Gilles lie on or very near the starting-points of the various pilgrim routes. Other equally important centres of pilgrimage lay along the routes themselves. On the road from Paris there had been Tours, Poitiers, Aulnay and Saintes. On the road from Vézelay were La Charité-sur-Loire, St-Léonard and Périgueux; on the Le Puy route lay Conques, Figeac and Moissac; and on the one from Arles, St Gilles and, above all, Toulouse.

Of all the possessions belonging to the abbey of Cluny along the pilgrimage routes to Santiago de Compostela, St-Sernin at Toulouse was the most valuable (though Cluny's authority over it was of brief duration). To many a Frenchman Toulouse was more important as a place of pilgrimage than Santiago itself, and certainly it possessed a longer history. As the capital of the kingdom of the Visigoths it was already a city of substance in the Dark Ages, and it continued to be one of the major cities in France under the

Franks in the early Middle Ages. Numerous sanctuaries and shrines were established there, the most venerated of these being the one dedicated to St-Sernin, who was the first bishop of Toulouse and an early Christian martyr of the 3rd century (though the name Sernin is an abbreviation of Saturninus, which readers of Robert Graves may feel throws some doubt on the Christian nature of his rôle). It was under Charlemagne that the church dedicated to St-Sernin rose to be among the leading places of worship in France, when the Emperor is reputed to have made a gift to the city of no fewer than six bodies of the apostles. These took their place in the lower crypt at St-Sernin and, as the pilgrimage spirit began to blossom later in the Middle Ages, a gigantic new church was soon required to hold all those who came to pay their respects to the six apostles and the holy martyr. This church remains substantially the same to this day, and is one of that small group of churches which conform to the same architectural pattern as the cathedral at Santiago de Compostela.

St-Sernin-de-Toulouse was situated on one of the main pilgrim routes to St James; but this was not all. It had a more specific link with the Santiago cult, one that must have confused not a few pilgrims, which was that among those six apostles presented by the Emperor Charlemagne was the body believed to be that of St James the Greater. In fact, when St James's body was also discovered in Galicia a few decades later there was a rival body already in existence in France, though a consensus of opinion seems to have been that the Toulouse body was apocryphal: had this not been the case, no sane pilgrim would willingly have trudged any farther than Toulouse. Not surprisingly, the *Codex Calixtinus* dubs the Toulouse relics spurious.

But the doubtful authenticity of one relic in no way impaired the reputation of St-Sernin as a holy shrine. There was so much else before which to genuflect, and throughout the later Middle Ages Toulouse continued to be enough of a rival to the Santiago cult for the abbey of Cluny, with its vested interests in the pilgrimage to Santiago, to arrange a take-over of St-Sernin in order to harness its considerable reputation to the cause of St James in Spain. The instrument of this operation was the Cluniac bishop of Toulouse who used his authority to expel the canons of St-Sernin and install in their place Cluniac monks. This was in the year 1082, at the pinnacle of Cluny's power and involvement with the Santiago pilgrimage. The take-over of St-Sernin, however, seems to have struck the Vatican as unscrupulous beyond the limit, and the original canons were reinstated. The Papacy was undoubtedly growing alarmed by its *protégé*'s empire, as well as by the burgeoning of the Santiago pilgrimage which that empire was successfully fostering. The Vatican had come to see in the growth and fame of Santiago de Compostela a rival not merely to Toulouse, but to Rome itself, and throughout the later Middle Ages relations between Santiago, now an archbishopric, and the Vatican remained, at best, cool. Rome had the reputation of its own martyrs to safeguard.

Most of the great treasure of St-Sernin was confiscated and lost in the French Revolution. We know from surviving inventories that it must have been among the richest of all in the Middle Ages. It contained eighteen caskets and a much greater number of precious statues and reliquaries of different descriptions, including one richly decorated reliquary depicting St James wearing a pilgrim hat. A very small proportion of this treasure has survived, but this includes a casket containing a piece of the True Cross, which is a splendidly enamelled object from Limoges, made during the 13th century specially for the church. Decorating it is the legend of the discovery of the Cross by St Helena, and of how this particular piece of it came to be brought to Toulouse by a pilgrim. A second survivor is the casket reliquary to St Saturninus himself, another 13th-century object, in silver and parcel-gilt, decorated with scenes of the saint's martyrdom. But most famous of the treasures of St-Sernin to survive the Revolution is the so-called Horn of Roland, which is undoubtedly a horn (or oliphant) of the period of Charlemagne, though the rich decoration on it looks likely to be 11th-century work done under Moorish influence. To pilgrims on their way to Santiago here was a romantic link with the legend of Charlemagne and Roncesvalles which many of them would have known from the *Chanson de Roland*.

St-Sernin is a textbook Romanesque church, and I confess I find it rather dull. It is obviously important—historically—and it has been much analysed and discussed, and roundly praised. For my taste it is simply too big, a modest conception of architecture blown up into something verging on the grandiose and the pompous.

Even the celebrated sculptures on the south portal, the Porte Miègeville, are coarse by comparison with other great sculptural complexes carved along the pilgrim routes. The ambulatory reliefs show a debt to those in the cloister of Santo Domingo de Silos, near Burgos, done late in the 11th century, but the Toulouse sculptor has managed to be sensitive to the least becoming characteristics of the Spanish carvings; and much the same is true where the stylistic comparisons are between Toulouse and Moissac. San Domingo will find its natural place later in this book; now is a good moment to turn to Moissac.

Here was yet another Cluniac abbey. In the latter part of the 11th century the abbot of Moissac was junior only to Abbot Hugh himself in Cluny's hierarchy. Sadly, the Romanesque church attached to the Cluniac abbey no longer stands, with the exception of one gigantically squat bell-tower and the supreme south portal—once the west portal but later moved. What also survives is the cloisters, which were completed in 1100 and remain among the most beautiful in France; though in the mid-19th century it was officially decided to demolish these to make way for the new Bordeaux–Sète railway. Only the intervention of the Beaux-Arts authorities got the decision reversed, and the railway authorities miraculously found a means of laying the tracks next-door. Oh, those 19th-century engineers: geniuses besotted with their skills, they approached their work like Michelangelo, and towards anything in their way they were Destroying Angels. I have more than a suspicion that if Moissac had stood in the path of Brunel's Great Western Railway, he would have done the same rather than diverge from the arrogant purity of his idea.

The inspiration of the Moissac cloisters came from Spain, Santo Domingo de Silos, and if Moissac is marginally the less fine of the two then it is a pedantic distinction. The Gothic arches in soft brick added between the line of double columns do alter the original proportions a little, though they blend to perfection, and some of the geometrical carving on the capitals—Moorish in origin—is only a shade less delicate than the best of the Spanish capitals. Santo Domingo, furthermore, is a two-tier cloister, while Moissac is only one. That said, however, the cloister of Moissac is glorious. The figure-carvings on the capitals are tender and earnest, though rather damaged: it is the geometrical carvings one tends to admire more, the best of them variations on a leaf-and-stem motif, wonderfully rhythmic and finely executed. There is a wealth of abstract invention here. In some of the capitals the surface is greyish but the incisions reveal a warm pink in the shadow, as if the stone were lit from within. Spreading a deep umbrella over much of the cloister is a single cedar-tree, of the kind that one feels might have evolved uniquely for such places of retreat rather than on the bare mountains of the Lebanon.

Much of the great portal at Moissac is from a different source. Here in the tympanum is the mark of Cluny. Though there is little left at Cluny to offer a direct comparison, it is clear from the style of carving that the Moissac sculptor looked to Burgundy rather than to Spain. What gives the Moissac portal its special character is the manner in which a Burgundian Last Judgment blends with the boldly Moorish features that accompany it. Cluny rises above Islam. On the lower level, to the left and right, the twin portal is toothed like an open jaw set sideways with, in the middle, a vertical column carved with three pairs of rampant lions, each pair crossed over one another, which seem to echo a pre-Islamic Orient of Assyrian temples, though no doubt a more direct source lies in those illustrations to St Beatus's *Commentaries on the Apocalypse* which we have already seen supplying the wilder beasts carved on the churches in western France.

This pillar of lions, performing a kind of heraldic circus-act, holds up a massive lintel carved with ten rosettes, and above this the superb Burgundian tympanum of Christ in Majesty. Christ is seated gravely in the centre. Around him are the four symbols of Matthew, Mark, Luke and John, writhing in tribute; while below him and on either side the twenty-four old men of the Apocalypse have set their musical instruments aside and turned their heads in astonished attention. They are rapt, incredulous, dumbfounded. The sculptor has created an atmosphere of stunned silence: it is a moment as dramatically poignant as the appearance of King Lear carrying the dead Cordelia in his arms. Below, the barbaric lions strain their throats, and the teeth of the portal are open like a steel trap.

On either side of the central column of lions, flattened into the stone so that they only become visible as you pass under the lintel to enter the reconstructed church, are two full-size figures of St

Paul and the prophet Jeremiah. Paul is stern, Jeremiah gentle: both have been carved in deep-grey granite with a delicacy that suggests they might be dressed in silk. They are elongated figures of the kind that art-historians irresistibly term "proto-Mannerist": the twist of Jeremiah's body is exaggerated to the point of coyness; the expression of benign sadness on his face, and the tilt of his head are equally emphatic. Is there anything in European sculpture which combines such refined elegance with such pure feeling, or which more cogently expresses the passionate nature of the mediaeval religious experience?

The flanking figures of St Peter on the left of the portal and the prophet Isaiah on the right pick up the same passionate movement. Their heads are turned inwards towards Christ; their arms are raised, their bodies twisted, their legs are represented in motion like an Indian temple carving; and the lines of their drapery are sharply cut in order to emphasise the shape and movement of the human form underneath. On the right-hand wall the high emotional key is again maintained, with panels representing the Annunciation, Visitation, Adoration and the Flight into Egypt. These carvings are more damaged than the others, but precisely the same rhythms are preserved, the same gestures, delicacy of carving, balance of figures, twist of bodies, expressions of tense excitement; and if the ecstasy is a little more muted than on the other carvings, then it is because the figures in these panels are engaged in a narrative, not responding to a revelation. Facial expressions are less theatrical, but a rich complexity of emotions is condensed in them. In the Annunciation panel, what promise of grace rests in the features of the angel, what delicacy of feeling in the face of the Virgin receiving the angel, what tender appreciation of a human predicament in the sculptor's treatment of the whole scene. This is sculpture from the soul, about the soul.

Facing the narrative panels on the western side of the door are a group of panels quite shocking in the contrast they offer to the ecstatic and humane carvings on the rest of the portal. These are scenes of damnation. The story of Lazarus is told as a kind of parable: emerging from this tale are the usual accounts of the torments of hell-fire, rendered more disturbing in this context because of the deeply civilised nature of the sculpture around. It comes as a jolt to witness the punishments awarded to the miser and the adulterous woman. How could a mind capable of such profundity of human understanding as is shown in the scenes of the Apocalypse and in the Annunciation panel, also be capable of recommending, as a proper punishment for sexual infidelity, a pair of snakes sucking at a woman's breasts and a toad feeding at her vagina? Mediaeval morality was made up in equal parts of profound compassion and leering brutality.

If some of the finest sculpture of the pilgrim routes is at Moissac, then the place (Santiago apart) retaining the most powerful feeling of the pilgrimage itself must be Conques. Some spell has kept Conques in the Middle Ages, a spell aided it is true by the efforts of Prosper Mérimée who came here while he was Inspector-General of Historic Monuments in 1837 to find the abbey in the process of demolition, its cloisters and outbuildings already gone. Like Moissac, Conques lay on the route from Le Puy, and pilgrims came to it after traversing the bleak tablelands of the Cévennes and the Southern Auvergne. It was Charlemagne who founded a Benedictine abbey in this isolated valley, and through the reputation of its treasures it grew into a shrine popular enough for the church to be torn down during the 12th century and rebuilt, greatly enlarged. For once Cluny had no hand in its affairs, and that independence is marked today by the west portal of the abbey church, where the carvings possess a narrative simplicity that owes nothing to the sophisticated and soulful artistry of Autun, Vézelay and Moissac.

The village of Conques is a huddle of grey slate roofs on a bony hillside, cordoned by stunted oaks. Climbing steeply towards it is the Rue Charlemagne. The modern road is just above it, and the original way into the village has been left as it always was. One's feet grip the knuckles of slate cobblestones. The narrow street, sloping into a central gutter, becomes the Rue Abbé and soon enters the village beneath the western gate, the Porte du Barry, built over with half-timbered houses. From here the old track curves up into the village between low fan-tiled roofs until, round a sudden corner, the massive abbey church presents itself on a scale quite different from the meagre buildings that press round it. It is the scale of a city. In the church square the houses and the hills close quietly round, and there is only the sound of hens. And of water. The 12th-century guide mentions an admirable spring that flows out in front of the portal of the abbey church—and there it is. Villagers still bring their buckets to fill and their horses to drink there. The abbey of Conques, like many of the holiest shrines, was built on a source of fresh water: a magic spring.

The theme of the Last Judgment, which occupies the tympanum above the main west door at Conques, presents an account of heaven and hell less moving and less artistic than many of the other great tympanums carved along the pilgrim routes; all the same, it is an account which is affecting because it is so literal. Here is paradise and there is damnation. Both are as factual and concrete as the square in which the pilgrim was standing or the inn where he would spend the night. Accordingly, the scenes of the torments of hell are disconcertingly lurid, while those of the pleasure of heaven are reassuringly comfortable.

The American scholar, Arthur Kingsley Porter, detected some close resemblances between these carvings on the tympanum at Conques and some of the sculptures on the earliest surviving door of the cathedral at Santiago de Compostela, the Puerta de las Platerías. He considered that it was the latter that inspired Conques, that two sculptors must have worked on both, and, furthermore, that Santiago in this way exercised a direct influence on the Auvergne school of carving which took its lead from Conques. I read such opinions with a cool fascination: no one will ever know for certain whether they are sound or not, but if they should be, then here is another striking example of the mobility of artist–craftsmen in the Middle Ages, and of the extent to which the pilgrim routes to Santiago provided a corridor—a two-way corridor—along which ideas and skills and styles could freely pass, halted by neither geographical nor national boundaries.

The Christ in Majesty at Conques is represented as a benign figure of authority: he blesses with one hand, pronounces judgment with the other. The figures to the left of him are equally unmoved. There is no shock of ecstasy as at Moissac, no gust of movement as at Vézelay. Mary holds her hands clasped in prayer, Peter grasps his keys, behind them stand the various donors who include Charlemagne: they are all impassive, rigid figures with round faces and staring eyes waiting in an orderly line. It is a literal and rather cosy scene. On the other side of Christ are the damned and their tormentors: figures being beaten, cleft with an axe, devoured, hauled up by their legs. How matter-of-fact it all is. The story continues below: Ste-Foy, to whom the abbey is dedicated, receives the blessing; the dead rise from their tombs; St Michael weighs their souls; demons wait expectantly. The elect, neatly arranged in pairs, are welcomed by Abraham to Jerusalem; the damned are thrust towards the mouth of hell where the Devil awaits them, eyes alight, and further demons press them into the flames. And that is it. This is not sculpture of human experience, but straightforward illustration. The pilgrim was expected to "read" the text, learn his lesson and go on his way strengthened in his purpose.

But first he would attend Mass in the abbey church itself. He entered a building of colossal height and labyrinthine construction, with arches stacked in tiers giving on to further recesses and yet further arches between which the light filtered from high up—a light less strong then, with the stained-glass windows in place, falling at varying angles and colours on flat and rounded stone, leading the eyes always upwards until the line of sight was blocked by a rough-stone ceiling. The abbey church of Conques employs few of the aids of art, but it is a place designed to wander in: through arches, past columns, from one small area to another, each area only half-visible from the next, everywhere the stone coloured with the subtleties of a Morandi canvas.

The choir is open, separated from the ambulatory by a semi-circle of columns and a Moorish iron grille from the 12th century which is made up of a simple coil motif repeated over and over again. The iron used for this grille was forged from the chains and shackles of prisoners, who had presented them to the church after their release, in thanksgiving to Ste-Foy one of whose special attributes was to deliver captives. The purpose of this grille was to protect what pilgrims had primarily come to Conques to see—the celebrated relics of Ste-Foy. These would be displayed round the High Altar where they would be visible to everyone in the nave, while a closer inspection was possible from the ambulatory, the choir being kept as open as possible for that purpose.

The statue of Ste-Foy was the most famous treasure in France during the Middle Ages, renowned for its miracles. Unlike nearly all the contents of mediaeval church treasuries it has survived, though today it is displayed with the rest of the sumptuous Conques treasure in a museum specially built in the ruins of the abbey cloisters. Aymery Picaud makes a point of recommending that Burgundians and Teutons on their way to Santiago from Le Puy stop here and venerate these relics of Ste-Foy, "virgin and martyr", but what he omits to tell is the 11th-century story of how her relics came to be in Conques at all, stolen from Agen by a monk who was planted there for the purpose and who remained at Agen for ten years before finding the opportunity to break into the tomb and remove the treasure in a sack while the community was at dinner.

The arrival of Ste-Foy ensured the prosperity of Conques and the decline of Agen. And no wonder. Even allowing for the fact that mediaeval churches were not originally stark and bare as we now see them, but decked out in rich colours and materials, the reliquary statue which is known as the *Majesté de Ste-Foy* must still have presented an overpowering sight displayed by the High Altar of that magnificent church: a diminutive and radiant torso of gold and precious jewels that stared out with hypnotic eyes under a giant canopy of stone. Here, supposedly, was the golden image of the saint herself, crowned and robed in yet more gold and precious stones, and the superstitious pilgrim—and what pilgrims were not superstitious?—would have seen in her an object more conspicuously magical than anything he had set eyes on. He was not aware or concerned that the taut, rather unfriendly and masculine-looking face was actually beaten over a carved head of the late-Roman period, or that the gilding had been undertaken at least five hundred years after the young Christian girl had been martyred in Agen. He saw it as a supreme dramatic presence, a reality rendered the more wonderful by all that costly weight of metal and jewels. The monks, too, had seen their *Majesté* sufficiently in terms of investment to enter her in the abbey inventory simply as "eight hundred grams of gold". She was an aid to salvation, but she was also money in the bank. The oldest mediaeval statue to survive in western Europe is a remarkable blend of opulence and magic.

By hiding it, the inhabitants of Conques saved the abbey treasure from the fate suffered by most of the other French monastic treasures at the hands of the Revolutionaries: and today there remains nothing in France which can quite prepare your eyes for what is on display in the treasury here. The *Majesté de Ste-Foy* rightly holds the centre of the scene, but what is equally astonishing is the wealth of other precious objects belonging to the abbey.

Conques received gifts of church treasures continually for one thousand years from the 8th century. The *Majesté* itself was given rich additions of gold and jewels in the 9th, 10th, 16th and 17th centuries. Among the oldest and finest of the other pieces is the reliquary of Pépin, dating from the 10th century and bearing a crucifix in gold relief surrounded by a delicate floral motif in gold filigree. Like other early reliquaries this is a richly ornamented golden box sprouting semi-precious stones like warts. More bizarre reliquaries here are shaped as human limbs, like the 13th-century arm-reliquary of St George; others are decorated in *cloisonné* and *champlevé* enamels mostly done at Limoges, in the Rhineland or in Spain. The treasury contains Moorish work too. These pieces were either captured in the Spanish wars, or they were the work of Moslem craftsmen in Christian service: all were the gifts of feudal lords, made in gratitude and thanksgiving. By such means did the abbeys of France grow rich, and the display of treasures enhance their reputation as holy places. The pilgrims came in reverence, in wonder and in hope. Art flourished in the cause of salvation, and in the interests of the wealthy: it honoured God and Mammon in a comfortable double-yoke.

The artist–craftsman of the later Middle Ages would have found it easier to define his art than would a painter or sculptor of the present age; at the same time he would have been quite bewildered by modern discussions on aesthetics and the nature of art. When we talk about the "art" of the Middle Ages we are employing an anachronistic term, and strictly speaking we ought not to use it. Art in itself was of little value in mediaeval times. Monuments were expendable, while objects were valued for the miraculous power they enshrined or for the materials of which they were made. A gold reliquary containing the rib of some saint was more likely to be preserved than a carved church portal or a painted ceiling. The burgeoning of what we choose to call "art" during the 11th and 12th centuries was in direct relation to the religious fervour of the times and to the economic and social stability which had settled (temporarily) on much of western Europe. Great Christian empires like that of Cluny, and popular Christian enterprises like the pilgrimage to Santiago de Compostela, provided unheard-of opportunities for craftsmen and craft workshops, and the result was a release of energies on a scale unmatched until the Renaissance in Italy several centuries later. Art, as always, blossomed with new opportunities for its usefulness.

Was there then an art of the pilgrim routes? Scholars have found little agreement on this. What is beyond question is that the pilgrimage to Santiago was a vehicle and an incentive in numerous fields of artistic production—architecture, sculpture, painting, metalwork, as well as music and poetry. It is probably true to say that many of the outstanding monuments of the Romanesque period would never have come into existence without the pilgrimage, and that the currency of artistic ideas and styles would never have become so widespread.

Artistically as well as politically the key was Cluny. The few choir capitals that survive from Cluny date from the last quarter of the 11th century, which was not long after the reappearance of full-scale stone sculpture in Europe for the first time since the Roman period. Only a little later than the choir capitals was Cluny's great portal which was the point of departure for several of the finest carved monuments on the pilgrim routes. This portal, we know, included an immense tympanum bearing a central figure of Christ flanked by four angels and, below, the familiar figures of the twenty-four elders of the Apocalypse.

The stylistic advances that were made in church carving at this time were another reflection of the growth in confidence and Christian purpose that took place during the 11th century. From being mean in scale and crude in execution, sculpture became an art-form practised with sophisticated skills and with a firm grasp of the potential of the medium as a way of expressing human sentiments and human ideals. Though what we term Romanesque emerged from the sculpture of provincial Rome, there is nothing in the art of the Romanesque period which echoes the wordly Classical spirit, least of all the Classical emphasis on perfection of form. In Romanesque sculpture form is the servant of expression, and each "school" evolved a different set of stylisations in accordance with whatever aspect of the religious experience it was felt urgent to express.

Both Romanesque and Gothic art are concerned with the inner man. The transition from Romanesque to Gothic during the late 12th and the 13th centuries represents the transformation in the nature and outlook of that inner man. From being troubled and imprisoned he becomes liberated. He sheds his overriding pre-occupation with damnation, and gains the confidence to explore and externalise his daydreams. The Romanesque sculptors expressed a rich human faith in God, without whom man was helpless, de-graded. But the Gothic sculptors found faith in the human spirit itself: they expressed a belief in the potential of man's imagination, and in his power to reach out and comprehend God. There are intimations of humanist thinking in Gothic art and architecture: the suggestion that God may only be there because man's spirit has proved itself large enough to perceive him. God therefore becomes the witness and champion of man's genius. This remains one of the foremost experiences to be gained from a great Gothic cathedral: it is also the real meaning contained in those new architectural features—the pointed arch, the rib vault and the flying buttress—which Abbot Suger introduced in the choir of his abbey of St-Denis between 1140 and 1144, and which came to their most triumphant expression in the cathedral of Chartres seventy years later.

"There are few subjects about which tradition is so defective as the aesthetic sentiment of past ages," wrote the eminent Dutch his-torian, Johan Huizinga, with a cautionary eye on people who vent-ure such speculative observations. But elsewhere in his historical masterpiece *The Waning of the Middle Ages* Huizinga permitted a provocative speculation of his own. "It is a general phenomenon," he observed, "that the idea which works of art give us of an epoch is far more serene and happy than that which we glean in reading its chronicles, documents, or even literature. Plastic art does not lament."

This observation seems to me only partly true. What is true is that, by concerning itself little with the anguishes of daily life, the plastic arts of the Middle Ages offer a view of mediaeval life more balanced and secure than the one presented by the written word. Documents are concerned with externals and raw facts, rather than with sentiments and dreams. What is serene about mediaeval art is the timelessness of those themes with which it deals, themes which, though timeless, are in fact far from happy. The religious experience displayed over and over again above the portals of Romanesque churches is a profoundly troubled one. The inner man with which mediaeval art is concerned is to the very roots pessimistic about the world in which he lives. His only hope is the prospect of what may come afterwards, and this is the principal content of the art found on the pilgrimage roads, and it is why the pilgrimages themselves are so representative of the mediaeval spirit. They were a long journey to heaven: and the art that worked out their course, far from being free of lament as Huizinga suggested, in fact offers a consistent lament for life. It was an elegy which accompanied and sustained refugees who were driven from their homes by fear, and by the conviction that the only ray of hope lay in making such a journey.

CHAPTER VII

Charlemagne Country

St-Jean-Pied-de-Port has the feel of a frontier town. Spanish
trucks clatter past the walls at night, lopsided with fruit and
vegetables from Navarre. By day the town is littered with dust-
coated cars abandoned in haphazard places: their occupants with
Spanish shoulder-bags and fat, bronzed faces are spread around
the café tables. There is a homecoming bonhomie amid the cigar-
smoke. St-Jean-Pied-de-Port does a roaring trade in being wel-
comingly French.

There were two pilgrim routes over the Pyrenees from here.
There was the mountain road over the Col de Cize, of which
Aymery Picaud writes. This was the ancient Roman road which
actually by-passed St-Jean to follow a rich valley up from St-
Michel to the east. Scattered along this way were numerous
churches, priories and hospices for the comfort of the pilgrim,
including the hospice of St-Vincent which belonged to the authorities at Santiago, and, at the pass itself, St-Michel-le-Vieux at a
height of 3860 feet. Here, Picaud claims, Charlemagne turned
towards the west and Galicia, and went down on one knee to say
a prayer to God and St James. And here, Picaud goes on, pilgrims
planted their own crosses in the ground, so that it was not uncommon to come across a thousand of them on the brow of the
Pyrenees at the gate of Spain.

Then there was the valley road straight up from St-Jean which
joined the mountain road just before the monastery of Roncesvalles at the crest of the pass, and which was less favoured by
pilgrims, perhaps because it was relatively easy. This way corres-
ponds to the modern road into Spanish Navarre. It is neither so
arduous nor so lovely as the track that leads up the next valley
over the Col de Cize, but if you are driving you have no choice.
And so, having seen Gillian off in the direction of Bordeaux and
London, and retrieved my car where I had abandoned it in

Peyrehorade a week earlier, I left St-Jean-Pied-de-Port on a cloudless early June morning and drove up into the Pyrenees. Within a few miles I was at the Spanish border at Valcarlos, where Charlemagne had been encamped with his army when he heard the horn of Roland blow—too late—and where my cantankerous literary companion and mentor, Richard Ford, had noted that "the frontier on both sides is marked by custom-house officers, those pests of travellers".

Spanish customs officials often give me the impression of an uncouth and mildly threatening thoroughness, as though they suspected my motives for entering Spain and wished I would not. Here at Valcarlos I was reminded how reluctant Spanish officials are to smile, or to seek anything to smile about. The one who dissected my baggage passed a dark thumb over my books, pondering on each with an aggressive silence. Jane Austen, Benvenuto Cellini, Alejo Carpentier, the poems of Sir Thomas Wyatt, a red-bound pamphlet on mediaeval roads in the Basque Country by Dr Clément Urrutibéhéty: I do not know what he made of such a hotch-potch, but the sullen face gave away no glimpse of an expression as he picked them up one by one. Was it pornography he was suspecting, or concealed pot, bank-notes, left-wing tracts? My box of notes for this book gave him further pause, and visions rose before my eyes of the customs official in Evelyn Waugh's *Vile Bodies* who had burnt as "downright dirt" the manuscript of Adam Fenwick-Syme's memoirs on his arrival at Dover, along with Dante's *Purgatorio*. Finally, Richard Ford's *Handbook to Spain* settled in his chunky hand; but the look of incomprehension held until the last, until with an unexpected flick of the head he dismissed me and my mysteries to the open road. I drove up a deteriorated highway sliced into the forest, the sunlight picking out spots of overnight rain on the leaves like tiny explosions of glass. A weasel scampered with its fore-and-aft movement across the road. Splashes of sapphire-blue columbines stained the grass verges. My customs officer already forgotten, it seemed to me an exhilarating kind of day to be going to Spain.

There is nothing dramatic about the Pass of Roncesvalles except the legend which hangs over it. The battle which engulfed Charlemagne's rearguard is supposed to have taken place at the highest point, now known as Ibañeta, a saddle between the mountains which is also where the two pilgrim routes join. The monastery of Roncesvalles itself lies a mile to the south, out of sight. Reputedly, Charlemagne founded a monastery at Ibañeta on the spot where Roland died. There was certainly a church there three hundred years later, the church of San Salvador. Today this exists only as a ground-plan pushing up through the turf. Nearby is a rubble of boulders any one of which might be mistaken for the rock Roland cleft in two trying to break his sword—not that guidebooks and tourists' couriers admit such doubts as to which boulder it was.

The mountain route from the Col de Cize slaloms down to Roland's split rock and the remnants of Charlemagne's church. It was midday—which is lunchtime for Frenchmen, but Spaniards eat at two in the afternoon—so I had a couple of hours to while away, and walked up the pilgrim road into the quiet mountains.

It was hot, suddenly very hot. I shed layers of clothes and tied them round my waist. Outcrops of rock glistened with iron in the sun. Huge beeches clustered in sheltered places, and vivid moss flourished in their shade. On the moss sat a grey-uniformed Guardia Civil, his improbable hat like a black bandage with wings pressed over a military hair-cut. He gazed at me and grunted when I said good afternoon. Self-consciously I went on at the same slow pace, half-expecting him to reappear from behind every tree, until the track zig-zagged up on to the open hillside. Clouds were sliding in from the east on invisible shelves. I sat and regained my breath, and watched six vultures circling below me on their slow control-lines, sinister in their silence. I wondered about their markings: seen from below inconspicuously brown so as to attract the least attention, but from up here displaying a vivid black-and-white signal like a marker-buoy to other vultures out of human sight in the sky. Perhaps it was the vultures that made me feel hungry; and I rose and walked down the mountain again. The Guardia Civil had gone. I felt less hunted, and much in mind of a bottle of red Navarre wine.

Aymery Picaud writes that there are thirteen stages between the Col de Cize and Santiago de Compostela. This is such a modest number for a journey two-thirds across the breadth of northern Spain that it is clear he was writing for the minority of wealthier pilgrims travelling on horseback: indeed, the millions who went on foot could not have read him since they would have been, for the most part, illiterate. At the inn in Roncesvalles I met a French-man of seventy-five who was making the pilgrimage on foot. His skin looked shrunken within his clothes, and his bones within his skin, and a scallop-shell dangled on a thong from his rucksack. He had been a bank manager in Le Puy, he told me. Now his wife was dead and his son was working on Concorde in Toulouse, had even offered him a flight in it, he said, elbowing his way into a lettuce salad, but that was not his pace at all. Lord no! His son ate too much and had a holiday flat in one of the new developments along the Languedoc coast; his grandchildren had long hair or else they took *la pilule*, and he didn't understand what was going on. The 20th century was slipping away from him, and he had taken to the road back to make his peace and affirm his values. He talked with the shining euphoria of one who had found his way, and as I listened to him speak of all the pain and sorrow and disappoint-ments of his life, something of the mediaeval spirit of pilgrimage came alive in this tallowy figure. The world had mostly failed him, and he accused it with all the venom of Alf Garnett. His views on every subject were rather horrifying, yet as a pilgrim he radiated humility and joyousness; he welcomed me as a friend until my own detachment made me feel guilty of failing him, and he spoke of love and goodness as though nothing else lay in his heart and he had not already thrown acid in the world's face. If I understood something more about pilgrimages from this man, I also realised that I should have made a rotten pilgrim in any age.

The Augustinian abbey of Roncesvalles was built during the century in which Aymery Picaud was preparing his guide. The Augustines had already concerned themselves with helping pil-grims before the Benedictines of Cluny became involved with the route to Santiago, and to an extent their activities were just as political. Roncesvalles, situated on what was already in Roman times the principal road into Spain, occupied a focal as well as emotional point on the pilgrimage route. It was the first major religious house after the junction of three out of the four pilgrim roads through France. It was at the gateway of Spain, the "promised land" which, with St James's aid, was in the process of being liberated from the Infidel. And it bore a name which carried the whole heady romance of the Charlemagne legend into direct associa-tion with the Santiago pilgrimage and with the liberation of Spain.

Roncesvalles grew wealthy and powerful on such reverence. I suppose that running on Charlemagne's ticket it could hardly fail to. The monastery's organisation was a factor in this success. From Bordeaux to the Pyrenees a chain of small convents and priories owed direct allegiance to Roncesvalles, and each of these kept a small hospice for pilgrims, to facilitate their journey, where they were no doubt primed with suitable information about the mother-house; and since much of that area lay in English hands during the Middle Ages, Roncesvalles was also able to extend its services to England itself, where it had "connections"—as we say —among the monks at Charing Cross, who could be relied upon to give a glowing account of the place and to acquaint would-be pilgrims with the deeds and legacy of Charlemagne.

The hospitality offered at Roncesvalles was indeed several categories better than that to which the pilgrim was accustomed. He would be welcomed by a monk who stood by the gate to the monastery offering bread to those passing by. (This custom was still observed in the 18th century.) There were separate houses for men and women, two hospitals for the sick, proper beds instead of straw on the floor, even baths. The food offered was of a corresponding standard; while for spiritual sustenance the statue of the Virgin Mary of Roncesvalles, set on the High Altar of the monastery church, was a famous object of veneration. The chapel of St-Esprit, contemporary with the original monastery, possessed a cloister until the 18th century, with thirty tombs which were not inscribed but which the monks of Roncesvalles were proud to show to pilgrims as the resting-place of warriors who had perished in the famous ambush on Charlemagne's army. Artists came to the aid of history by painting murals illustrating this battle, and included the names which history had omitted—Roland, Oliver and other legendary heroes—in their re-enactment of the scene. These paintings were actually no more than illustrations of songs that were popularly sung about Roncesvalles in the Middle Ages along the pilgrim routes, but they supported the impression that pilgrims were privileged to revere the relics of heroes who had served the champion of Christendom and had perished at the perfidious hand of the Infidel. It was all a pack of lies, but even the monks are unlikely to have known that.

The chapel of St-Esprit still survives, a low, deep-roofed

building crowned with corrugated iron and with little that is legendary about its plain squat features. Next to it stands the 13th-century chapel of St James, the pilgrims' own chapel, in grey simplicity by the gate of the monastery. There are solemn beech-woods all around, the sound of mountain streams and the scream of swifts; but disillusionment sets its roots here. The guidebooks, expansive on the history and legend of the place, do state that the monastery of Roncesvalles has since been much changed in the Gothic period, during the Renaissance and in the 17th century. What they do not say is that time has thoroughly gutted it of its life, its function and its spirituality. Roncesvalles today has the feel of a run-down boarding-school of spartan character where the boys are hanging around to leave and the masters hanging on to retire.

The very first impression is an ugly one: driving down through the beech-woods from Ibañeta one is confronted by acres of corrugated iron, which is practical roofing material in a snowy climate, to be sure, as I imagine it might be useful to coat the Port-land stone of St Paul's Cathedral with a pollution-resistant plastic skin—perhaps a pink one against glare. Below roof-level Ronces-valles is no more inviting: an unloved, secular-looking place, its institutional buildings of stone and whitewashed plaster backing into the hillside, its courtyards scratched by chickens and threaded with laundry. A few surly monks mutter by. A tourist shop sells views and knick-knacks.

The early Gothic cloister retains a certain chill beauty in decay, its wooden shutters broken, damp plants sprouting from its walls: off it an equally gloomy chapel serves as a pantheon for the colossal sarcophagus of King Sancho VII of Navarre, who was seven feet tall and hero of the conclusive battle against the Moors at Las Navas de Tolosa in the year 1212. The monastery church itself, a hand-some French Gothic construction with Romanesque origins, is as cold and bare as winter, and the statue of the Virgin of Ronces-valles on the High Altar glimmers between electric candles.

I wanted to see the famous treasury. A notice invited me to knock. Anxious not to rouse the monks from their contemplation, I knocked delicately and waited. Then I knocked again more boldly. Still nothing. Not a sound through the monastery. I returned to the lady in the postcard stall and explained. She put down her knitting and mumbled something about the idle bastard upstairs. She shuffled to the door in her slippers and banged loud enough on it to rouse the porter in Macbeth's castle; then she heaved on a great chain which set a bell clanging and clanging within the silent house. I began to wish I had given Roncesvalles a miss, and muttered apologies for causing so much trouble to the good monks; but she only cursed some more, and clanged again, shouting this time the most unfriendly threats, until at length slow footsteps could be heard on the stairs. As I prepared my most obsequious expression in greeting, the wooden door squeaked open just enough to reveal not a tonsured reverend at all but a youngish janitor who, it seemed, was her husband and from whose manner, it seemed, might not have been too good at it.

The treasury is a monument to the Charlemagne legend, and to the success with which that legend was harnessed to the dual cause of the Holy War and the Santiago pilgrimage. Here are the slippers of Archbishop Turpin of Reims who is supposed to have accompanied Charlemagne on his Spanish campaigns but who in all probability did not. Here are Roland's war-clubs, which may conceivably have belonged to Sancho VII over four hundred years afterwards, but which are more likely to be anonymous relics from the battle of Las Navas de Tolosa. From the same battle is an oriental emerald by tradition worn in the turban of the Moorish leader defeated by Sancho. And here is Charlemagne's chess-board, so-called, which is in fact a very handsome reliquary in gold, silver and enamel, dating from the 14th century, 600 years later. This reliquary houses two pieces of the True Cross, set into it on a gold disc like some enshrined hot-cross bun. I came away bemused by this half-hearted display of make-believe.

The popular link between the Charlemagne legend and the pilgrimage to Santiago was the *Chanson de Roland*. Epic poems were regularly sung by poet-minstrels, or *jongleurs*, for the entertainment of pilgrims at inns along the way. *Jongleurs* also sang at fairs, outside the doors of churches, and accompanied parties of pilgrims on their travels. The exact origins of the *chansons* they sang are obscure since it was not until the latter part of the Middle Ages that they came to be written down. They certainly existed in numerous versions, and in general took some heroic legend as their theme. In Spain the exploits of Rodrigo Díaz de Vivar (El Cid) yielded the first Spanish epic poem known to us, the *Cantar de mio Cid*, composed about the middle of the 12th century; while on the French side of the Pyrenees it was the campaigns of Charlemagne which provided the most popular themes and resulted above all in the *Chanson de Roland*, the first French epic poem, which was set down at approximately the same time.

The classic instrument of these vagabond singers was the hurdy-gurdy, and illustrations of them playing this instrument appear on the carved portals of a number of mediaeval churches along the pilgrim routes. At the beginning of the 16th century the Flemish painter, Hieronymus Bosch, gave it a place of prominence in his masterpiece, "The Garden of Earthly Delights", now in the Prado Museum in Madrid; and by including it in the panel devoted to the torments of hell he expressed what may have been the official church view of the entertainment it supplied. A more sympathetic view of the instrument was taken a century later by the French artist Georges de la Tour. I like to think that for his salty portrait of a "Blind Hurdy-Gurdy Player", which is one of my favourite works in all French art, the painter may have used as his subject one of those vagrant rogues who attached themselves to the pilgrim roads when all else in their lives had collapsed but a love of sweet music and strong liquor.

The pilgrims also journeyed to the accompaniment of more devotional music. There were the *chansons de St-Jacques*, which dwelt on the miracles the apostle had performed, his deeds in the rout of the Infidel, and the salvation he offered to the traveller who would go in search of him. Several of such "hymns" that were chanted by pilgrims to keep their spirits up on the way to Santiago are included in the *Codex Calixtinus*. They are among the earliest pilgrims' songs known to us, and to judge by the recording recently made of one of them, *Ultraea*, by the Société des Amis de St-Jacques in Paris (as part of a record of mediaeval songs devoted to St James), they were touching in their simplicity and vigour, and must have made a stirring sound from the lips of a hundred or more pilgrims as they approached Roncesvalles across the open mountainside, or caught sight of the towers of Santiago from the Galician highlands.

It has been claimed—without any supporting evidence—that it was the monastery of Cluny which was responsible for attaching the Charlemagne legend to the cause of the Santiago pilgrimage. It has even been suggested that the *Chanson de Roland* was actually "sponsored" by Cluny, in order that the history of Charlemagne's exploits in Spain might be rewritten in a popular form and suited to the requirements of the pilgrimage which that monastery was pledged to support, thereby providing a legend that would rival in its appeal the story of the liberation of Jerusalem by the crusaders. From a position at some safe distance from the facts, I must say this sounds highly unlikely, and I would recommend anyone who may favour such a view to take himself to the city of Nantes and to contemplate Georges de la Tour's "Blind Hurdy-Gurdy Player"; then to ask himself whether the predecessors of such a putrid old vagabond would have been likely to accept or receive the sponsorship of the most civilised and powerful monastic institution in the western world.

A much more likely explanation is that the authorities at Cluny, who were nothing if not resourceful politicians, seized on the legends that were already current, and the epics that were already being sung, and turned them into official history. If the *Codex Calixtinus* is the work of Cluniac propaganda which many scholars have believed it to be, then the account of Charlemagne's experiences which is contained in the fourth book of the *Codex* is a vivid example of that exploitation of popular legend at work.

Book Four of this *Codex* is the so-called chronicle of Archbishop Turpin—*Turpini Historia Karoli Magni et Rotholandi*—otherwise known as the *Pseudo-Turpin* for the good reason that it has no connection with Turpin whatever. The chronicle of Turpin recounts how Charlemagne, after a long life of campaigns and troubles, saw a starry road in the sky that crossed France and Spain towards the end of the world. Since—as I described in Chapter I—the body of St James had not yet been discovered in Galicia, Charlemagne was deeply perplexed. (For the purposes of this story one has to assume that Charlemagne never previously had time in his busy life to notice the Milky Way.) Some nights later Charlemagne was visited by a man who addressed him thus:

I am James the Apostle, servant of Christ, son of Zebedee, brother of John the Evangelist, appointed by God's grace to preach His law, Whom Herod slew: look you, my body is in

Galicia, but no man knows where, and the Saracens oppress the land. Therefore God sends me to recapture the road that leads to my tomb and the land wherein I rest. The starry way that you saw in the sky signifies that you shall go into Galicia at the head of a mighty host, and after you all peoples shall come in pilgrimage even to the end of time . . .

This scene is also recorded on Charlemagne's shrine at Aix-la-Chapelle, now Aachen.

Accordingly, Charlemagne is reported to have made three expeditions into Spain. The first of these expeditions took him to Pamplona, thence westwards to the Atlantic coast at Padrón (where, according to the legend soon to become widespread, St James's body was brought ashore); on the second, he founded an abbey where the town of Sahagún now stands, to the east of León; and it was at the conclusion of the third expedition that his rearguard was ambushed from the heights above Roncesvalles and one thousand of his knights died in the attack, including Roland and Oliver. Charlemagne, according to the *Pseudo-Turpin*, sorrowfully buried them at Blaye on the estuary of the Gironde, at Bordeaux, at Bélin a little to the south, and at Les Alyscamps in Arles; he also founded churches dedicated to St James at Béziers, at Sorde (where Picaud described the villainous boatmen), at Paris and at Toulouse (where he presented the bodies of six apostles).

This is not an account which agrees in all respects with the one given in the *Chanson de Roland*, and it agrees in very few respects with the facts of history as we know them. Where historical facts diverge from it most crucially is at one key point—Charlemagne never went to Galicia or anywhere near the tomb of St James. The *Pseudo-Turpin* and the *Chanson de Roland*, both rooted in popular legend and both concerned with the epic stature of their heroes, contrived to establish Charlemagne not simply as the defender of Christendom, which he was, but as the first pilgrim of St James, which he unquestionably was not.

The clouds sliding in from the east had built up into rain and mist. Roncesvalles looked more bleak than ever under a grey sky. It was late afternoon. Outside their derelict-looking barracks, members of the Guardia Civil were listening to English pop-music on transistor radios. Farther down the road a pilgrims' cross stood back among dripping Christmas trees. The original one, known as Roland's Cross, was destroyed by Napoleon's armies, even though it had been mostly for the reassurance of French pilgrims that the cross had been put up in the first place. This was the mildest of the acts of pillage and desecration performed by that barbarous crew. The present cross—14th century in origin—was put up almost a hundred years later, by now grown as mossy and ageless in appearance as though it had grown here in its bed of violets. I drove on towards Pamplona, my exhilaration of the morning more than a little dampened by the day.

Pamplona is the capital of Navarre. Now, the area of the French Basque Country I had come from is also known as Navarre—Old Navarre—though the people who live there call themselves Basques and the majority of them speak Basque. To add to the confusion many of the people in Spanish Navarre also speak Basque, but Navarre not being one of the three official Basque provinces of Spain, they call themselves Navarrais instead. The Basques are also an intensely nationalistic and private race, which the Navarrais do not appear to be, though since the two are, for the most part, synonymous, I am puzzled as to how this can be, and where national boundaries and loyalties may reside. I doubt if General Franco knows either, though clearly he wishes they would go away. I sidestep the puzzle, except to say that Pamplona in my experience is among the most rumbustious and outward-going cities in Europe, with a hat-in-the-air vitality that is in stark contrast to the sullen dignity of Castilian Burgos only a hundred miles away to the west. In Pamplona you feel people fear to take life seriously; in Burgos that they fear not to.

Ernest Hemingway of course loved Pamplona and the Navarrais. Richard Ford was more snooty, though he did permit himself to suggest that one should "observe the buxom peasant girls". Aymery Picaud, by all accounts, observed them a good deal too closely. In certain regions—not admittedly in Pamplona—when the Navarrais of both sexes got heated, Picaud vouched, they frankly exposed themselves to the opposite sex, the women as shamelessly as the men; and if no pleasure was forthcoming in this direction then the men openly fornicated with their animals, even going so far as to fix chastity-belts on their mules to keep them from their lascivious neighbours.

For a pittance, Picaud goes on, a Navarrais will kill a Frenchman. Altogether they are "full of wickedness, dark in colour, ugly of expression, debauched, perverse, perfidious, disloyal, corrupt, sensual, drunken, experts in every form of violence, ferocious and wild, dishonest and untrue, impious and impolite, cruel and querulous, incapable of all worthy feeling, attuned to all the vices and iniquities". The very name Navarrais, he claims, derives from the Latin *Navarrus* meaning *non verus*—untruthful. With just such a prospect of welcome did the mediaeval pilgrim make his way down from Roncesvalles.

At the approach to Pamplona the pilgrims' bridge over the River Arga is hidden among poplars. The main roadway into the city passes nearby. A stone font showing Moorish influences has been placed by the side of the old bridge, next to a modern cross, and near it stands a convent. From here pilgrims made their way under the massive walls of the city to the Puerta de Francia, which is the north gate and leads directly into the oldest part of the town. Charlemagne insisted on demolishing the original walls of the city for fear of having to encounter a fortified bastion on his journey back to France, and it was in return for this threat to their pride and their safety that the Navarrais, or Basques (at any rate, not the Moors, as legend relates) chose to ambush his army at Roncesvalles. How often, I wonder, do the roots of epic lie in such small local politics?

The walls of Pamplona have been rebuilt and razed again many times since then. The present walls are ringed on the north side with the remains of many of their predecessors, and their wreckage is a witness to the hazards of living on the strategic path between France and Spain, between Islam and Christendom, between northern Europe and southern. The Navarrais always got it in the neck. On this damp evening in early summer the colossal ramparts served no more martial a function than a promenade for elderly couples exercising tiny dogs and, in one place, a pelota court where four young men had peeled off their jackets on their way home from work and with bare hands were slamming a hard ball against the far wall amid the city rubbish that had blown there.

There were many churches for the pilgrim here. San Saturnino is often referred to as San Cernin and is a 13th-century black hulk rising out of the side streets, built under Cluniac influence and in fact named after the same dubiously Christian martyr who gave his name to St-Sernin in Toulouse. A figure of St James stands in front of the church porch. The interior oozes with Spanish Baroque glimmering in the gloom. Pamplona, I was reminded, was also the city where St Ignatius Loyola had set his steely mind to the Counter-Reformation, and to the conception of the Jesuit Order.

The original Romanesque cathedral is no more. Neither is the 11th-century hospice of San Miguel which was much frequented by pilgrims and which endured until the last century. The building that has replaced the old cathedral is a Gothic construction of the early 15th century, with a blunt neo-classical façade of columns reminiscent of the British Museum, and put up in 1783 "during the pseudo-classical and Royal Academical mania", sniffed Richard Ford. "The cathedral library is tolerable," he acknowledged, with the air of one who had read it all and found the Arabic to be less verbose than he expected.

Inside the cathedral the sun diluted darkly on to gilt *retablos*. The kings of Navarre lie buried here in the nave: on their tombs their alabaster features wear a look of frozen piety. Behind the choir, golden caskets—safely locked and barred—are illuminated in the walls of the ambulatory. The caskets contain fragments of forgotten saints once considered memorable enough to warrant the skills of the finest Arab craftsmen to enshrine them. One of the caskets can be dated 1005: it is the earliest piece of Christian ivory carving in Spain—except that everything which makes it distinguished is not Christian at all but Moorish. I found it exceedingly doubtful whether these early Spanish kingdoms were more than superficially dedicated to the cult of Christianity, so imbued were they with a culture and a civilisation that was in every way superior to what Christendom then had to offer in western Europe. What is more, co-existence seems to have worked in much of Spain for several hundred years, and religious tolerance been practised. Moorish masons built Christian churches: Christian craftsmen acquired from them such skills as tilework, mosaic, ivory-carving, the science of perspective, an understanding of mathematics, above all, a sense of abstract design. A hybrid culture was already in existence in Spain when something happened to Christendom. It acquired a spirit of zeal. It grew militant. It wanted to beat the world. From that moment onwards there could be no more co-existence, and the Christian conscience would not rest until the last Infidel had been swept from the Spanish peninsula, and the armies of righteousness had crossed every known sea to hack all unsuspecting pagans to their knees.

CHAPTER VIII

◆

Hermits of Castile

"There are four roads which, on their way to Santiago, become one at Puente la Reina." So wrote Aymery Picaud. Puente la Reina lies fifteen miles south-west of Pamplona, and the fourth pilgrim road which joined the others at this point was the one from Arles and St-Gilles. It had cut directly westward across Languedoc to Montpellier and St-Guilhem-le-Désert, taken in Toulouse, then swung southwards through Gascony over the High Pyrenees to Jaca, thence west again, hugging the foot of the mountains until it joined the other routes and became a single road all the way to Santiago—the *camino francès*, the way of the French.

This fourth road involved a mountain journey a good deal more arduous than that through Roncesvalles. Picaud calls it the *Portus Asperi*: today it is the Somport Pass, and at nearly 5000 feet it is almost twice the altitude of Roncesvalles. Not surprisingly one of the most celebrated hospices in mediaeval Europe was waiting to receive pilgrims not far from the summit: this was attached to the priory of Santa Cristina, which today survives as a few scattered stones only. Then there was Jaca, already an important city in the 11th century, and where St Francis of Assisi halted on his way to Santiago. There was much French influence in Jaca, too: King Louis VII stayed here as a pilgrim to Compostela, and the style of local church architecture—particularly in the marvellous Romanesque cathedral—came from across the mountains, from Languedoc and south-west France, along with the pilgrims.

But where was French influence *not* marked in these northern kingdoms of Spain? Forty miles past Jaca stands the monastery of San Salvador de Leyre, whose church was substantially rebuilt by monks from Cluny during the early Gothic period. In the Middle Ages San Salvador de Leyre had been the most important Spanish monastery and hospice on the entire pilgrim route, and after it was wrecked by the Moors, and reconstructed, some of the kings of Navarre used it as their pantheon.

I drove out there from Pamplona. The road descended to a river valley that sucked the wind and dust off the plains of Aragon to the east. A rough shoulder of rock shut off the north, and a track climbed up towards it among box-wood and gorse and a gale strong enough to blow me to Burgos.

Of the old monastery predating the attentions of the Moors little remained. The crypt had been deep enough in the ground to survive: steps led down to a forest of chunky columns dramatised by concealed lighting. In the forecourt above, excavations were in the process of uncovering some foundations, it was impossible to tell what of, but a heap of bones and skulls was being piled up on one side to the delight of several parties of Spanish tourists. Every now and then, interest was rekindled by a new femur or jawbone tossed up on the pile from below, and I felt that given a small miracle at this moment the party might fall upon the bones and enshrine them in brass and plastic beads.

The monastery church of San Salvador de Leyre is one of the most enchanting in Spain. It has a carved portal reminiscent of those squat churches of the Saintonge I had been admiring some weeks earlier: the familiar beasts crowded into the arches above the door, and a central column dividing the entrance. Inside, the broad nave is scored by delicate 14th-century vaulting; beyond, the neatest of Romanesque choirs is flanked by three arches, each diminishing in size as they recede towards the apse, to produce a theatrical illusion of greater distance than there is, as well as a feeling of intimacy framed by grandeur.

A tall American standing next to me introduced himself quietly as an architect and said, "That is what I call architecture." We agreed how rare it was in Spanish churches that architecture was allowed to have its say uncluttered. I did not feel quite patronising enough to add how rare it was to find an architect taking an interest in historic buildings at all; so I merely asked him why American architects in general seemed to possess a broader outlook than those in England. He said he thought that, if this were so, it was because their professional scope was so much less restricted and their viewpoint accordingly less mean. He spoke as a man who would have looked the architect of Chartres squarely in the eye.

The American went off to find his son who was more gripped by the bones of Cluniac monks than the charms of Cluniac architecture. I drove quietly down the track towards the main road again, and followed the slab of high rock in the direction of Pamplona. Here and there the pilgrim road could be seen hugging the base of the cliff, no more than a cart-track now. Soon it reached a point where a tributary of the River Aragon had eroded a gorge through the rock; and, there, in a setting reminiscent of a vintage Western, were two single-span bridges, old as the pilgrim road, high over the canyon. The larger bridge had collapsed, and the smaller was still intact, though when I left the car by the roadside and made my way up to it I convinced myself that, since one bridge had given way, there was no good reason why the second should not also. A hoopoe perched on the slender span and raised its crest at me as if in reproach, and I turned and retraced my steps through the shale and the scrub of bright yellow jasmine.

A mile or so down-river lay the town of Sangüesa. Here the Knights of St John of Jerusalem established a hospice for pilgrims in 1131, and here the church of Santa Maria la Real still displays a portal richly carved with figures of heaven and hell. They are primitive, vivacious carvings, some of them sculpted into pillars that were to me a faint echo of the great figures on the west door of Chartres—more evidence, I thought, of wandering craftsmen bringing ideas and skills with them across the Pyrenees, though in this case the sculptor probably came from Burgundy. St James leans upon his staff above the tympanum.

It was another Sunday: one half of Navarre I had seen getting ready for a picnic by the river-side. Much of the other half I now found packed into the Bar Las Navas, where the sounds of singing and drinking spilt into the main street and swirled round the groups of young girls, scrubbed and primped in white, making their way to church. Handsome Renaissance houses bore gigantic heraldic coats-of-arms beneath carved wooden eaves. From the church of Santiago burst a cacophony of bells, and fireworks sizzled into the morning sky.

I turned off the main road to Pamplona to follow the pilgrim road direct to Puente la Reina. The outlines of fields looked roughly-cut with scissors and slapped down in a patchwork on this scrubby landscape. The wind was rasping the plateaux, tearing at the soil

The first town after the four main pilgrim roads meet: Puente la Reina, named after the bridge built for pilgrims in the 11th century by Queen Urraca

(*Above left*) Basque Country: view from the point where three of the main pilgrim roads become one

(*Above right*) The old pilgrim road in Spanish Navarre, west of Puente la Reina: the road was paved along much of its length, and five metres wide, an indication of the heavy traffic it took

(*Below*) Hornillos del Camino, a village to the west of Burgos built for and around the pilgrim road

The Spanish Church continued to glorify St James as the saviour of Spain from the Moors: witness this extravagant 18th-century statue on the side of the church of Santiago in Logroño, Old Castile

(*Above*) Scene depicting the
fight between Roland and the
Moorish giant, Ferragut,
carved on a capital of the
Palace of the Kings of Navarre
in Estella

(*Left*) A masterpiece in a cave
in Old Castile: detail of the
12th-century alabaster
sarcophagus of a hermit who
founded a monastery south of
the pilgrim route through this
region

The Cathedral of Burgos, its inspiration drawn from the cathedrals of the Rhineland

(*Above*) West door of the church of Santiago at Carrión de los Condes: detail of a frieze

(*Left*) Carrión de los Condes: statue of St James on the façade of the church dedicated to him

(*Above*) Mozarabic convent chapel of San Miguel de Escalada, approaching León

(*Right*) The great Pantheon of the kings of León, off the cloisters of the church of San Isidoro, León: the Romanesque murals represent one of the most complete cycles of 12th-century painting in Europe

One of the columns of the cloisters in the monastery of Santo Domingo de Silos

The great monastery of Santo Domingo de Silos: the two-tiered, 11th-century cloisters possess some of the finest stone carving in Spain, a blend of Moorish and Christian influences

wedged precariously with vines, spinning it into slender coils of dust. Navarre—country of wind and wild roses, prayers and picnics. Then I came to Eunate.

The 12th-century chapel of Eunate is octagonal and stands in the middle of a field. It is surmounted by a twin-arched belfry and ringed by an open colonnade set within a low wall to keep the cornfield out. Light squeezes into the building through windows of alabaster, and between each of the walls rise slim columns which become arches and meet in the centre of the roof in an eight-pointed star. I have visited Eunate twice in my life: on the first occasion it was desolate and chill, with not a glimpse of life save a golden oriole swooping between the poplar trees. This Sunday, at a hot midday, it was transformed into a Spanish Hampstead Heath. Young Pamplona had emptied upon it equipped with barbecues, wine and the inevitable daytime fireworks. (Is there some law or superstition forbidding fireworks at night in Spain except on civic occasions?) Again I was reminded of the fizzing exuberance of the Navarrais. There seemed no reason why this remote hermitage chapel should have been selected—unless it be a tradition of making Sunday excursions to church, with a party to swill the service down. In any case, that was the stage it had reached when I arrived. About a hundred teenagers were dancing round the outside of the colonnade, dressed in half-Navarrais costume of berets and tasselled jackets and half-discothèque gear of jeans and tee-shirts with Mustang Cobra Jets and Elvis printed on the front. Some of them were playing what sounded remarkably like a Scottish air on an instrument that resembled a piccolo; others beat a quick rhythm on a drum, and there was much hand-clapping and hopping about in Highland fashion. There was some particularly light-footed dancing over a skipping-rope, while the younger men engaged in athletic leaps. The wine was passed from hand to hand, and the smell of woodsmoke and lamb grilling on charcoal drifted over the fields. Eunate was a glorious place to be that Sunday morning, and I guessed they would all be there till evening.

Puente la Reina was just down the road. The junction of the four routes which Picaud wrote of lies at the approach to the town, and from here a single pilgrim road, the *camino*, passes beneath an arch between the church of El Crucifigo and a former monastery-cum-hospice which is today a college. This complex of buildings looks more heavily restored than it is, disappointingly so. How conditioned we are to respond to ruins. Fountains Abbey, Stonehenge, the Colosseum, the temples of Karnak: had the plunderers respected their perfect state, would our sensibilities ever have been so quickened by them as by their sweet elegance in decay? Henry Moore has said that the Parthenon complete was a building, but in ruins it has become a piece of sculpture. We have been conditioned to prefer the sculpture. In a sense, the pilgrims may have been similarly conditioned: a saint's rib or toe-nail had them genuflecting in reverence, but what would they have done if they had met a flesh-and-blood apostle on the road? Asked him the way to the tomb?

The porch of the church of El Crucifigo is freely decorated with scallop-shells among very Moorish stone tracery: some terrifying beasts of hell are included there, in case the pilgrim had by now lost sight of the cause of his journey amid the hazards of the Pyrenees and the wilder habits of the Navarrais. Appropriate to the first place of prayer which united pilgrims from all the four routes, here was a truly international church. Travellers from every nation in Europe came here, and, what is more, it seems the tradition is still maintained. Confession may be heard in six languages today, though on the day I visited the church there was no one to say or receive even a good afternoon.

From El Crucifigo the pilgrim road, now the Calle Mayor, strikes directly through the middle of Puente la Reina. "A tidy place," acknowledged Richard Ford. The main street is sunless, flanked by tall severe houses and a finely arcaded main square, and by the church of Santiago from whose belfry the bell still rings forty times at nightfall. Inside is a 14th-century statue of the saint halting to pray. Then, at the end of the long street, the western gate of the town leads directly out on to the finest bridge to be built for pilgrims along the whole route to Santiago—built near the end of the 11th century at the command of Queen Urraca, the daughter of Alfonso VI who had captured the Spanish capital of Toledo from the Moors in 1085. Queen Urraca's great bridge stands unchanged, still mostly for foot-passengers and animals, since a new roadbridge nearby takes through-traffic via a ring-road outside the walls.

Once I was across the River Arga, the old road climbed steeply on to the low *sierra*. The dry-stone walls marking its course struck across open, gravelly countryside under the larks and clouds. There were poppies in the corn, and wild roses looped over the verges of the ploughland. To the left, a line of olive-trees had sprung from the rootstock of trees that must have been old enough to give shade to the earliest pilgrims. I decided to leave the car for the remainder of the day and to go on foot through the afternoon. Instead of the damp pasture of France I had walked through the week before, there was now a footing of stones, sand, scrub and thyme. The road took its time along the contours of the dusty hills—and so did I.

The next village was always in sight, a pattern of dun-coloured roofs on the hill ahead, matted round its church. Cirauqui was like this. The road had stumbled down between high banks and over boulders displaced from walls which once flanked it. Bursts of broom and honeysuckle half-blocked the way, until the track emptied into a field and I could see it cutting across the main road and curling up the far hill to disappear under a stack of roofs. Modern roads, by swishing past them, leave old villages like this behind in the past, until they become peasant Bantustans, shop-windows of the Middle Ages. Cirauqui might have been just such a place in any other European country; but Spain has so much that is mediaeval in its looks and ways that, by and large, passers-by do not stop and ogle at Cirauqui. That was left to me.

Within ten minutes I was in the shadow of its roofs. The track had become paved once more—five metres in width, precisely that of Queen Urraca's bridge at Puente la Reina which I had measured. The stones had become deeply grooved by metal wheels and the tramp of feet; at the edges the flag-stones were a full metre across. A green lizard raised its head above one of them like a miniature dragon, and was gone. Then the road ducked into the village under a narrow arch. The street climbed steeply. On either side the eaves were deeply carved—a reminder that I was still among Basques—and gutters ended in the rusted heads of beasts. Women with silent faces sat in broad doorways watching with their cats, just as their ancestors must have sat watching the pilgrims plod in—watched them, peered at them from upstairs windows, greeted them, set them up with provisions, directed them to the church, wished them well, wished them gone. Cirauqui was more that kind of village than any I had seen. I climbed up to the church. It had a Moorish portal and primitive carvings, and preserved a ruggedly antique appearance from the outside with its bell-tower open to the winds and the lichen and the screaming swifts; but the inside was dainty and antiseptic, ornamented with Baroque *kitsch*. A pelota court occupied the church square. A few houses farther on and the village ended abruptly at the summit of the hill; and there was the rest of my day's walk spread out ahead. I stepped out of Cirauqui by the attic window. On either side of me, blue butterflies were being blown about over the corn.

I waited for a flock of sheep to huddle and nuzzle each other across a ruined bridge at the bottom of the hill. The shepherd, blanket folded over his shoulder, conducted them across the main road like a children's lollipop man; then they fanned out over the bare fields. A mile or so more and I came to a second ancient bridge, worn to a pair of stone hoops. Here, I realised from the notes I carried in my rucksack, was the place where Aymery Picaud warns that the water is particularly fatal, putting the words into the mouth of Pope Calixtus to lend them due weight: ". . . take good care not to put your mouth to the water," he writes, "or to water your horse, because this river brings death." And he proceeds to re-count a characteristically ghoulish tale of how he noticed a pair of Navarrais men whetting their knives on the bank, and asked them if the water was sweet. Being assured that it was, he watered two of the horses in the party, which promptly died, whereupon the two Navarrais ceased whetting their knives and flayed them on the spot. Peering into the river from the shell of Picaud's bridge, I saw the water seething with trout of all sizes, while from the riverbank came an enthusiastic gurking of frogs: clearly pollution was often a worse problem in the Middle Ages than it is now, which was reassuring.

At Estella, on the other hand, says Picaud, the River Ega is sweet and excellent to drink; also "the bread is good, the wine excellent, meat and fish abundant", in fact it "overflows with all delicacies". In the 20th century he would have awarded the place a squad of crossed knives and forks, perhaps even a rosette or two. I wished I could have shared his enthusiasm about Estella. I know it was late and I had walked many miles since noon, but my frayed (and fried) condition could not entirely explain my disappointment with this town. It was partly that, unlike Picaud, I found it hard to obtain anything to eat at all—except in the concrete suburbs or in a Rotary Club atmosphere on the first floor at the end of a corridor painted landlady's green. And it was partly that my car, back in Puente la Reina, was littered with Spanish tourist office pamphlets on Estella that had prepared me for a town to rival Verona in its convivial charm and in the grace of its monuments. Worse still, it so obviously could have been a gem had the authorities taken care of it in due time; instead, it has been ravished by bad taste and mean exploitation, and what remains has been left in decay. Estella means star: a fallen star. Odd corners and back streets offer reminders of what Estella was and might have been: and there are, it is true, a great number of surviving monuments.

Entering Estella from the eastern gate of San Agustín, pilgrims crossed the River Ega and made for the *francos* quarter of San Martín, where French merchants and traders had been encouraged to settle from the 11th century, to help re-establish the town after the depredations of the Moors. The Plaza San Martín was the heart of this French quarter, and where the pilgrims gathered. On one side of the square stands a Romanesque building known as the Palace of the Kings of Navarre—a small palace for a small kingdom —which is of no particular splendour save for a carved stone capital depicting Roland unhorsing the Moorish giant Ferragut with his lance: yet one more instance of the Charlemagne legend being shackled to the Santiago pilgrimage, and a piece of sculpture that would have been clearly visible to pilgrims as they prepared to leave the town along the Calle de San Nicolas and out by the Puerta de Castilla towards those lands only recently liberated from the Moors.

The main place of worship for pilgrims was the church of San Pedro de la Rúa, at the head of a long flight of steps up from the Plaza San Martín. They clambered under the shadow of a massive belltower of Tuscan proportions to one of the most handsome Moorish portals on the pilgrim route. How aware were they, I wonder, of just how many shrines they venerated were the work of the Infidel of whom their revered apostle was the renowned "slayer", *Santiago Matamoros*? After such a dramatic exterior, the inside of San Pedro comes as a disappointment. At least it did to me. A party of local schoolchildren was being given the familiar indoctrination by a paper-white priest. A 19th-century drawing-room chiming clock added a comically discordant note, and my attention was then drawn to a single extraordinary pillar next to the choir, carved in the shape of three entwining serpents rearing upwards and supporting keys and a mitre. Here was a mediaeval touch amid the white-gloved fragrance of the place.

Pilgrims would leave an offering here at the altar of St James; and at the rear of the church was a secluded cloister where those who died here on their journey could be buried. Two sides of the cloister have since been demolished and the town by-pass now runs almost literally overhead, which has somewhat blasted its character. The columns of the cloister are arranged in pairs, as I had seen them at Moissac, and in the middle of one colonnade a group of four columns had been carved in a twisted formation that put me in mind of two pairs of old-tyme dancing partners executing a waltz. The sculpture on the capitals were much damaged, many of them rather academic floral motifs that were less engaging than the jungle of roses and syringa all around. Workmen were trundling barrows of cement and stone in from the lane outside, and by now I expect nature has been firmly uprooted and the whole place is spick and span. Who knows, there may even be a chiming clock in the cloister.

Nuestra Señora de Rocamador on the southern edge of the town was a sanctuary that many French pilgrims would have recognised, since it was a brother foundation to that of Our Lady in Rocamadour in central France. Nobody, I should add, is clear who St Amadour actually was, but a cult nonetheless grew up round her shrine, and the figure of the celebrated Black Madonna of Rocamadour became the object of the most fervent veneration from the later Middle Ages, and has remained so. Attached to this Spanish outpost of the cult there used to be a pilgrim hospice. The apse of the original 12th-century chapel survives, much restored, now part of a neo-classical building of amazing anonymity.

On a hill at the northern edge of the town stood another shrine of French origin: the Real Basilica de Nuestra Señora del Puy. Our Lady of Le Puy is in fact the town's patroness, and the statue of her enshrined here is supposed to have been discovered in the ground through the agency of a magical star. I walked up to it among scented pines next morning, having had to spend the night in Estella, and found the famous treasury closed and the building itself apparently constructed of concrete, glass and rust. Below extended a tatty belvedere that caught the dust and supplied a panoramic view of how the town has been thoroughly messed around.

My sour mood did not begin to disperse until several monuments later and a cup of superb coffee in the main square. What really restored some warmth to my feelings about Estella was the last of the churches I had the strength to visit. This was the largest in the town, San Miguel Archangel, set in a rubble-strewn area by the old market-place. I waited while a party of schoolgirls popping bubble-gum were being told all the right things about the church, then went and had a look at the Romanesque portal, which turned out to have some of the finest carvings in northern Spain. In the centre of the tympanum was the figure of Christ in Majesty, with a row of carved capitals on either side. I was taken back to Burgundy and to those partly-humorous sculptures that told the Bible story to the illiterate. Both on the capitals here, and in the larger relief-carvings and free-standing figures to the left and right of the door, was a quality of artistry and sophistication I had not seen since crossing the Pyrenees. I do not know who carved them—probably no one does—but he was a man who could have kept company with Gislebertus of Autun and with the sculptors of Vézelay and Moissac without bowing his head. He possessed a rare wit, skill and humanity. Later as I made my way to the bus-stop to return and collect my car from Puente la Reina, I retained before my eyes a recollection of one figure above all: a carving of Joseph asleep, wearing one of the most benign smiles in all art.

Driving back through Estella an hour later I was now heading south-west towards the River Ebro which is the boundary of Navarre and Old Castile. But first, there was yet another reminder of France and of those little churches of Poitou and the Saintonge I had warmed to early in my journey during the spring. This was the monastery church of Irache, Santa Maria la Real, one of the earliest Benedictine houses in Navarre with a pilgrim hospice attached that was once famous all along the pilgrim route and is today a priests' seminary. Santa Maria la Real was standing on a hill among a feast of scarlet poppies. After the severe Gothic cloister, the 12th-century church seemed on an altogether more human scale, as though it belonged elsewhere—as in a sense it did. Diminutive carved arches ran round behind the High Altar in a semi-circle, their geometrical patterns and lacelike trimmings producing an effect of such delicacy that I began to imagine how Aymery Picaud, who would have been just too old to know it, might have appreciated such French refinement, and how it would have reminded him of the gentle plains of his Poitou.

Beyond Irache the patchwork countryside continued: vines, almond groves, olive-trees of vast age. First to Los Arcos, where the Renaissance church of Santa Maria was so encrusted with gilt and glistening *retablos* that it was like sitting within a jewel-box. Then to Torres del Rio, with its octagonal chapel reminiscent of Eunate but crowded around with buildings, and with a fortified tower forming the eighth side, slashed with arrow vents. To Viana, a mere village on the map, but where every other house bears a coat-of-arms, and where the church of Santa Maria guards the remains of Cesare Borgia who relieved the world of his presence here. And finally over the last bump of the Pyrenean foothills to the plain of Castile, and to Logroño, where the waters of the River Ebro, so Picaud remarked, were full of fish and which, as far as I could see, still are.

In the earliest days of the pilgrimage the journey to Santiago was an undertaking that only a Marco Polo might have tackled with confidence. The road system introduced by the Romans had deteriorated: where roads existed they were frequently impassable at certain seasons, and there were generally no bridges. Neither was there any assurance of personal safety. Roman order had broken down along with Roman rule, and travellers were the natural prey of bandits. The social system was too unsettled, and authority too dispersed, to keep much check on outlaws, least of all to ensure adequate services for the benefit of those moving from one place to another—whether merchants, musicians, priests or pilgrims.

Towards resolving this state of confusion, one small group of individuals made a contribution out of all proportion to the authority they wielded or the funds at their disposal. These were the hermits. It is hard to look back over such a span of time and be precise in one's mind as to what sort of people hermits were in the

Middle Ages. Many were unquestionably odd: drop-outs and mis-
fits and self-styled mystics of one kind or another, who were more
or less outcasts from society (very likely regarded with the kind of
amused suspicion with which western society of the late 1960s
regarded "hippies"). When hermits were killed for their oddity
they became "saints". But there were many devout Christians
among them, monks or priests, men who chose the lonely and
ascetic life dedicated to poverty as a means of purifying the soul
and clearing the mind for the tasks they set themselves to achieve
—theological work, teaching or physical tasks of one kind or
another. These people were the direct heirs of the earliest Christian
devotees in Italy who, following the example of the Copts in the
Middle East, retreated from society and set themselves up in
religious cells. Hermitages were pockets of calm within the storm.

Such a man was Santo Domingo de la Calzada, St Dominic of
the Causeway. He acquired his name on his reputation as a builder
of roads and bridges in the 11th century. By origin a shepherd, he
is reputed to have been refused entry to a Benedictine monastery
on the grounds of illiteracy, whereupon he built himself a hermitage
and chapel in a forest between Logroño and Burgos on a particularly taxing and bandit-infested stretch of the pilgrim route. Here
he offered travellers the comparative safety of a roof for the night,
and set himself to clear an area of the forest and construct a proper
road where none existed.

The activities of Santo Domingo came to the attention of King
Alfonso VI. Alfonso had high political ambitions to be overlord
of the Iberian peninsula, and even awarded himself the title Emperor of all Spain. It was important for any Spanish ruler to encourage French support for the struggle against the Moors and to
encourage the Santiago pilgrimage which brought into Spain the
craftsmen and merchants the country needed, besides the wealth and
know-how of the French church. It was Alfonso who permitted
settlers to establish their own Frankish districts in Estella, Logroño,
Burgos and other towns along the route to Santiago, and who saw
to it that the way was, if not entirely freed from bandits, at least
relatively safe. And so it was that Santo Domingo found himself
accorded special funds and privileges in order to pursue his construction work. Other hermits followed Santo Domingo's philan-
thropic example, notably his disciple San Juan de Ortega, and

within two centuries Christian hermits were numerous and important enough for Pope Innocent IV to enrol them into a new order
adopting the rule of St Augustine. (The Augustine or Austin
Friars trace their origins to this new order.) In order to qualify, it
was first necessary for a man to obtain land on which to build his
hermitage, and the consent of his bishop. Anyone who consults a
detailed map of Old Castile today will find again and again the word
Ermite printed over the bleaker areas of countryside. But the
traditional picture of the bearded sage dressed in a goat's skin
contemplating the desert is only part of the truth. Hermits such as
Santo Domingo were fired by a pioneer spirit: with their per-
tinacity and their practical skills they helped to open up the
country like true frontiersmen.

The bridge over the Ebro that led pilgrims into Castile was built
in the first place by Santo Domingo, and it endured until the 19th
century. It had twelve arches and was guarded by three stone
towers. Once across it, the pilgrim was in Logroño. Since then
the town has expanded into a noisy prosperous centre of business
and minor industry, but the network of dark alleys close to the
river still retains much of the feeling of a mediaeval town. It looks
prosperous, Logroño. No time for folk-lore and face-painting. I
walked down a shaded street that was blowing with poplar-down
from across the Ebro. Shop-windows were hung with red hams
and coiled with yards of livid sausage. I bought presents for my
children, sent a brassy postcard to Gillian and felt for the first
time since Pamplona that I was surrounded by the 20th century—
far from relics and rubble, far from that depressed life of rural
Spain scratched on to the surface of the Middle Ages. How am-
bivalent were my feelings towards it all, towards the journey I
was making, towards the subject of that journey, towards this
book. Perhaps I had done too much of it, too intensely, too quickly.
I needed a reprieve.

The mood lasted only minutes, and what pulled me out of it
more than anything was, finally, nothing to do with the 20th century at all, but a sight that greeted me at the end of the street I
had turned down towards the river. Blocking the way ahead was
the tall Baroque chunk of the church of Santiago el Real, and high
on the north side which faced me was poised a monument to St
James such as I had never hoped to see. It was a colossal equestrian

statue in stone of *Santiago Matamoros*, with our hero thundering
into the attack like Don Quixote in drag, sword flailing, his billow-
ing robes destining him for certain to the fate of Isadora Duncan:
he was mounted, what was more, on a stallion equipped with the
most heroic genitals in all Spain, a sight to make any surviving
Moor feel inadequate and run for cover.

So, as recently as the 18th century—the statue was carved in
1733—the church authorities in Spain were still inflaming their
congregations with tall stories of St James and his feats in battle,
though there were no more scars to show on Crispin's Day and
there had been no Moors to slay for at least three centuries.

Nine hundred years had passed since the birth of that legend,
and it had begun only a few miles from here. I left Logroño now,
in the highest spirits, for the place marked in tiny letters on my
map—Clavijo.

The makers of myth could not have chosen a more stirring site
for the first appearance of *Santiago Matamoros* than Clavijo. Here
was where the King of the Asturias, Ramiro I, deeply ashamed of
his ancestors who had bought off the Moors by sending them an
annual tribute of one hundred virgins, is said to have marched
from his capital at León in the year 834 to engage the enemy in
head-on battle. And this is where, as the outcome of that battle
was looking black for Ramiro, St James is said to have appeared
for the first time at the head of the wilting army of Christendom
and put the Infidel to rout, personally killing 70,000 of the enemy.

There has long been disagreement over whether any such battle
ever took place, with or without St James. But looking down from
the extraordinary pinnacle of rock on which the ruins of the castle
of Clavijo today stand, there could be no doubt even to a mind as
unmilitary as mine that command of the heights of Clavijo must
have been crucial for any army determined to hold the Ebro
valley and therefore the main east–west highway of northern
Spain. All that is most fertile in Castile lies open to the north of
Clavijo: green terraces descend into the plain, with only the wild
Cantabrian mountains in the distance between a defender and the
sea. To the south lie the high *sierras*, sliced by a few tortuous
valleys whose rivers are a dry gutter in summer and a torrent in
winter. Any army reaching Clavijo from that direction would have
felt in sight of the promised land; and Ramiro I, if there be any

truth in the legend, must have sensed from his rich pastures and vineyards that hundreds of thousands of eyes were peering down at him from the desert, and a hundred thousand curved knives being whetted for the kill. No wonder he decided to keep his hundred virgins and try to push the enemy back out of sight once and for all.

It needed only the lightest lift to the imagination to envisage a tremendous tussle and carnage in the slender breach in the mountain far below this high rock at Clavijo : and the pious, who sought to boost legend with fact, can be forgiven for searching that valley for scallop-shells that would prove their apostle had truly been at their army's side—shells (or some sort of shell, at least) which they found in thousands. And not being geologists they could hardly have been expected to recognise that the land they stood on was fossil-bearing rock capable of furnishing a thousand armies of pilgrims to Santiago with the emblem of their saint, or something resembling it. I must say, I looked and found none, which may devalue my thesis, unless of course the armies of the faithful have long since made off with them all.

Another mighty battle was fought in the plain below here in the year 1367. This was nominally a local scrap between Pedro the Cruel of Castile and his brother Henry of Trastamara, except that both protagonists had managed to engage the support of the two outstanding military champions of the day, and of their armies. These were Edward the Black Prince, heir to the throne of England and commander of the English forces in Aquitaine based on Bordeaux, and Bertrand du Guesclin, the Breton warrior who was his principal enemy in battle and was dedicated to driving the English from French soil, a feat which he all but accomplished. The outcome, chronicled by Froissart in the 14th century, was a victory for Pedro and the Black Prince. The great du Guesclin was taken prisoner, and French plans for the liberation of their country dealt a temporary blow. I consulted several accounts of the Battle of Nájera, as it is sometimes known: in Spanish guidebooks it is referred to as a mighty victory for Pedro of Castile over the foreign invader backed by his own treacherous bastard brother (the English army is scarcely ever mentioned); in English it is represented as one of the Black Prince's most famous feats in Europe; while to the French it is an insignificant setback in du Guesclin's triumphant campaign for the liberation of the motherland (and indeed the French warrior was freed for a ransom the following year and proceeded to defeat and slay Pedro, south of Zaragoza, on his way to liberate most of English Aquitaine).

It is not French blood but Rioja wine that is the red of Nájera today. Here San Juan de Ortega built a bridge over a fast-flowing tributary of the Ebro at the point where it had widened a cleft in the magenta sandstone, and where the *sierras* gave way to the rich plains of Logroño. And it was here, a century earlier, that the monastery of Santa Maria la Real was built for the monks of Cluny who were then being invited into northern Spain to strengthen the Christian church and to service the pilgrim route to Santiago. Nothing is left of San Juan's bridge or of the early monastery in Nájera. The present building dates from the Renaissance period, while the lofty church attached to it is 15th-century. A severe cloister of slender columns adjoins the church with, between the columns, stone lattice-work which filtered the early morning sunlight and cast maze-like patterns on to the inner walls along with a thousand shadows of bees nesting in the stonework. Beside the church the pilgrim road pursued a shallow valley up on to the *sierra*; while the main road circuited the old town before cutting west towards the town which takes its name from the engineer-hermit, Santo Domingo de la Calzada.

But first I made a detour south into the foothills of the Sierra de la Demanda to see another of the great abbeys of the Rioja, secluded in a green valley near the village of Berceo, which was the birthplace of the earliest known poet of Castile, Gonzalo de Berceo, who was writing during the same period that Santo Domingo was constructing the pilgrim road to the west. Gonzalo wrote principally on the life of another of the Castilian hermits of this region, San Millán de la Cogolla. It was San Millán who had founded the original monastery here, during the 6th century, round the cave and hermitage where he himself lived. He worked many miracles and, it is said, wrestled with the Devil and (like the Basques) got the better of him.

Today there are two monasteries of San Millán. There is San Millán de Suso (meaning above) and San Millán de Yuso (below). By the 11th century the Benedictine monks of *Suso* felt in need of a more comfortable and spacious house and so built *Yuso* in a setting that was less insistent on mortification of the flesh. The present San Millán de Suso survives as a national monument and dates from the 10th century. Its shape complements the curve of the rock-face round which it is constructed, and which is perforated with the original cave-dwellings of the saint and his followers. The hefty rounded arches have been added to the columns of a Visigothic temple of an earlier period, and these were subsequently given a "kink" or "lip" to transform them into a Moorish design, shaped like a row of broad keyholes.

There was a piercing chill about this church constructed into the damp rock. A healthy Eskimo might have suffered frostbite. I felt for the Benedictines who decided God might be worshipped more warmly down the valley. It was early June and still I dragged five layers of clothes from the car. Those hermits, I reckoned, must have possessed amazing powers to endure this place summer and winter. The guardian of Suso was something of a hermit himself. I could see him watching me closely as I was still some way from the monastery, and he walked down the slippery path towards me with an expression of delight and astonishment that made me feel I might be some early visitor to Mount Athos. He then led me into his cell and before long was reading aloud some verses of Gonzalo de Berceo in a raptured incantation, one hand pressed to his heart, the other stretched out towards the chestnut forest below. Then he read me several of his own poems, mostly composed to local saints, and including one to the Spanish heavyweight boxer Urtain whose photograph heaving rocks was pinned up on the wall.

The guardian, who knew he had got me for the day, led me round his church with deep pride and a great deal of knowledge, supported by the names of no doubt eminent Spanish professors of architecture and archaeology. To all of it I listened attentively until we came to the tomb of San Millán himself, and from that moment his voice became only a distant drone to me. I had known nothing of this extraordinary Romanesque sarcophagus, carved during the 11th and 12th centuries in a sea-green alabaster which is kept almost perpetually moist by the atmosphere of the cave in which it shelters. The guardian lent me his torch to examine it more closely. There lay the full-length image of the saint, carved with an air of massive majesty, and flanked by groups of smaller figures of monks in attitudes of worship and with expressions of agonised devotion, while by the feet of San Millán knelt other small figures of the blind and the afflicted who had come to the saint to seek a miraculous cure. The shining green tomb was supported on the heads of further grimacing figures, and the entire complex of carvings seemed to have been done from a single block. It was a masterpiece that was totally unexpected to me, stunning in its impact.

I paid only a brief visit to the lower monastery, San Millán de Yuso, which is now occupied by the Augustines. The present buildings date from the 15th century, and looked very institutional and bare except for the usual Baroque embellishments in the church. Some birdy cloisters took my eye for a while, but there was nothing else to distract my mind from what I had already seen that day—until the friar led me to the treasury. Here were kept what remain of the 11th-century ivory shrines donated at the time of the rebuilding of the monastery by Sancho the Great, and containing the remains of San Millán and his disciple San Felipe. (The great carved sarcophagus which had so astonished me at Suso is in fact empty.) These two reliquaries, and principally the one known as the Arca de San Millán, were for many centuries among the earliest and finest examples of Christian carving in western Europe. Unhappily they fell victims to Napoleon's avenging armies as he retreated northwards before the Duke of Wellington, and now fragments of their exquisitely worked panels are in collections all over the world, and those that remain have been painstakingly reset into new reliquaries. These were what I saw: and even in this state they were a moving sight. The fourteen tiny panels illustrating the life of the saint are of a delicacy of craftsmanship which stone does not yield to. Mere hairline scratchings conveyed so much feeling, and I appreciated how ivory, because it is soft in texture and fugitive in colour, offers a subtlety of tone—darkish where it has been incised and pale where exposed to polishing hands—which I have never seen obtained in sandstone or granite.

It was close to evening when I took the by-road through Berceo and forked left in the direction of Santo Domingo de la Calzada where I intended to stay the night in a pilgrim hospice built by Santo Domingo himself in the 12th century—not that there would be a straw mattress on the stone flags for me tonight, nor prayers at dawn, nor bread dipped in whey for my supper. The pilgrim hospice at Santo Domingo is now the property of the Spanish state, whose tourist authorities have included it among a collection of historic buildings they have converted—and beautifully converted—into semi-luxury hotels, *Paradors*. The original stern entrance on to the pilgrim street is closed off, and a new façade and entrance built at the side opening on to the cathedral square. The great vaulted interior has been softened by low lights and deep sofas: a finger on the bell will bring you a high-ball or a Scotch-on-the-rocks where exhausted travellers once sipped raw wine from wooden bowls. Only three-star pilgrims need apply; though as I came down early next morning the silhouette of a knight in full armour standing by a stone column momentarily dropped me into the Middle Ages. I hoped the interior designer for the tourist authorities had placed it there for the irony.

As in Puente la Reina the pilgrim street cuts straight through Santo Domingo de la Calzada. In the centre of the town stands the cathedral which was finished in 1180, and as such is among the earliest Gothic buildings in Spain, French in origin and inspiration. Richard Ford comments that it has an "overloaded belfry", which is a fair description. Inside, the usual obscenely ornate Baroque *retablo* rears up behind the High Altar. Santo Domingo's tomb is in the crypt, and a folkloric touch is provided by a twee wooden cage in the south transept containing a live cock and hen. These peck around on a shift basis, relieved by two others periodically so that they shall not perish from the cold. The origin of this nonsense is a now-famous local legend (first recorded by an early 15th-century pilgrim, Nompar de Caumont, in his diary) of a German youth hanged for a theft he did not commit. Divine intervention kept the young man alive on the gallows until a cockerel, which the local justice was about to carve for dinner, jumped up and crowed. The justice was disturbed, not unnaturally, and in seeking the cause of this irregularity he discovered the miraculous survival of the man he had condemned to death. A cockerel and his mate have occupied a place in the church ever since.

On either side of the pilgrim street, west of the cathedral square of Santo Domingo de la Calzada, rose impressive mansions emblazoned with heraldic coats-of-arms, many of them incorporating scallop-shells. Spanish teenagers strolled by in their obligatory blue-

and-white gym-slips, skirts at a decent length, hair squeezed back
into an elastic band. I chewed on the idea of bubble-gum as a
virginity symbol. On the edge of the town a pair of storks prodded
at invisible young on one of those Baroque belfries that look as
though they were designed to the birds' specifications. (Where did
storks nest before Christianity?) Beyond the church lay the sixteen-
arched bridge over the River Glera which was another of the con-
structions of Santo Domingo, today scarcely recognisable as an
antiquity, so thoroughly have the authorities imposed a disguise
by broadening it, adding reinforced pillars and a new surface to
take the main-road traffic to Burgos, and by allowing the site
to be used as the municipal rubbish-tip.

Beyond Belorado, ten miles westwards, the pilgrim road appeared now to the left and now to the right. Soon the old road ran
beneath a sandstone cliff where a priory had been built slap on to
the rockface, presumably on the site of another hermitage. Earlier
I had passed through Castildelgado, a typical village on the pilgrim
route, by-passed by the main road and now slowly crumbling into
the once-paved mud street. The shell of a former convent and
hospice, painted a fading blue, survived at the approach to the
village. Unsmiling faces peered through broken upstairs windows.
Silent children and frantic dogs lingered in doorways. The single
street emptied down a gully into a cornfield.

Other villages were even more deteriorated. Villafranca Montes
de Oca, as its name suggests, was founded by French pilgrims who
were encouraged to settle in Spain by Alfonso VI at a time when
the country was recuperating from the Moorish devastations. It
grew important enough to become the seat of the regional bishop
before this was transferred to Burgos. Today it is just another
tattered village of livestock and muddy streets, with some handsome half-timbered houses faced with plaster glimpsed down
slender alleys and half-hidden flights of steps.

Villafranca lay on the edge of the mountains of Oca, one of the
most dangerous regions along the whole route during the Middle
Ages, notorious for wolves and bandits. Today it is a favourite
site for picnics. In the Montes de Oca, Santo Domingo's disciple,
San Juan de Ortega, set up, in the 12th century, his hermitage,
where pilgrims could pass the night in safety and prepare for the
next day's trek to Burgos. The present road passes a few miles to

the south, and in about the time it takes to chew a peppermint one is in the outskirts of Burgos, with its wild and slightly mad cathedral roof-line which seems to hang by invisible threads above the city.

But I did not want to stay in Burgos yet. I had set myself another hour or more to drive that afternoon, south and east again round the other side of the Sierra de la Demanda. I intended to spend the rest of the day at a place I had read and heard much about, the place that had been the inspiration of the cloisters and carvings at Moissac. This was the Benedictine monastery of Santo Domingo de Silos, whose cloister is generally regarded as the triumphant climax of Romanesque art in Spain, and where—so I discovered—the monks have also revived the mediaeval Gregorian chant. This I had only once before heard one late winter's morning in the north of France, on my way to begin this journey, at the monastery of St-Wandrille in Normandy, as the mists of the Seine had begun to melt away. Now the *sierras* were the colour of cement-dust laid flat against a wall of heat, speckled with the occasional white cistus among the gravel. I had run out of bad weather, and run out of most signs of life too. What an extraordinary landscape this was—so dead today, so full of the spirit of life yesterday. Ruined hermitages and priories were scattered here and there. Christian asceticism had flourished in the parched discomfort of this wilderness; and the Moors, who in the end proved softer in their habits, lost these dominions for ever.

The road wound and narrowed into a gorge, red and grey, spotted with low furze. Erosion had done spectacular damage to this countryside. Then, surprisingly, there were green fields, water, trees, a village. And in the middle of the village the bastion-like walls of the monastery. The first impact of Santo Domingo de Silos is disappointing because everything that is visible of it is severely 18th-century. Nothing remains of the original monastery—except the cloisters.

But what cloisters! This elegant quadrangle of double columns nestled within the bulwark of monastery buildings. The sun was low and had smeared the walls and one side of each column the colour of honey. Each carved capital was lit against violet shadows. Diagrams of light and dark, drawn by the sun's glare as though with the sharpest pencil, demonstrated the calculated subtleties of the building: the balance of upper and lower cloisters, the slight swelling in the centre of each stone pillar, and in the upper cloister the merest concavity in each alignment of stones so that from the four corners every column was retained in view—just. As for the capitals themselves, I had considered at San Millán the previous day that no stone-carving could match the delicacy of ivory. I began to reconsider that view. Some of the leaf and animal patterns incised in relief here seemed to defy the brittleness of stone, achieving the effect of filigree gold-work or the finest embroidery. Textures—of fur or feathers—were scratched in as though with needles. Clearly oriental in origin, these writhing, sinewy animal patterns may have been the work of Persian masons according to my guide, Padre Agustín Ruiz, who had been a boy here when Arthur Kingsley Porter was carrying out his momentous research on the sculpture of Santo Domingo during the early twenties. The Persians, I realised, belonging to a different Moslem sect from the Arabs, were not similarly prohibited from treating living forms.

At the four corners of the lower cloister stand large panels over five feet high and carved in low relief—flattened I imagine so that nothing should be allowed to protrude beyond the alignment of the columns. Perfection of geometry was the first consideration. These sculptures are close in style to the astonishing relief-carvings on the portal at Moissac: at their best they appeared to me very nearly as fine, though one of our most intelligent scholars, John Beckwith, has described them as "pale, attenuated, stiff spectres in comparison with the apocalyptic visions of the artists at Moissac . . .", a view which strikes me as prejudiced. The Santo Domingo reliefs are emotionally cooler, by intention less ecstatic. The Entombment panel, and the Crucifixion, throw the emphasis upon a balance of rhythmic shapes which are formed by the angle adopted by the faces, hands, feet and by the graceful elongation of the bodies. The Moissac carvings, on the other hand, concentrate on the passions projected by the individual figures. The sculptures at Santo Domingo are a controlled dance; at Moissac they are something much closer to a bacchanalia.

In the superb panel at Santo Domingo, Christ with his Apostles, the left arm of Jesus is thrust out in a way that is at once distorted and physically awkward: but as a mime gesture it is arresting and powerful, and the same stiff rhythm is picked up in the faces of the apostles, in threes, all tilted the same way; and by the legs of the lowest three crossed over one another like the limbs of puppets. The fourth outstanding panel, the Journey to Emmaus, is the most delicate and emotionally withdrawn of them all, relying for its impact almost entirely on the snake-like curving of the three forms. And here, on the wallet of Christ, is carved a scallop-shell. Christ represented as a pilgrim. Another journey.

That evening, talking with Padre Agustín, there was no doubt at all in my mind that the cloister of Santo Domingo de Silos was among the most radiantly beautiful places on earth. Should I perhaps have been disturbed by my own very peace of mind? Here was I, after all, an atheist, brought up tepid C of E and now standing in a Roman Catholic monastery chatting to a monk who referred to my home city of London (albeit chucklingly) as "Babylon", and I dared to experience such a thing as peace of mind. But the thought did not disturb me. I merely became aware of how few secular buildings in the world were capable of inducing such a condition of peace. Why, asked General Booth, founder of the Salvation Army, should the Devil have all the best tunes? And why, I felt, should God have all the best buildings?

Professor Kingsley Porter points out that documentary evidence dates the earliest part of the Santo Domingo de Silos cloisters to the years following the death of the saint himself—who was abbot here—in 1073. By his assertion, the impact of these sculptures was felt first at Moissac, at Souillac a little farther north, at Arles in the cloisters at St-Trophime, at St-Guilhem-le-Désert, and thence on much of the sculpture of the 12th century. "It is the art of the pilgrimage," he concludes. Scholars have not always found Kingsley Porter's dating convincing: Beckwith for one doubts that the Santo Domingo reliefs were carved before about 1130. But I have never encountered an opinion worth listening to which did not acknowledge that the pilgrim routes supplied the currents which carried these artistic ideals and skills throughout Europe, only disagreement as to which way those currents flowed.

What I find harder to decide is the extent to which pilgrims themselves exerted an influence on the sculpture of the pilgrim routes. We know that master-craftsmen travelled these routes: Kingsley Porter wrote that "the pilgrimage road may be compared to a great river, emptying into the sea at Santiago". We know of the existence of *ateliers voyageurs*. How likely is it, then, that many of these travelling craftsmen were themselves pilgrims? Émile Mâle thought it very probable, and that they offered their professional services on the return journey. John Beckwith has pointed out an ivory relief of the Deposition done in the mid-12th century by a carver of the school of Hereford, which clearly reflects the artist's own journey to Santiago. Unfortunately we know next to nothing of the minds of artists in the Middle Ages. We have their work and sometimes their bills, and that is all. But I should be mightily surprised if the men who travelled from afar to carve the portals of San Miguel Archangel at Estella or Santa Maria la Real at Sangüesa, or these cloister reliefs at Santo Domingo de Silos, were just doing it as a job of work because they were paid to leave home and travel half the western world. Whether or not these craftsmen were pilgrims in fact, they were surely pilgrims at heart. Their vision was moulded by the same faith and the same fears. And they journeyed in much the same way.

The closer one examines these currents along which the art and architecture of the pilgrim routes were borne, the more diverse seem to be the springs that fed them. I have cited the importance of France, in particular the church of Cluny; I have mentioned the contribution of the Moors, often conveyed by Christians—Mozarabic craftsmen—who had worked under the Moors; and I have quoted the importance of Spanish ivories, early French and German enamels, bestiaries, the illustrated versions of Beatus's *Commentaries on the Apocalypse*; even the likelihood of Germanic and Celtic as well as Persian sources. But there is also Byzantium to take into consideration.

We know that illustrations of the church of the Holy Sepulchre at Jerusalem circulated on the pilgrim routes: this was of a round design—a rotunda erected over the tomb—and may well have influenced the design of certain early pilgrim chapels such as the octagonal sanctuary at Eunate in Navarre. The church of the Holy Apostles at Constantinople may have been another model: this was founded in the year 536 by the Emperor Justinian and housed relics of three apostles, Andrew, Luke and Matthew. Rather closer to the west there was Venice, where the great church of St Mark was of course entirely Byzantine in design and had housed the relics of the apostle Mark since these were brought from Alexandria in 829. From the east, in other words, two currents converged on Spain: a Moslem one along the southern coasts of the Mediterranean, and a Christian one along the northern shores.

As to the Romanesque currents, it is generally agreed that Romanesque art emerged in France and Spain more or less simultaneously. But from these twin springs where did the currents flow? Émile Mâle was a true Frenchman and saw it all lucidly in terms of craftsmen–apprentices spreading the culture of northern France along the pilgrim-routes to Bordeaux and Bayonne, Burgos and León, and to Santiago itself. Arthur Kingsley Porter, with the advantage of having methodically studied the sculptures in question, saw it as a two-way traffic, with Santo Domingo de Silos occupying as seminal a role as Burgundy and Languedoc. He considered that "the completion of the cathedral of Santiago in 1124 ends the great creative cycle of the pilgrimage school". Porter went deeper. Finger-prints could not have led him to distinguish more minutely the different hands at work on the monuments of the pilgrim routes, or to track by means of stylistic similarities the vast (and sometimes improbable) journeys apparently undertaken by these master-masons. Notwithstanding the admiration I have for his work, some passages in it steer towards a kind of fantasy peculiar to art historians. For example, "If the animals in the scene of the Money-Changers at St-Gilles, and the sheep at Chartres be all placed together, we shall at once feel that the animals at Chartres and of the Money-Changers belong in one group . . ." Even distinguished scholars have to count sheep sometimes to send themselves to sleep.

John Beckwith, like Mâle, places his weight on the primacy of France as a source of ideas. In the Miègeville tympanum at St-Sernin, Toulouse, and the sculptures at Moissac and Souillac, likewise from the early 12th century, he detects the emergence of a "great new school", one that "operated at various stages on the pilgrim route to Santiago de Compostela, in the town itself, and exerted an influence which radiated out to northern Italy and the Île-de-France".

I have quoted the views of merely three scholars, one from our own day, two from earlier in the century when the pioneer studies were carried out, to give some idea of the complexity of the subject and the variety of interpretations it has yielded. Whatever its sources and its currents, the art of the pilgrim routes remains quintessentially an art born of great hope, great fear and great faith, and sometimes of great love. There are few artistic achievements of mankind that have moved me so deeply. I left Santo Domingo de Silos and Padre Agustín with some reluctance that evening, the sound of Gregorian chant in my ears, as the light was beginning to pale and sharpen, and the rocks were taking on the hard, unnaturally real look of an early Flemish painting. I drove slowly through that wilderness of eroded fields and abandoned hermitages towards Burgos, that old and miniature city founded almost eleven hundred years ago as a bulwark against the advancing Infidel, where Spain's national hero El Cid was born in 1026, and where, even then, the roads into the city were straggled with pilgrims from every corner of Europe.

CHAPTER IX

◆

A Feast of Bones

One area of Burgos Cathedral attracts more kneeling figures than any other. It is a long chapel to the right of the west entrance, dimly lit except for the area round the altar. Here giant candles illuminate what I feel sure is the most macabre piece of religious statuary in Spain. It is known as the *Santísimo Christo*. This is a figure of Christ on the cross which is still widely believed to be covered with human skin, and to have been copied from the actual body of Jesus. Spanish taste for the *farouche* has been responsible for a further legend that the face requires shaving every eight days. Indeed the hair under the matted crown of thorns probably is human, but the skin is the hide of a water-buffalo killed a good 1300 years after the Crucifixion. At all events, during the later Middle Ages the *Santísimo Christo* became an object of the deepest reverence and wonder, as well as the author of innumerable miracles, and the Augustinian monastery in Burgos where it was originally displayed attracted every pious pilgrim on his way to Compostela. The monastery itself was destroyed in 1836, since when the ghoulish statue has been housed in the cathedral, its air of phantasmagoria dramatised nowadays by a purple backdrop and by the puzzling addition of a full skirt of vivid hue.

The *Santísimo Christo* may give one the creeps. Yet to comprehend the spirit of mediaeval pilgrimage one has to overcome a distaste for mawkish cult objects and try to understand the magnetism and meaning they held for the mediaeval mind: understand, too, what Huizinga described as "the vehement pathos of mediaeval life". It was a way of life that "bore the mixed smell of blood and of roses", with people oscillating "between the fear of hell and the most naïve joy, between cruelty and tenderness, between harsh asceticism and insane attachment to the delights of this world, between hatred and goodness, always running to extremes". It was a way of life supported by a belief that each man, whatever his status or degree, possessed an immortal soul to be saved.

Hence the importance attached to penitence. In the Middle Ages most pilgrimages were made in a spirit of penitence. There was a universal preoccupation with *remissio peccatorum*, the remission of sins, and unless you were rich enough to found or endow a monastery, this was available only to the man who absolved himself by private or public penance. Without the promise of *remissio peccatorum* the First Crusade would never have got under way. Neither would the pilgrimages to Rome, to Santiago and to countless other shrines across Europe ever have become such established features of mediaeval life.

The pilgrim routes were the roads to heaven, and the art and architecture of the pilgrim routes were signposts to guide a man there.

Later, works of art were to embody more exclusive sentiments, serving the aggrandisement of the ruling classes and the authority of the church; but this was not generally so in the Middle Ages. One of the strongest appeals of mediaeval art remains its universality. By and large, the painting and sculpture of the Middle Ages is the art of Everyman; and in just the same way the relics of saints, and the representations of saints, served their function for feudal lord and humble pilgrim alike. A man from any walk of life could beg these saints to intercede with the Almighty on his behalf. A common belief in sin was a great leveller.

No one had to search very far in the Middle Ages for the prevailing stain of man's sin. Evidence sounded from the bell of every leper on the road, and from the creak of every cart bearing victims to the plague-pits. Disease was widely held to be a punishment which man had brought upon his own head, and much of the pervading horror of sin in mediaeval Europe was the expression of a revulsion felt against the miseries and appalling decimations which attended men's lives no less regularly than the pleasures of love and the satisfaction of a full belly. It was the mixed smell of blood and of roses again.

Disease, doubt, recurrent poverty and spiritual insecurity: these all contributed to a malaise which manifested itself in restlessness. It is hard to imagine, within the relative comfort of our own social and national barriers, that in the Middle Ages there might be little enough encouragement for an ordinary man to stay put; that he might actually have a better chance of survival without roots at all than with roots embedded in a society quite so insecure.

The mediaeval fondness for pilgrimages is one outcome of this spirit of restlessness. Pilgrimage was a kind of escape, a controlled escape which took the form of a search, and equally the form of a punishment: for large numbers of pilgrims undertook these lengthy journeys not of their own free will but as penalties imposed by the Church, and later by civil authorities too. As early as the 9th century a system of fixed penances was in force in Ireland. These consisted of periods of fasting or of exile; and with the widespread establishment of Church authority this form of punishment extended to other parts of Europe, culminating in the rigid penalties laid down by the Inquisition founded in the early 13th century. Indulgences were available to those who visited certain sanctuaries. It was not until the late Middle Ages that the wealthy could obtain the easier option of making a payment instead (like the gentleman from York mentioned in Chapter IV). A number of these redemption tables have survived, establishing a fixed scale of payment that was considered appropriate to each shrine according to the distance and hardships involved in getting there. Thus we know that to avoid making a pilgrimage from, for example, Flanders to St-Wandrille in Normandy the price was under a pound (or the equivalent); while the journey to Santiago or to Rome was rated at £12, and to São Thomé in Portuguese India, as high as £60.

The average sinner, needless to say, had about as much chance to avail himself of these options as a press-ganged sailor of buying himself out of service. He had to go and that was that.

Not surprisingly, the fervour to revere saints, and to obtain a remission of sins by so doing, led to the most intensive programme of religious building that Christendom has ever known. The chronicler and monk, Radulph Glaber, writing in the 11th century, noted that after the Millennium had passed "one saw in almost the whole world, but mainly in Italy and Gaul, the rebuilding of churches, although the majority being well-built had no need of it. A veritable contest," Glaber contended, "drove each Christian community to have a more sumptuous church than its neighbours. One would have said that the world itself was removing its vestments and replacing them with a white mantle of churches, episcopal seats and monasteries consecrated to all sorts of saints, and even the little chapels in the villages were reconstructed by the faithful more beautiful than before."

Consider the profusion of saints whose relics could be venerated along the principal routes to Santiago de Compostela alone. There was St-Trophime at Arles, St-Seurin at Bordeaux, Ste-Foy at Conques, St-Gilles and St-Guilhem at the places bearing their names, St-Isidoro at León, St-Léonard near Limoges, St-Front at Périgueux, Ste-Radegonde and St-Hilaire at Poitiers, St-Facundus and St-Primitivus at Sahagún, St-Eutrope at Saintes, Ste-Véronica at Soulac, St-Sernin (as well as questionable remains of St James himself) at Toulouse, St-Martin at Tours, Ste-Marie-Madeleine at Vézelay; and of course St James at Santiago. And this is the shortest of short-lists which could be stretched to the length of a modest telephone directory were it to include them all. It was in fact illegal in the Middle Ages—according to church law—to consecrate any new church which possessed no relics; and bishops who did so could be threatened with loss of office and even excommunication, according to a decree issued by the 7th General Council of Nicaea in the year 787, a decree which has never actually been annulled.

The relationship between a church and a particular saint was more than a mere formal dedication. In the Middle Ages a saint was thought of as dwelling in his church, just as the Egyptian sun-god Amun was considered by the people of Thebes during the New Kingdom to inhabit his great temple at Karnak. A saint's relics were evidence of his physical presence; and they were tangible objects to which the superstition and mystery of the mediaeval Christian faith could attach itself. By means of relics and imagery a commonly shared store of beliefs was cast in a perceptible form: it became real, in the same way as the mediaeval notion of sin became real when embodied as the Devil, a creature against whom one could actually wrestle. And the urgency of that combat with the Devil, and the currency of fear upon which it relied, was brought home to the faithful by propaganda that the end of the world was approaching and the Last Judgment unavoidable.

The presence of tangible evidence of a dead saint was a source of profound confidence (because he was a saint) as well as of profound insecurity (because he was dead). His remains were invested with godlike powers. They could influence the course of events on earth. In the 12th century Abbot Suger described how King Louis VI of France, when the Holy Roman Emperor invaded his kingdom and attacked Reims, went first to Suger's abbey of St-Denis with gifts and prayers, placing the relics of the saint on the High Altar "to conduct the defence", and then went out to lead his army into battle. And when the invader had been successfully driven off Louis returned to St-Denis with more gifts for the abbey, and himself bore the holy relics from the High Altar back to their resting-place. Allied generals in World War Two and American generals in Vietnam regularly invoked the support of God for their cause, too, but I never heard of one setting holy relics on the High Altar of Washington Cathedral, or returning from battle to endow the Church with gold and lands. In the Middle Ages it was not enough to genuflect and be faithful; it was necessary to placate a tangible intercessor and to reward him for his support with tangible goods.

Thus relics came to acquire a morbid sanctity. The example of the all-conquering Moors contributed to the cult: in Córdoba the rulers of Moslem Spain kept an arm of Mohammed in a vault, and in the eyes of the beleaguered Christian armies this revered limb seemed to give their foes an advantage which was only cancelled by the subsequent discovery of St James's body in one of the few areas of Spain not yet overrun. That the relic of a mere Infidel should seem to possess divine power over the fortunes of Christendom is of course an illogicality, except that this particular area of faith has its roots not in doctrine but in superstition. A belief in the power of holy relics presupposes a trust in magic.

The degree of sanctity awarded to holy relics depended not only on the importance of the saint, but on their antiquity. Those closest in time and place to the Crucifixion were the most potent. Early martyrs rated more highly than late ones. Though the cult of relics rose to its fervent crescendo in the Middle Ages, a respect for objects associated with the early church was already present at the time of the Emperor Constantine's adoption of Christianity early in the 4th century. It was Constantine's own mother, the Empress Helena, who at the age of seventy-nine took herself to the Holy Land and claimed to have discovered the remains of three buried wooden crosses, including most of the one she identified as that of Christ, which she brought to Constantinople. Part of her find was later borne to Rome.

The growing asceticism of the Church in the age of Jerome brought with it, besides an insistence on the celibacy of priests (who without heirs would also be unable to hand on valuable church property to their sons outside the church), a growing love of such relics. St-Martin, the soldier–hermit who became the first bishop of Tours and died in AD 397, was the most famous of these early Christian ascetics: his cloak came to acquire the most potent magical properties, and in battle the Frankish kings of the 8th century took care to have it with them. By now the export of holy relics from Rome to other potential centres of pilgrimage had become something of an industry. Pope Gregory the Great, in the 6th century, formed the practice of sending to foreign potentates keys which contained a minute proportion of iron from the chains of Peter and which, he claimed, would bring untold aid both to the body and the soul.

The proliferation of relics continued throughout the early Middle Ages. Their fragmentation, too. Within a few centuries of the discovery of St James's body in Spain, part of his arm was in Liège, his hand in Reading and a fragment of his mastoid in Pistoia, besides the further relics claimed by Toulouse. At a solemn feast in the year 1392 King Charles VI of France ceremonially distributed among his guests the ribs of his ancestor, St Louis. The most distinguished members of the company, like the Duke of Berry and the Duke of Burgundy, were awarded entire ribs; lesser mortals received a mere splinter.

Inevitably, fragmentation led to multiplication. Estimates have been offered of the number of cargo-vessels which could be built from the assembled pieces of the Holy Cross. There are several shrouds of Christ, and an inordinate quantity of the Virgin's milk. There is the story of a 16th-century visitor to various shrines in France being shown the skull of John the Baptist on two successive days at two different monasteries, the custodian of the second offering as an explanation that the one he had seen the previous day must have been the skull of the saint as a young man. At the same period the printer, Henry Stephens, recalls how one monastery had on display a phial containing Christ's tears, while a church he had come across possessed a glass containing the breath of Our Lord.

From the 11th century onwards the cult of curious and improbable relics burgeoned. Chartres, which is the most ancient sanctuary to the Virgin in France, possessed a reliquary purporting to contain the robe she wore on the day of the Annunciation. The church of Santa-Croce-in-Gerusalemme, in Rome, formed a truly remarkable collection—which I believe it still has. This included three pieces of the Holy Cross brought from Constantinople (originating in Helena's dig in Palestine), some blood of Jesus, two thorns, one nail and a piece of cord (likewise from the Crucifixion), one of the coins which Judas was paid to betray Christ, a phial of Mary's milk, a wisp of her hair, some bones belonging to Mary Magdalen, a finger of St Thomas, Peter's tooth, a part of the head of John the Baptist and a piece of Aaron's rod. If these could not obtain a man redemption then I imagine hell must have been as certain as night follows day.

Chartres no longer has its skirt of the Virgin but it still possesses a reliquary of the Circumcision. Reims has a reliquary of the Holy Thorn, Toulouse a reliquary of the True Cross, Conques an arm reliquary of St George, Boulogne a reliquary of the Precious Blood, and Évron a reliquary of Our Lady's Milk (the source of Mary's milk was actually a supply of white dust from the cave in Bethlehem which traditionally is the scene of the Nativity). Small wonder that men with a scrap of scepticism sought refuge in ridicule. Boccaccio tells the tale of the Archangel Gabriel's feather left behind after the Annunciation. Chaucer's Pardoner carried around with him, besides a small copy of St Veronica's handkerchief, a piece of the sail used by St Peter on the Sea of Galilee. There is the story of another pardoner who carried a vial containing the sound of King Solomon's bells.

But is the satirical any more fanciful than the serious? Hardly. Is there indeed a sharp line dividing them at all? Amid what Huizinga has described as that "everlasting call of *memento mori*" in the Middle Ages, were not Boccaccio and Chaucer as near to the true spirit of mediaeval life as the gloomy prognostications of the theologians?

Politically, holy shrines were of the utmost importance. They were a primary source of revenue to their owners, an investment the dividends from which depended upon the celebrity of the relics. This made them as vulnerable to theft as expensive paintings are today—except that unlike paintings they could not be stored conveniently in banks or no one would revere them and all revenues be cut off. They had to be shown, whatever the risks involved. Conques, as we have seen, acquired its fame and much of its wealth by stealing the relics of Ste Foy from another monastery, though the operation took ten years. If disaster threatened, the first objects hurried to safety were a monastery's relics. A church, after all, could be rebuilt and its lands recultivated, but a treasure once lost was lost for ever and its owners plunged into penury. The entire pilgrimage industry, relatively no less important in the Middle Ages than the tourist industry today, depended upon relics as tourism depends upon the sun. A rainy season in Benidorm could be no greater disaster than the theft of a holy molar from Toulouse.

Naturally, the more a saintly relic could be seen the greater the revenue to be had from it. Abbots anxious to raise funds for building or other purposes would take an abbey's most notable shrine or reliquary on a tour of the district, and at each stop the appropriate relic would be placed on public display before the sick and the sinful, who would pay for the honour of offering up prayers. The same motive prompted the habit of removing holy relics from the crypt for important religious services and placing them on or near the High Altar: pious motives doubtless played their part, too, but piety that could be weighed in gold was doubly satisfactory to the abbeys concerned. The generous prospect of the High Altar offered by pilgrim churches in the Middle Ages was in expectation that such generosity would be reciprocated.

Once indulgences became available to those who visited shrines the status of relics was enhanced still further. In origin the responsibility for such a fever of superstition lay with the Vatican. In the first half of the 13th century there had emerged one of the most extraordinary doctrines ever to be spawned by mediaeval Rome, which was that of the Treasure of the Church. This doctrine was confirmed by a Papal Bull of Clement VI in the year 1350, and it sponsored the belief that Christ's merit, and that of the saints, could actually be made available to the Christian through objects, access to which he could obtain at a price. Within fifty years of Pope Clement's Bull no pilgrim road in Europe was free of a new breed of men—official pardoners, who were men like Chaucer's Pardoner, less endearing perhaps, but scarcely more honest. These people hawked their wares like travelling salesmen and those wares were generally phoney. Their so-called official letters, and dubious relics of some remote saint, were the mediaeval equivalent of the panaceas offered by quack doctors in the 18th century and some of the cut-price insurance policies offered in the 20th.

The Council of Trent abolished the office of Pardoner in 1562, though the doctrine of indulgences remained. It was too profitable a levy for the Church to discard lightly. Nonetheless, in most of Christendom a spirit of change was afoot. In northern Europe the impact of Protestantism hastened the decay of many of the more rotten props on which the mediaeval Church rested, and in Italy and France the Counter-Reformation was re-invigorating the Church of Rome on more contemporary and rational lines.

Only Spain seemed impervious to this change in spiritual climate and, as so often in its history, chose to go fervently in the opposite direction. The impact of Jesuit thought was not quite what it was elsewhere in Europe. It served to reinforce precisely those hysterical and irrational aspects of Spanish faith which in other countries were being weakened by Renaissance inquiry. The fervour of Jesuitical teaching cast an untouchable sanctity over Spain's legendary history of saints and martyrs and, what is more, threw up a new race of scholars who chronicled this bogus history and presented it as fact. It was in this period, during the 16th and 17th centuries, that many of the richer elaborations to the Santiago story appeared. Spain entered a phase of martyr-mania. Every town longed to hear that some saint's blood had been spilled within its walls; and amid an *aurora borealis* of strange lights and beckoning stars, visions of decapitated martyrs were revealed to amazed virgins and senile archbishops. How far away it all was from that new spirit of the Renaissance which Huizinga described with such simple accuracy as an "inner ripening" of the mind. "Europe," Huizinga went on, "after having lived in the shadow of Antiquity, lived in its sunshine once more." But not south of the Pyrenees. The cathedral at Burgos may be an amalgam of Rhenish, Flemish and French influences, but it is Spanish in one unmistakable respect. It admits no sunshine.

Burgos Cathedral, says Richard Ford, is "a superb pile of florid Gothic". Gothic architecture could no more have germinated in

Spain than cricket could have germinated in the West Indies. Indeed, the Spaniards seized on Gothic in much the way the Barbadians and Trinidadians seized upon our gentle English summer game: with a gusto that soon wrought a transformation inconceivable to its originators.

On a windy afternoon in early summer I stood where Ford's Gothic "pile" looks most "superb", and gazed upwards at that bristle of extraordinary pinnacles which raked the clouds into loose strands overhead. Here, from the high terrace to the north-east of the cathedral, an armoury of spires thrust into the pale sky, each spike hollow, the stone wafer-thin. The man who crowned this place with spires was a dreamer from the Rhine, and his name was Juan de Colonia—John of Cologne. The richest inspiration of Burgos Cathedral was that airy and intricate Gothic style of building which German architects had perfected during the late 13th and early 14th centuries in the minsters on or near the Rhine: the cathedral of Cologne and, in particular, Freiburg Minster, its octagonal western tower as light and open as a cobweb.

The foundation stone of Burgos Cathedral was actually laid twenty-seven years earlier than the one at Cologne, in 1221, and the basic shape of the building was modelled not on a German but a French cathedral, St-Étienne at Bourges. So all the major phases of Gothic are present in Burgos, which is appropriate for a city that in the Middle Ages was considerably more international in flavour than it is today. The cathedral was built in the international Gothic style brought south of the Pyrenees by the Cistercians, and the city itself lay at the crossroads of international trade routes. With trade came pilgrims, mainly along the principal route from Navarre but also along the coastal road which ran down from Soulac near Bordeaux, through Bayonne and St-Sébastien, and then crossed the mountains into Castile. This route brought French pilgrims from the western regions of France, as well as many Englishmen who had crossed the Bay of Biscay to the estuary of the Gironde on those wine vessels returning to pick up a fresh cargo.

The Pilgrim Gate to the cathedral of Burgos is the north entrance. The present north transept dates back only to 1515, and the original pilgrims' stairway leading down from street level outside has been replaced by a pompous Baroque double staircase. The traditional pilgrim street of St John approaches the cathedral on a high level from the north-east, past the terrace where I had been gazing at that armoury of spires. Once this street was lined with hospices all the way from the city gates and the little chapel of San Lesmes within the walls. Today shops lean out towards the cobbles, and in the doorway of one of them my eye fixed upon an alabaster figurine of some half-naked martyr whose affiliation to the Santiago legend was advertised by the scallop-shell which he wore as a cod-piece. The pilgrim street sweeps up to the cathedral on the north side, and as it slides into the dusty shadows the finest of the cathedral's carved portals looms over it. Here the pilgrims entered. Today the north entrance is by a Classical entrance below. On the steps in the sun grubby children were grinning for *pesetas*. Over to the west this pocket-sized city ended in fields of ripening corn. With its bustle, its boulevards, its open-air cafés, its well-dressed women, its faces of well-bred disdain, Burgos belies its size, still wears the sullen authority of Franco's capital city—which it once was.

Burgos gathered Santiago pilgrims into the city's hospices at least from the 11th century. The Hospital de San Juan on the east side of the city already existed in 1091, and to the west the much larger Hospital del Rey was founded by King Alfonso VIII in the 12th century. Royal patronage ensured for it wealthy bequests, and in the 16th century under the Emperor Charles V the entire place was rebuilt in Renaissance style, including a Classical entrance gate over which St James still presides with the air rather of one preparing to sip a nice cup of tea.

To stay at the royal hospice the pilgrim first had to produce documents signed by his local bishop, and on his return from Santiago he had to show his *Compostela*—the certificate given to prove that a pilgrim had duly completed his mission. If all documents were in order he was then permitted to stay at the Hospital del Rey for two days. Here he would be looked after by a staff of knights attached to the Cistercian Order, and provided with rations consisting of twenty ounces of bread, twelve ounces of meat and sixteen of red wine.

The main buildings of the Hospital del Rey have been reduced to stubs of massive columns protruding from a patch of green. Village life has taken over: a handsome side-gate to the hospice is now squeezed by crumbling dwellings. What does survive more or less intact is the front courtyard with its colonnade of slender arches, which was being extensively restored when I visited the place, and its former elegance could only be guessed at through an entanglement of pulleys and ladders, ropes, planks and buckets. We may not know what the dormitory and sanitary conditions were like, but for two nights the penniless and footsore could enjoy the environment of a prince. Places like the Hospital del Rey were truly showpieces of patronage.

The king placed the Hospital del Rey under the authority of the abbess of the royal abbey of Las Huelgas, nearby. This monumental complex of buildings on the dusty outskirts of Burgos was founded by Alfonso VIII in 1187 as a convent for nuns of the same Cistercian Order. Under royal patronage it received the inestimable privilege of exemption from taxes, and in consequence it grew wealthy and powerful in a manner that had not at all been Cistercian practice according to the teachings of the founder, St Bernard of Clairvaux, who preached the spartan life. The kings of Castile were buried here at Las Huelgas, and these included Alfonso himself who reclines in a double tomb shared with his wife Eleanor of Aquitaine, who was the power behind the abbey and was in fact English (or as English as were any of the Plantagenets), her father being King Henry II of England and her brother Richard Cœur-de-Lion.

The present abbey church of St Catherine is a lovely, cool Gothic structure, and one of the aisles has been shut off to form the pantheon itself. Here the tomb of the founders keeps company with splendid Gothic and Mozarabic tombs of fifteen later monarchs and protectors of the abbey. Las Huelgas is among the earliest monastic foundations in Castile. Its association with the Santiago pilgrimage is marked not only by the responsibility of its abbess for the royal pilgrim hospice in Burgos, but by a curious rectangular chapel within the abbey complex itself, built in Moorish style. The chapel is dedicated to St James and contains a 13th-century statue of the apostle, dressed in a polychrome tunic, whose right arm has been designed to move in order—it is thought—the more effectively to dub knights of the Order of Santiago.

Nowhere, I think, in all Burgos speaks so richly of the past of Castile as the abbey of Las Huelgas. The vigour of royal authority, the violence of mediaeval politics, the blossoming of artistic ideas brought across the Pyrenees, the passage of pilgrims and men of scholarship, a new self-confidence and a sense of permanence staked out in the form of great monuments to show the world: these were impressions which passed through my mind as I wandered from the proud tombs of the kings into the Cistercian cloisters that were like a plain flower opening cautiously into the sun.

But most of all Las Huelgas spoke of that ambivalence towards the civilisation of the Infidel which characterises so much of the mediaeval history of Spain. Here hung the magnificent Moorish ensign captured in 1212 at the battle of Las Navas de Tolosa, the victory which had opened a breach into southern Spain for the Christian armies to exploit, and which led ultimately to the reconquest of the entire Iberian peninsula. And yet, enter the Gothic cloisters a few paces from that captured ensign and gaze up at the ceiling. What answers that gaze is an example of plasterwork breathtaking in the delicacy of its geometry, and of a sophistication centuries in advance of anything that could have been conceived within Christendom at that moment in time. The right hand of Christianity wielded the sword, while the left was extended in respect and homage. Such was the true spirit of the *Reconquista*.

I left Burgos by the road west, under the railway-bridge—two railway-bridges—then up on to the *sierra*, starved of trees, the few trees starved of water, the tired old soil dragged by the wind into spirals that spun and dragged across the plain and into my eyes as I stepped from the car into the glare of that June morning. A Great Bustard rose in a flurry of brown and white wings from the crown of the road ahead and circled low and fast over the corn before sinking out of sight. I stalked it for a while, wondering how a bird the size of a turkey could hide amid a crop in which a field-mouse might have felt exposed. Then it burst out of the ground a few yards ahead, long neck craned, a target my five-year-old son Jason might have hit with a bow-and-arrow as easily as a huntsman with a gun. Fortunately, neither was around, and my thoughts went out with affection to that most amiable of romantics, Aylmer Tryon, who right now is dedicated to the project of reintroducing the Great Bustard to its native Salisbury Plain.

It was no longer the main road. Some miles to the west of Burgos the *camino* strikes through the scrub and rock of the high plain. I had taken a minor road along a shallow valley to see whether I could find a point where it came down off the *sierra* and across my path. There was no mistaking it: nothing more than a broad cart-track but straight as a Roman road—which it must once have been. And as it crossed in front of me I turned to follow it into the nearby village.

Like so many of the villages along the route this one acknow-ledged the pilgrim road in its name: Hornillos del Camino. The name means small stoves of the pilgrim route. Hornillos was created for and by the pilgrimage, and in consequence it was quite unlike other Castilian villages around in both style and spirit. Instead of the usual muddle of plain houses which the roads circuit or squeeze between, here in the dip of the plain rose stone mansions, many of them bearing massive lintels inscribed with crosses or with motifs; and through the twin ranks of these mansions swept a highway fit for a procession of arms or the passage of royalty—except that the village was empty. The surface of the road was mud-baked where the spring rains had modelled it, and only the odd hen occupied the broad spaces between facing doorways. I felt rather like John Wayne as I strode into the silence of Hornillos between those rows of peering eyes and black shawls.

But Hornillos is un-Castilian in another respect. Centuries of accepting and caring for travellers from who-knows-where have bred a manner towards strangers which is free of that sullenness I had grown used to since leaving Navarre. I had scarcely walked fifty yards from my car before each of the houses behind me seemed to be sending a representative to catch me up and accompany me— where to, I wondered? Then, as if waiting for the boldest to lead, all the men of my cortège began to make international drinking signs to me, thumb towards the mouth. Within minutes I was being led a guided tour of the stone *bodegas* which every householder in this part of Spain keeps within thirsting distance of his home. And so, as hoopoes and golden orioles swooped between the walls of an old Benedictine convent, I drank the hospitality of Hornillos until the *camino* might have been the road to Mandalay for all I knew and the afternoon broke apart in splinters of laughter in the sun.

Out of Hornillos the pilgrim road becomes once again a cart-track. Only some unusually solid stone walls half-buried in the bank on either side distinguish this from any other track as it winds up on to the crest of the *sierra* again. The *camino* leaves the high plain some five miles farther west to follow a shallow stony valley past the villages of Castellanos de Castro and Hontañas: a mourn-fully evocative stretch of road, this, the valley steadily deepening and widening to contain the broken fingers of old shrines and way-side chapels, until it levels out among poplar trees and fertile meadows. There in the midst of this rivulet of cultivation between parched hills—straight ahead—stood a soaring double arch strad-dling the road. To the left of the arch rose a grey gutted mass of stone nave piled with bales of hay and littered with tractor tyres. Behind the buildings, low walls broke away into the fields. This was the 14th-century Gothic convent of San Antón, an incongru-ous sight in this scraped landscape: an invader from the Île de France, beheaded, gutted, abandoned to decay between these alien hillsides of wild lavender where sheep nibbled a subsistence and found shelter in the evening within its Gothic bones.

I walked over the fields behind and, when I turned to look back, the convent in its ruins seemed to be decaying into the ruined hills beyond. In time there would be no distinction. Rock and rock. Erosion of land, erosion of culture. There was the persistent drag of sheep-bells among the rocks, and the song of an evening night-ingale was amplified within the dry cup of the valley. Offerings to the wind.

I wandered back towards the car, stamped the dust out of my sandals, and set off for Frómista where there was the promise of an inn for the night and, with any luck, a bath. But first there was Castrojeriz, another ruin, on another parched hill, propped there ahead of me against the evening skyline, ringed by a collar of houses and mouldering churches—all that remains of a once important centre of power, trade and devotion along the pilgrim route to Santiago. The old road ran straight towards the stubby fingers of the castle, then veered left along the slope of the hill through the main village cemented between the dusty hill and the dusty plain. Past the tower of the church of San Juan walked a tall and radiant girl, her glossy hair tied back, her severe clothes tailored in the manner approved by numerous aunts. She kept her eyes lowered and her face set as she passed, but from her shoulder swung a bag with the letters printed across it—Carnaby Street. The sun began to settle into a shawl of dust thrown around the hills.

Before Frómista the Castilian landscape rolls out into a mono-tonous plain stretching all the way to León. It is veined and kept modestly fertile by numerous rivers that bring silt and mountain water from the Cantabrian highlands to the north, in return taking their fee of Spanish topsoil down to the River Duero, which then steers it through Portugal to deposit it finally in the Atlantic at Oporto, a process of spoliation that has been in operation seasonally ever since Spain was once a rich and fertile land.

In Frómista a family of storks was nesting on the church tower outside my hotel window. The church itself bore a French dedication, to San Martín, and architecturally too, it was French, owing much to those carved and compact little churches south of Poitiers I had so loved what already seemed half a year ago. The church of San Martín de Frómista, though much altered since, is among the earliest in Castile, indeed one of the first pilgrimage churches in all Spain. It was begun in the 11th century, came under the authority of Cluny during the period of Cluniac reform, and is all that remains of a Benedictine monastery founded by the widow of Sancho the Great during the early years of the Reconquest of Spain. During the 12th century the monastery merged with that of San Zoílo in Carrión de los Condes ten miles to the west, and gradually ceased to exist. Not a great deal has happened at Frómista since.

Pilgrims who left the protection of San Martín next sought the shelter of the Knights Templars, who built an important fortified church a few miles to the west of Frómista at Villalcázar de Sirga (*Sirga* has the same meaning as *camino*: the road). A heavily sculptured east door displays five rows of figures carved in yellow sandstone with, above them, a Christ in Majesty and a figure of the Madonna to whom the church is dedicated. And on either side of the door have been scratched those Greek and Latin crosses by which pilgrims in the Middle Ages notched their passage to salvation, just as they did at every shrine along the pilgrim routes of Europe from Castile to Saintonge to Gloucestershire, from Villalcázar to Echebrune to Stoke Orchard; and the vast space of this church interior, chill with emptiness now, brought home to me once again the scale and urgency of those journeys of pilgrimage. A chapel of Santiago remains at Villalcázar, and so do some handsome relics in the form of three magnificently carved and painted stone tombs of Castilian rulers, one Romanesque in style, two proto-Gothic. They lie full-length in their curiously oriental costume and headgear, the stone beneath them cut into panels representing Biblical scenes, and into a frieze of coats-of-arms that are interspersed with splashes of red—the emblem of the bloodied sword of knights pledged to the service of St James.

And what other enterprise, save the liberation of the Holy City itself, could so powerfully have enflamed the soul of mediaeval chivalry? The Santiago pilgrimage possessed all the ingredients required of a knightly cause. In particular, of course, it offered physical danger and hardship, and an unrelenting fight against the Infidel; but it also offered the ingredient of Romance. Not exactly the rescue of damsels in distress, but something very like it. The town of Carrión de los Condes stands beside one of those tributaries of the Rio Duero which irrigate the Castilian plain. This was already an "industrious and prosperous town" in Aymery Picaud's day, as well as roughly halfway along a particularly dusty stretch of the pilgrim route between Burgos and León. And it was at the entrance to Carrión de los Condes, on the spot where the church of Santa Maria del Camino now stands, that the hard-pressed rulers of Christian Spain are said to have paid annual protection-money of one hundred virgins to the Moorish lords. How true is the legend, and how true the location, we do not know; but the story of the hundred maidens, of that mournful ceremony at Carrión de los Condes, and of the Battle of Clavijo at which St James made his first victorious appearance (see p. 13), were, nonetheless, central to the whole Santiago legend and crucial to the command it held over the mediaeval imagination.

The spirit of the stonemasons who carved the main door of the church of Santa Maria del Camino was scarcely in keeping with so tearful an occasion. Whoever worked on these stones must have seen—and perhaps worked on as an apprentice—some great carved portals on other early churches; and either he aped them here for laughs or (more likely) his primitive perception of things and clumsy hand rendered the required apocalyptic scenes as best he could: those devils and angels, virtues and vices, follies and ecstasies, visions of bliss and damnation, all of which seem to have animated his spirit very much as a man might be moved to recite from *King Lear* after ten pints on a Saturday evening.

St James's own church in Carrión fared better at the hands of the stonemasons, a great deal better. Time, however, has treated it worse. All that remains is the sculptured façade whose frieze of apostles from about 1165 was described by Kingsley Porter as "one of the great achievements of the 12th century". The carving is of a sensitivity and a solemnity I had not seen since Santo Domingo de Silos, though the figures themselves have the down-to-earth vigour of Burgundian carving rather than the ecstatic quality which makes the sculptures at Santo Domingo feel so removed from our own physical existence. Is it mere accident that Santo Domingo should lie hidden from the traffic of life amid the parched *sierras*, while the church of Santiago in Carrión stands full-face on the busiest street in the town?

I drove on through a decaying and evocative landscape. At Cervatos de la Cueza the bones of an old bridge carried the pilgrim route precariously over water hidden by a white veil of flowering crowfoot. A stork planed down among the washerwomen and donkeys on the river bank, and the frogs' concert abruptly ceased as they plopped for safety. On farther, the pilgrim road cut through the fields, gathering in the villages left and right, villages that were now Moorish-looking, yellow-brown with mud walls matching the colour of the street, and very quiet: villages with inflated names like San Nicolás del Real Camino and Terradillos de Templarios: villages with squat brick churches rubbed by the wind. A disused convent—everything is disused round here—displayed a coat-of-arms above the door and gave shelter to some antique harrows that had seen long service in the dust. A collapsed dovecot stood in a nearby field. A red kite perched on a tree, tense as a trap. I came to Sahagún.

Nothing epitomises the decay of this region more than Sahagún. It was once a power in the land. During the Middle Ages it had a monastery second in importance to none in Christian Spain. In the year 1083 Abbot Bernard of Sahagún received in Rome from Pope Gregory VII many of the same privileges already awarded in France to Cluny; and, as a result, over fifty priories and abbeys became dependent upon the abbey of Sahagún. The autonomy given to Bernard became an effective instrument for the expansion of Christian authority in Spain—and, indirectly, papal authority too. Bernard himself was one of the prime agents in the Reconquest, becoming the first archbishop of Toledo in 1086, following its capture from the Moors. Ironically, there is no town in all northern Spain whose architecture is more profoundly Moorish. Sahagún is the centre of what has become known as Mudéjar art: that is, work (generally of the late Romanesque period) done for the Christian Church by Moorish craftsmen, and not to be confused with Mozarabic art which is work executed by Christians who were living under Arab rule and were influenced by Islamic ideas or were converts to the Moslem faith.

Of Bernard's great abbey at Sahagún nothing remains except some lumps on the hill where it once stood—lumps which may one day, I suppose, reveal to a scrupulous archaeologist some immaculate foundations. The great treasures of the abbey, too, are dispersed. The 11th-century Virgin of Sahagún, which is among the finest examples of early sculpture in Spain, is now in the National Archaeological Museum in Madrid. Other sculpture from here is in the San Marcos museum at León. What does remain, semi-ruined, is the gaunt brick chapel of San Marco that was attached to the abbey, and which dates from about 1100. Its onion-shaped Mudéjar arches contain delicate patternings of brickwork that contrast with the ungainly wreckage of the building as a whole. But what a position this abbey must have commanded. The plain rolls away westward towards León; and only from here does the former prominence of Sahagún grow clear. Of its nine great brick churches standing in the Middle Ages five have perished. The four that remain thrust magnificent perforated bell-towers proudly above the mean roof-line of the modern town: the churches of El Trinidad and Santiago near the pilgrim road on the outskirts; San Lorenzo to the north, bulging among the low mud walls around it; and San Tirso, already restored and primped up in its tumble-down square. I got the feeling in Sahagún that the tourist party was about to begin, with all hands engaged on piecing together the old place as a respectable and orderly monument to receive it.

A final stretch of plain separates Sahagún from the rich river-valleys around León. Once this region was notorious for wolves: today only the odd brace of partridge disturbs the prospect of nothing. I drove through Mansilla de las Mulas, a town shrunken within the gigantic stumps of its old walls, now empty as the cavity of a tooth. Past the Rio Esla, in full spate, the river marshes spread out before me. Somewhere in this wasteland lay sanctuaries, hospices, abbeys, churches, places that provided shelter for the pilgrim. How did they know where to find them? Equipped with a car, roads, maps, money, some Spanish, I still managed to grow help-lessly lost among those unnamed villages and endless water-meadows screened by poplars and criss-crossed by canals. It made me understand what a remarkable intelligence system existed among mediaeval travellers.

My last stop before León took me a few miles upstream from Mansilla. Here, tucked into the fold of a rocky hill overlooking the threads of the River Esla, lay a tiny convent chapel by the name of San Miguel de Escalada and built in the 10th or early 11th century during some very dark days for Christianity in Spain. The Moors were still everywhere. Indeed, a hefty colonnade of Moorish arches greeted me as I turned off the road: here was Christendom by courtesy of Islam. And what did pilgrims make of this relationship, I wondered, when they knelt here and offered prayers to their saint and *Matamoros*, St James the Moor-slayer?

A cross of St John of Jerusalem—the cross of the Knights Hos-pitallers, patrons of pilgrims—was carved over the lintel. It was the evening of a long day, heavy with bird-song and the scent of summer. I think few simple buildings have filled me with such a sense of peace as this hybrid place. I stood for a while and thought of friends and people I loved. Sometimes, just sometimes, travel can be a vehicle for thought. I watched the colour of the land grow gold then palely violet. The sound of the car felt like a wound on the surface of the evening.

CHAPTER X

Bagpipes in the Rain

"Like other ancient capitals," wrote Richard Ford, "León is dull, deserted and decaying"; though he acknowledged that it had "a casino, a theatre, and a Plaza de Toros".

In more than a century since Ford was there León has grown—and grown anonymously—into a city of almost 100,000, mostly by the addition of those stark tower-block suburbs which register the new prosperity of tourist Spain. Nonetheless León, when all is said, remains a city finer than the lugubrious Ford was prepared to admit in the mid-19th century. It is an ancient city: its name is a corruption of the Latin *Legio*, referring to the Roman Seventh Legion, *Gemina*, quartered here by the Emperor Augustus during the 1st century AD. The city subsequently grew into the capital of Christian Spain during the height of the Moorish invasions, and was in fact sacked by the dreaded Al-Mansur in 966 following a siege lasting a year; the Moorish war-lord then pressed westwards to take Santiago de Compostela, too, and transport the bells of the cathedral in triumph back to Córdoba.

Like Siena in Italy, and Winchester in England, León lost its political importance early: like them, too, it acquired a kind of elegance in decline. Being on the main pilgrim route to Compostela it attracted travellers from all over Europe and became a centre of hospitality for them. It became something of a cultural centre. And it came to boast what was—and is—arguably the loveliest cathedral in Spain. This was consecrated in 1303 and is purely French, architecturally as well as in spirit, derived as it is from the early Gothic cathedrals of Reims and Amiens. Unlike the cathedral of Burgos it is too homogeneous in style to have acquired over the centuries any strongly Spanish flavour—except in one remarkable respect: its glass.

It is not simply that León Cathedral has the best stained glass in Spain—which it does: to enter the chill, twilit interior of this place and look around in the gloom until, by chance, the sun chooses that moment to come out is, I felt, to comprehend something of the hold which the Christian faith has been able to retain over so many people and for so long. Man contrived here a revelation: a revelation of light. In general, Spanish churches are exceptionally dark, and in my view exceptionally oppressive; and León is no exception—until the sun comes out. Then, more than any building I have ever set eyes on, it seems to burst into fire, a fire which enflames the very soul. Suddenly it is like standing diminutively in the heart of a fire-opal; for this glass, installed most probably late in the 13th century, may indeed be French in tradition and in craftsmanship, like the cathedral itself, yet in range of colours it is as Spanish as a fiesta or as the burnt *sierras* in summer. Torches of red, or orange, gold and yellow appear to burn up the dry interior of this great monument until you want to shield your eyes. I walked from this dazzling interior out into the sunlight in a state of the purest exhilaration. I was astonished, and moved. God, it seemed, had been invented by the glassmaker's art.

León Cathedral is a bulwark. It looks more solid in its stance than the northern basilicas upon which it is modelled. Chateaubriand, who regarded Gothic cathedrals as the embodiment of religious daydreams, would not, I think, have detected many dreams suspended between these substantial towers. Even the flying buttresses reaching out to the walls of the nave manage to look extraordinarily earthbound: mere struts holding it all in one piece, rather than the divine architecture of dreams that Chateaubriand admired at Chartres and Bourges.

Like many of the greatest French cathedrals, León concentrates its purest artistry on its western portal: the place where a man entered. The western portal of León contains some of the most stirring sculpture to be found anywhere along the Spanish pilgrim route. Amid the ranks of apostles to the left and right of the entrance stands St James himself, in his pilgrim hat complete with scallop-shell, his beard aged into an avuncular whiteness by the action of time on the pale sandstone. And he wears a smile on his face. Here is not James the scourge of the Moors, but rather James the teacher, James the benevolent Latin master—kindly, good, a little remote perhaps, a little dull certainly. James the preacher to the converted. James the country vicar. Or perhaps James who is one among a procession of university dons chuckling their way comfortably towards the port. Yet within feet of this benign figure, above the same entrance to the cathedral, are scenes of damnation of a sadism such as I have never seen depicted on the outside of a church. And, as so often on this journey, I was made to wonder at the polarity of the mediaeval experience of human life: at that mixed smell of blood and roses again, each enriched by the other, made more heady by the certainty that the one could so easily become the other, and perhaps *was* the other but for the grace of God.

It was hard to remember that St James, this gentle doctor of learning as he is represented on the west front of León Cathedral, was the same warrior-saint who inspired the armies of the Reconquest in his glistening armour.

There were other saints, too, who enjoyed such a double rôle, like the 7th-century archbishop of Toledo, San Isidoro, who unlike the apostle James really was a doctor and yet in León is represented in St James's traditional rôle of Moor-slayer. This particular confusion of rôles appears on the finial of the Collegiate Church which was dedicated to San Isidoro, built two centuries earlier than the cathedral and which is principally famous today for its Royal Pantheon. It was the burial chapel of the kings of León. This chapel was completed between the years 1063 and 1067 and the area above the level of its stubby columns is entirely decorated with paintings in such perfect condition that it requires an effort of the will to recognise them as original, so readily do we associate antiquity with decay. The Royal Pantheon of San Isidoro is to Romanesque painting what Altamira is to cave art: one of the foremost treasure-houses in Spain.

Executed in nothing more than the colours blue, terra-cotta and white, these scenes from the New Testament, assembled round a central figure of Christ Pantocrator, possess the jewel-like quality of miniatures that have been enlarged, which in a sense they were, since most early church painting originates from illuminated manuscripts. But what is overwhelming about this complex of art, more so even than the quality and condition of the paintings themselves, is the manner in which they harmonise and enhance the design of the building they distinguish. And the agent of this harmony is quite simply the use of the decorative borders. These borders contrive to unite the painted surface with the form of the actual building—the simplest of structures—by playing a dual rôle: they emphasise its architectural features, and by doing so they supply a kind of frame for the picture. Every scene is framed by the arches and vaulting of the room. This was a harmony of art and architecture scarcely ever achieved by church painting during the Gothic and Renaissance periods which followed: later buildings tended to offer paintable surfaces for artists to cover with their designs. Pictures became stamps on the wall. Giotto's Scrovegni Chapel in Padua or, even more so, the Sistine Chapel in Rome, are instances of this. It was not until the evolution of Rococo ceiling painting in the early 18th century that something of the same balanced partnership between painting and architecture was restored, on a lighter note.

As striking as the cathedral in León, and San Isidoro, is the former hospice and convent of San Marcos. This was founded in 1168 for the Knights of St James, and it became their principal house and show-piece. In the 16th century it was embellished with one of the finest Renaissance façades in all Spain, so that it must have looked more like a palace to be approached with a fanfare than a refuge for pilgrims grimy from the roads. Indeed, a kind of palace it became, to the greater glory of the Knights themselves and of the Church Militant in the person of *Santiago Matamoros* who rides in holy wrath above the main entrance, sword raised, enemies crushed, the rule of righteousness restored. Richard Ford, when he was here, raised his quizzical eye higher than the figure of St James over the door of San Marcos and noted that part of the façade was in fact "a clumsy modern construction by Martin de Suinaya, 1715–19, whose Fame blowing a trumpet adds very little to his". So be it; but a lot more than the occasional clumsiness would be required to spoil so magnificent a spread of formal stone.

The pilgrim hospice and convent of the Knights is now the Hostal San Marcos, run by the Spanish tourist authorities. I would personally submit it in any competition for the most beautiful hotel in the world, and quite possibly the best—its cost, by the way (at least off-season), roughly the same for the night as a room equipped with coin-meter heating overlooking the railway near West London Air Terminal. And should you wish to take afternoon tea in the chapter-house under a Moorish sandalwood ceiling, should you prefer the decadence of sipping martinis in a Gothic cloister, should you enjoy breakfast overlooking a convent garden extending down to the river, then the Hostal San Marcos may be your scene. It is— I feel no shame in saying so—mine too. Or it was for one luxurious night.

Separated from the five-star pilgrims only by a wall of plate-glass is the Museo San Marcos. This is composed of a small but exceedingly fine collection of sculpture and ornaments that formerly belonged to various religious houses in the León area. And in this select company there is, let me say, one absolute masterpiece. This is a figure of the Crucified Christ, carved in ivory during the 11th or 12th century, and it was once in the Leónese monastery of Carrizo, where presumably it formed part of a small altarpiece. It stands no more than fourteen inches high, as I recollect. The hands and feet of the carving are disproportionately large, and so is the head. The eyes are wide and staring: a figure of awkward gravity. It is not a representation of suffering, neither is it an object of reverence; but a figure of humility, of resignation. It is overwhelmingly touching, and this is because it embodies an attitude to reality which is of the very essence of the best early Christian sculpture, and which may offer a clue to much of the appeal of such sculpture today. Nothing in the way this piece has been carved is elevated above the simplest but strongest feeling of an ordinary man. Sophistication has yet to enter man's devotions. Implicit in this gentle ivory carving is the suggestion that even an after-life is no more than may be comprehended in terms of our own life. Christ lived, Christ suffered, died, lived again: the cycle is a plain one, the message common, the manner of its representation accessible to all. That is something which European art tended to lose in its subsequent grandeur. Reality is not here the reality of appearances but the reality of emotions; and the sculptor could allow himself a freedom in the treatment of appearances because mere physical accuracy did not particularly matter. This figure was carved not in imitation of external realities but in order to convey internal ones. It was carved, so to speak, from the inside. A comparable approach to reality is one that has been adopted by many of the principal carvers of our own century. Brâncuşi, Henry Moore, Barbara Hepworth, Arp: they also have tried to create forms "from within". Maybe this is why Romanesque sculpture tends to

The prize exhibit of the museum attached to the Hostal San Marcos, León: small ivory figure of Christ Crucified, 11th or 12th century

(*Left*) The scallop-shell symbol emblazoning the superb Renaissance façade of the Hostal San Marcos, León, built as a convent and hospice for pilgrims and now among the grandest, most beautiful hotels in Europe

(*Below*) The Gothic cloisters of the convent built by the Knights of St James in León, now part of the Hostal San Marcos: you can order your gins and tonic on the upper gallery

(*Right*) Cebrero in the Galician highlands on the toughest stretch of the pilgrim route: the houses are built to keep out the savage climate, having no chimneys and virtually no windows

(*Below*) Ponferrada, on the edge of Galicia: castle of the Knights Templars

León Cathedral, west front: sadistic and erotic representation of the tortures of hell

León Cathedral, west front: the benign figure of St James

South door, known as the Portico de las Platerias, of the cathedral of Santiago de Compostela: King David playing the lute (12th century)

Former monastery church of Vilar de Doñas, Galicia, used by the Knights of Santiago as a place to bury their dead killed in battle against the Moors

(*Above*) Santiago de Compostela: one of the four quadrangles of the Renaissance hospital built for pilgrims by King Ferdinand and Queen Isabella in the early 16th century – now a 5-star hotel, the Hostal de los Reyes Catolicos

(*Below*) All that remains of what was once the most powerful monastery in Spain, on a hill above the town of Sahagún

Maestro Mateo's great west door of Santiago Cathedral, known as the Portico de la Gloria (late 12th to early 13th century): the figure of St James stands above the Tree of Jesse on the central column, beneath the feet of Christ

A final object of veneration for pilgrims to Santiago de Compostela: gilt and jewelled statue of St James, above the high altar of the cathedral, which pilgrims approach from behind to kiss and embrace him

register a more intimate connection with our own sensibilities than does much of the sculpture that has filled the intervening centuries.

Beyond the museum lies the church of San Marcos—the convent church—deep, solemn and pale, with an ambulatory on either side of the nave linking a series of private chapels where knights and pilgrims sought the strength to undertake the last and most arduous stage of their journey. Soon the hot plains of Castile would give way to the highlands of Galicia where only travellers from Scotland or the Mountains of Mourne might be expected to feel at home. Among those rainswept hills lay the long last march, under damp skies blowing in from the Atlantic, towards the ultimate goal of a city built around a tomb and a legend, close to where the ocean gave up a harvest of shells for the weary pilgrim to string round his neck, just as Watteau observed many hundreds of years later. And it was as if to give jaded travellers a final boost of spirit that the Knights of Santiago emblazoned the outer wall of their chapel in León with images of those same shells: the image of the scallop, symbol of St James.

Symbol too of Venus. The earliest examples of the scallop-shell in European art are related to the goddess of Love, not to St James. One early legend relates that she was born in a shell, and was carried across the sea to the island of Cythera. Botticelli's "Birth of Venus" in the Uffizi, painted in the 15th century, is the best known representation of this legend. Watteau's painting in the Louvre called "Departure from the Island of Cythera", executed in the early part of the 18th century, playfully associates the tale of Venus's island birthplace with the idea of pilgrimage. Watteau's *galants* are themselves immaculately tailored as pilgrims, hat, scrip, staff and all; but they have become *pèlerins de l'amour*. Watteau's people (as Michael Levey has written) are "pilgrims of the only god the eighteenth century really believed in". Before long the wearing of a pilgrim outfit was to lose even that trivial significance. When a contemporary of Watteau, the French painter Jean-Baptiste Oudry, undertook the portrait (now in the National Gallery of Warsaw) of King Stanislaus Augustus of Poland, the monarch who had surely never risked limb or thought in the direction of Santiago, chose nonetheless to be represented with pilgrim's staff in hand, scallop-shell on his left shoulder, wigged and powdered, flounced cuffs, royal orders and all. The pilgrim's garb had become a mere piece of regal dressing-up.

The association of the legend of Venus with the Santiago pilgrimage clearly predates the frolics of 18th-century courtiers by a long way, though it may be impossible to pin-point when and precisely how that association took place. The symbol of the scallop-shell appears in early Coptic churches (probably of Hellenistic origin.) Since the basilica plan of the earliest church at Compostela derives from Coptic and Byzantine churches, and various legends tell of the apostle's body being brought to Spain from the Middle East, it is not impossible that the shell symbol made the same journey. Well, not quite impossible. What is a great deal more certain is that the shell symbol, relating specifically to St James, can claim an antiquity no earlier than the 12th century, and that the picturesque legends claiming a miraculous association of the scallop-shell with the apostle (such as I related in Chapter II) are relatively modern. They may mask a truth now sentimentalised beyond recognition. There must be some reason, other than his journey by the sea, why the first Christian martyr after Stephen, and champion of the Reconquest, should have become symbolised by a shell—not a conch-shell or an oyster-shell or a clam-shell, but a shell actually known as *venera*, a shell therefore traditionally associated with Venus, a shell even considered to be an emblem of the vagina. I have never heard a convincing explanation of why this should be so. What does appear certain is that the scallop-shell (*Pecten maximus*—the great scallop) is first represented as a badge of pilgrims on the west doorway of Autun Cathedral, in a high-relief of the Last Judgment carved during the middle of the 12th century, and it is first referred to as such, in writing, by Aymery Picaud in his pilgrims' guide of much the same period, where he notes that such shells were offered for sale to pilgrims on the north side of Santiago Cathedral.

But how did the emblem become widespread? Whatever its significance, in origin it seems likely that the scallop-shell image gained currency in response to a need for a recognisable badge to distinguish the pilgrim from other wayfarers, and therefore, to some extent, to protect him from the hazards frequently attending mediaeval travellers. A pilgrim, after all, was a privileged figure. There were laws safeguarding his progress—laws of hospitality, tax laws, church laws, moral laws. A pilgrim's costume marked him out no less than did that of a knight, a monk, a minstrel, a beggar or a leper. And the scallop-shell was his badge, or token; just as pilgrims returning from Jerusalem after the liberation of the city from the Moslems in 1099 bore a palm leaf; and the more faithful of Chaucer's pilgrims, as they wended their way from Canterbury back to the Tabard Inn, may well have carried each of them a metal ampulla containing, supposedly, a grain of dried martyr's blood and bearing the legend "St Thomas makes the best doctor to the worthy sick"; and just as from Rome the faithful carried with them a badge representing the kerchief of St Veronica, those from Amiens a brooch representing the head of John the Baptist, those from Rocamadour an image of the Virgin. And so on. Even at Mont-St-Michel in Normandy, far distant enough from Galicia, there were booths at which scallop-shells were offered for sale during the late 14th century—as we know from an ordonnance of King Charles VI of France—and the same emblem even appears in the abbey's coat-of-arms. Well, Mont-St-Michel acted as an important link between England and the main pilgrim routes south to the Pyrenees; but there is evidence that by then, even by the 13th century, the emblem of Venus and of St James had become adopted as the badge worn by any pilgrim anywhere, as soldiers today sometimes wear regimental badges upon their uniforms incorporating battle-honours which not a campaigner among them could have been aged enough to have won, or witnessed and very possibly not even heard about. What remains is prestige; and the dignity of history.

From León the plain edges towards cold mountains to the north and the west. Soon we are in the area of the Maragateria. Local guidebooks, all too apt to explain in a tone-deaf English what must have had little enough meaning in Spanish in the first place, make much of the Maragatos. They live, so we are told, in the region of Astorga, and folkloric occasions endeavour to impress upon us passers-by the unique nature of their culture. George Borrow, writing in *The Bible in Spain* in 1843, claims the Maragatos to be the descendants of those Goths who identified with the invading Moors to the extent of adopting many of their habits and dress. These consisted of remaining and marrying strictly within their own tribe, and of sporting a tight-fitting jerkin, wide bloomers, gaiters, a slouch-hat and a broad belt equipped with a pouch. It has even been advanced that such a costume may link them with the Berbers. Recent historians have preferred less ornate theories such as that the Maragatos may be no more exotic than an Asturian tribe of some antiquity who chose to retain conservative habits long enough for their fellow men to mark them out as alien. I have to admit that I did not detect in the jeans worn by farmers in their boggy fields round the Rio Orbigo and the Rio Tuerto any mark to distinguish them from men tilling the land in Palma or Picardy or Pennsylvania, though I am sure the local tourist board would have been pleased to convince me otherwise.

At Puente de Orbigo, a few miles before Astorga, stands one of the finest, and certainly the longest, pilgrim bridges in Spain. The fact that it is still in its original state is thanks to a new main road which skirts the village half a mile to the south, hurrying tourists as rapidly as possible across the monotonous Leónese plain. In origin this was a Roman bridge, the very length of it testifying to the marshy and undoubtedly malarial terrain it traversed. The river-banks have recently been laundered into picnic-grounds. Iron seats were holding the stance of yesterday's conversations in the afternoon sun, in twos and threes. Children paddled in lurid canoes, their mothers swollen into deck-chairs, their fathers fishing with an air of Anglo-Saxon resignation. One old church-goer who straddled my passage along the bridge claimed this to be the king of trout rivers in all Europe. Did I not know, he asked. Did I not know that cabinet ministers from Madrid came here for such sport, as did foreigners from Paris and Rome, even the British consul? And he spread knotted arms slow and wide, white cuffs bulging, to indicate a trout the size of a young shark such as might be mine if I had a mind to join such exalted company. No wonder the family of storks who were preening out the clanging of the Matins bell on the baroque belfry of Puente de Orbigo looked uncommonly spruce and complacent about that Lord's-day scene spread below them. A pile carpet of down from white poplars was puffed in the breeze across the useless fields. I switched on my car motor for the thousandth—ten thousandth—time and snarled out of earshot of the insistent bell to prayer and of the lulling radio in the grass. A stork was retching up some reptile on the roof.

Astorga left me with a confusion of impressions. It was early. I had passed the day before wandering along river-banks exercising away a gloom that had settled on me since leaving León, only half-aware that the orchestra of sound burbling from every bush was in fact the song of nightingales. And so I reached Astorga early enough for the café chairs to be stacked upon the tables, and the floors scrubbed and slippery. I felt hungry. Miserably, there was nothing on the aggressively bare counter that one might conceivably eat, save a slice of sweet pie at which I peered until it was thrust at me as though in challenge by a lady whose red hair, I had the feeling, expressed more eloquently than any words her thoughts about her son, her life, her lot and her husband.

I paid the lady what it occurred to me her pie and her temper might be worth, and left just as the painted carts, the braided donkeys and the shawled women with their high black boots were taking their time to market. I followed. I love markets. It was June, and Astorga still felt the sting of distant snow in the wind driving from those unfriendly mountains to the west and north where, as I remembered from my Henty and from some unlikely days as an instructor in military history, Sir John Moore's light infantry had clawed its frozen way towards Corunna and the sea, which most of them never reached. North-west Spain is not the Spain of castanets and Ambre Solaire; for all its broad prospect of the plains, which would be wearing their skin of green for a few weeks longer, for all its cats tiptoeing over pantiles in the sun, Astorga is no place to warm the imagination and nourish thoughts of Hemingway. Spain can be mighty dull, and here was a little and ordinary town with a taste for plastic geraniums and morose barmaids, which somehow seemed to deserve one another.

But then there is Gaudí: Antonio Gaudí. And whatever was he doing here? Anyone familiar with Barcelona and that inspired dream of the impossible which is the church of the Sagrada Familia, could have identified at once the hand responsible for the Bishop's Palace here in Astorga, which the magnificent Catalonian eccentric had put up in 1909 at the request of a local patron, doubtless to the astonishment of local opinion. This is no moment to explore the virtues and oddities of Gaudí's genius—because genius he was—except to admit that the Bishop's Palace at Astorga was not his happiest invention, but the kind of Gothic fantasy which appears shrunken by the very elaboration of its ornament until it would come as little surprise to see a small pantomime witch sweeping the doorstep with her broom. Inside, though, all was much happier: the spaces, which managed to appear so much larger than the exterior dimensions should have allowed, have been turned into a Museo de los Caminos (a Museum of the Pilgrim Roads) such as exists nowhere else, and within whose unlikely walls documents, emblems, civil badges, registers, garments, statuettes and a hundred and one other trophies and trinkets of the journey are preserved. I browsed contentedly.

If Astorga gives the appearance nowadays of a place history has touched with a light and eccentric brush before passing on to greater topics, it was once, nonetheless, a town of substance on the route to Santiago. There were monasteries and hospices here, the largest being the Hospital San Juan where St Francis of Assisi rested during his own pilgrimage to Santiago in 1273. And there was the cathedral. The one St Francis knew no longer exists. The present one, as the guidebook informs you, was rebuilt between 1471 and 1693, which is another way of saying there is no architectural style known to man—except Romanesque—which has not elbowed its point of view somewhere into the red and yellow sandstone. Not my favourite cathedral, Astorga. In the interior, laden with the customary Baroque furniture to weight the soul, Mass was in full sound and ceremony for the edification of a congregation of three. Yet there, behind its 18th-century façade to the left of the cathedral, lay a glimpse of an Astorga not especially old, yet of a character such as St Francis might have recognised—a quiet monastic courtyard of the Hospital San Juan with its glazed-in balcony and the passage of nuns stooped in thought.

It was rough going for the pilgrim after Astorga. He had two choices, and in neither case could he avoid the Montes de León. The harder and more favoured way took him over the Rabanal Pass through the heart of the Maragatos country I have already mentioned. The road today, such as it is, follows the Rio Jerga, then climbs to Rabanal del Camino among the heights of Foncebadón, at which point those so inclined could take their lives and their discomfort in their hands and hump it optimistically in a westerly direction towards a cluster of thatched houses called Acebo. Thereafter the monotony and the rough going continued until before unduly long a road led to the village of Molinaseca which today could scarcely invigorate the human spirit more in this wilderness were it Las Vegas. Then from Molinaseca to Ponferrada is only a few miles more; and there the pilgrim was on the doorstep of Galicia.

The second way from Astorga is, and I suspect always was, marginally the easier. This took the pilgrim north-west, not directly west, over the Manzanal Pass, and it is by this route that the hitherto sealed honeypot of Galicia is now being opened up by a multi-lane highway which slices and strides across a high mountain pass in order to speed the tourist to Santiago and the Atlantic beaches in time for tea. At the roof of the pass I turned off the highway on to the old and now pitted road which once linked the huddled villages of the Maragateria. Never in their centuries of life have they felt and looked so isolated as they do now. For so long they were nothing much, certainly; nonetheless, those who crossed these mountains called there, sheltered there, needed these roofs and the hospitality they offered. No longer. Motorways open up a country, but they also shrink it, isolate it, and they impose upon those who have traditionally humanised those hard regions a new irrelevance. As a local you either live in a backwater or you get out.

Between Manzanal and Ponferrada by the northern route lies a mean and scurvy landscape, stubbly and rough as an old elephant's hide. Here and there its bones break through. Blades of coal. Mists smear a black grease over the road, over the heather, over the rock-roses that push up between the cracks of the rock. Open-cast pits lie like cavities in the dead face of the mountain. The new concrete *camino* that slaloms down the shale of the Montes de León eventually hurtles one towards a town in the river-valley by the name of Bembibre. Here I stopped for a brandy and a coffee—and where is coffee better than in northern Spain? And so fortified and cleaned of the coal-dust and the wet wind I encountered a most uncommon pleasure in the centre of the town, one that made all that dreary journey worthwhile. This was a concrete figure of Christ high on his belfry, of ambitious scale and of pious intent, though the latter was impossible to tell on this occasion since the figure's arms were stretched just wide enough to contain within their embrace a nest of white storks. The head of the statue was lost among a bundle of twigs, and the hands protruded from the sprigs in blessing, in a manner suggestive of blunt knitting-needles.

The road to Ponferrada might be the road to Wigan Pier. And as I drove down into the industrial smog that bathes this jerry-built heap of modern Spain my heart sank into the kind of stupefied disbelief I associate with American television entertainments. It was, I have to admit, something of a triumph for the local tourist bureau (closed on that day, I like to imagine out of despair) to have photographed Ponferrada from the air. This has the effect of minimising, even glossing with a sort of charm, the squalor of the new town, and of raising to a spectacular prominence the truly splendid castle which during the 12th century the Knights Templars built high upon a rock over the gorge spanned by the iron bridge that gives the town its name—Ponferrada. Around the wreckage of the old castle lay surprising old arcaded squares, enclosed by rickety houses whose glass loggias leant, as if in gossip, across the street, and by the old town gate under which the pilgrim road passed towards the panache of turrets and saw-blade battlements that the Knights had thrown up as their proudest monument to the crusade of the sword.

There were numerous orders of knights. Their members swore the strictest vows to defend Christendom with their lives, often living in closed communities—or commanderies—which were half-fortress and half-monastery. They flourished throughout that period of militant Christianity during the 12th century which witnessed the emergence of both the crusades and the pilgrimages; indeed the spirit of both the crusades and the mediaeval pilgrimages was to a large extent an outcome of the upsurgence of the knights. The emergence of the chivalric figure as a hero of romance and of love was a later and largely artificial embellishment, and it is doubtful if the highways of Christendom would have been so secured had the policing of them been left even to the likes of Chaucer's gentle Knight.

The Order of the Knights Templars, architects of that swaggering bastion in Ponferrada, was founded ostensibly for the protection of pilgrims in the year 1119. So great did its territorial power, influence and wealth become, however, that they were forcibly dissolved in 1314. Meanwhile, upon the example of the Templars were based many other orders of knighthood, one of them being the Order of St James of the Sword in other words the Knights of Santiago, who were essentially a Spanish organisation established to defend the frontiers against the Moors in the early days of the Reconquest. The Knights of Santiago were affiliated with the much larger and international Order of St John of Jerusalem (founded during the First Crusade), who were the Knights Hospitallers and who became the principal chivalric order in western Europe after the abolition of the Templars in the 14th century. The Hospitallers, internationally, cared for pilgrims on their journeys across Europe, which is why the Cross of St John of Jerusalem—known later as the Cross of Malta—is everywhere to be found scratched or engraved on doors and lintels along the pilgrim routes to Santiago. The cross of St John was as universally recognised among poor travellers in the Middle Ages as are the initials YHA today; and it served a not dissimilar purpose.

The Knights of Santiago were specially motivated in their military role. *Rubet ensis sanguine Arabum* was the motto of their order: "The sword is red with the blood of Islam." Their badge, likewise, was a blood-red sword shaped in the form of a cross together with a white scallop-shell. But the strength of the Knights of Santiago grew in inverse proportion to the menace they were pledged to remove. They became a political organisation; and by the end of the 15th century they were responsible for no fewer than two hundred commanderies in Spain, and approximately the same number of priories, apart from villages, castles, hospices and other properties.

By this time the knightly pilgrim could scarcely be said to be one who drew his strength and purpose from the monastic life: he was more likely to be a man of substance, of standing, who embarked upon pilgrimages where his sword was little likely to be unsheathed in anger, who travelled in a pleasant enough fashion enjoying the diversions and pursuits of the countryside, paying courtly visits to other noblemen, taking part in tournaments, entertaining bored ladies with accounts of his travels and sampling the wines. To be a Knight of Santiago was the thing to be. In the 17th century Velasquez, when he included a modest portrait of himself in that account of the royal princess and her attendants, "Las Meniñas" (now in the Prado), was pleased to portray himself as a Knight of Santiago—though in fact the last Moor had been hounded from the land a full two centuries before he painted it. One year after the fall of Granada in 1492, which marked the virtual conclusion of Arab power in Spain, the Order of Santiago had already ceased to be an independent power in the land. By tradition the Knights elected their own Master, and, when a vacancy occurred in 1493, Queen Isabella had the wit to go to Uclés, the headquarters of the Order, and request the Mastership for her royal husband King Ferdinand, a request which could scarcely be refused. Thereupon naturally all the titles and possessions of the Knights became the property of the Spanish Crown, and the sign of the blooded sword became a coveted symbol of courtly favour to be worn by royal ministers and ambassadors—and by royal painters like Velasquez.

To the west of Ponferrada rise the highlands which are known as the Bierzo. But first comes the little town of Cacabelos which Ford, I noted, pronounced "a wretched hamlet", and which a few years earlier than Ford was there had been the scene of a disastrous episode in Sir John Moore's retreat to Corunna during the Peninsular War. Then at the very ankles of the Bierzo comes the rather larger town of Villafranca (clearly a version of Freetown, which appears in many European languages, but which, as the name suggests—particularly on this route—was originally a Frankish settlement). The town turns out to be far richer in character than Ford gave it credit for. An "abode of dirt, misery, and picturesque poverty", he called it. Here in Villafranca stood wooden buildings that were soon to become familiar to me in Galicia over the mountains: houses with deep eaves and precarious balconies, a jostle of whitewashed walls that sat like weights anchoring the steep vineyards laid down across the hillsides like mats.

The church of Santiago, too, is a French church. How it must have gladdened Aymery Picaud's heart to see a west portal and rounded apse looking quite so like those of his native Poitou. Here among the apple-trees—for the climate here is already cooling under the snows of the Bierzo—and among the green and orange slate of this Frankish church, the pilgrim whose strength could carry him no further than Villafranca could hobble into the north portal known as the *Puerta del Perdón* and here obtain the same absolution as he would have gained had he reached Santiago de Compostela itself. History has not handed down to us what manner of health-test an ailing pilgrim might have to undergo to obtain this privilege, nor how many Frankish doctors prospered in Villafranca by knowing how to call an ague the plague: what is certain is that the prospect of that formidable heap of hills rising between them and the city of St James must have tested the most devout heart. "Never," to quote Ford again, "was nature more enthroned in loneliness than here . . ."

Or, he might have added, in loveliness. The Bierzo, I imagine, can look no more beautiful than it does in June. I drove up the valley of the Rio Valcarce, and the hills on either side were sugared with white broom, iced here and there with limp white cistus flowers, their throats stained yellow and magenta. Fishermen braced themselves against fast water. The sky was a cold blue now, clear of haze; contours sharp. Farmers were riding homewards on donkeys through lavender that looked as though it had been dipped in concentrated indigo. Castile seemed as far away as Africa. This was the north. I turned off the fan-cooler in the car for the first time since entering Spain. I felt I might be in Scotland.

There were even bagpipes. Not folkloric bagpipes: no tourist in his senses would have found himself where I was at that moment, shivering on the crest of a pass called El Poyo where my country lane had led me since I turned off the main road at Piedrafita to follow the old route across the mountains into Galicia and the Atlantic gales. It was Sunday, about 4.30 in the afternoon. Directly to the north the landscape was still held in winter under the snow of the Cantabrian mountains. Heather dyed the deep valleys between; stone walls separated the sheep. And as I struggled with the car against the buffeting of the wind I could see the pilgrim road sheltering under the lea of the hill between boulders: a stony track now, a path between farmhouse and farmhouse.

While I was gazing down the valley, there spilt out of one of these farmhouses a group of five young men singing. They were some distance away but the wind was hurtling my way, carrying their voices up the path to where I stood. An older man stood at the door and waved them up the hill. They had been enjoying Sunday lunch, perhaps at an uncle's farm, and the wine and music must have been flowing while the gales battered outside. One of them I could now see carried a football under his arm, while another a small bagpipe of brilliant scarlet. They kicked the football from one to another until the track grew too stony and they began to clamber in a chain up the slope; and as they did so, the boy carrying the pipes started to play and the others to sing. And the music he played was a high-pitched dirge that stretched and wandered like the pilgrims' path itself among those northern mountains as if some unseen Celtic hand had floated them—men and music and landscape—down the Irish Sea and across the Bay of Biscay, and provided them with the lightest veil of rain to disguise where they had come from. Finally the group climbed the last bank of shale and joined the road near where I stood, whereupon the bagpiper put his scarlet pipes under his arm and the five of them became young supporters of Real Madrid once more, flicking the football from one to another across the road until they disappeared over the crest of the hill.

A short distance from the El Poyo Pass, and back a little along the mountain road, stands Cebrero. What exactly Cebrero is evades an easy description. It is a village built near the height of the pass exactly where the most violent nastiness of the Galician weather must strike it from every angle. Cebrero is also a monument to poverty. It was right on the main pilgrim route across the Bierzo. It has a 10th-century church, now much spruced up with plaster-work and plastic flowers, and a hostelry likewise made acceptable for visitors who drive up in fine weather for a purified sniff of the Middle Ages. Cebrero is a village maintained by the Spanish authorities as a memorial to a vanishing Spain and, of course, as a tourist attraction of a minor kind. It consists of a cluster of low and more or less circular thatched cottages, built heavily of stone, as well they might be, but virtually without windows. These houses are called *pallosas*, and all that admits light is a low door and the occasional window so minuscule that its only practical purpose seems to be to emphasise the pervading interior gloom. Those *pallosas* that are still inhabited—and the people who live in them are subsidised to do so, I was thankful to learn—are choked by smoke from a central fire, since the builders of these deep thatched roofs made no allowance for anything like a chimney. So the smoke and smells of living stay put. Tourist literature is fond of referring to Cebrero as *típico*, though *típico* of quite what I am not sure. In the terminology of tourist authorities it is a word that generally means they have found one example surviving and have done it up.

Fragments of sunlight were quilting the hillsides of the Bierzo orange and green between the ragged heather. To the left the Sierra del Orinio bore the look of a region which summer never reached or, if it did, then it departed leaving no mark. This was a rough last lap for pilgrims: and yet it was here, in this most unwelcoming of regions, chiselled by water into raw valleys, waterfalls and sawn-off rocks, that as early as the 10th century communities of Cenobite monks built monasteries for themselves—Samos, Sobrado de los Monjes among them. These monastic communities cheered many a chilled pilgrim on the road to Santiago with the sight of some holy relic, but were the very opposite of those anchorite hermitages which had been a feature of the parched Castilian landscape round Burgos. These were establishments of learning and enlightenment, spacious in architecture and powerful in lands. San Julián de Samos, in particular, owned one of the richest libraries in northern Spain; and though, alas, the monastery was gutted by fire in 1951, the restored hulk of the place still looms prison-like over the road that leads to Sarria (the site of one of the most important pilgrim hospices in Galicia) and on through valleys so infernally wet and fertile that many a pilgrim from the north decided to settle there for good; finally to the valley of the Mino, a river which cuts Galicia vertically in two, and where today stands one of the strangest monuments to the pilgrim route I found in Spain.

This was Puertomarin, once a mediaeval sanctuary linked to the eastern bank of the Mino by a bridge built in 1120 by a man known as Pierre le Pèlerin, or Pedro Peregrino, who also constructed a pilgrim hospital here six years later on the bank of the river. A third feature of Puertomarin was a church built as a fort in the same century by the Knights of St John, who further secured their position here by constructing a palace nearby. Today old Puertomarin has entirely vanished, engulfed in a reservoir which holds back some of the plentiful rainfall of Galicia against its traditional dispersal southwards towards Portugal.

But the church the knights built, and which they named after their patron saint, John of Jerusalem, was a fine one, and when Puertomarin was placed under sentence of flood the authorities agreed to move it, stone by stone, and to rebuild it in the heart of what has since become a new town on the hillside above the reservoir. And there it stands, this great bulwark of newly chiselled battlements overlooking an ornamental garden that would do credit to Eastbourne were it not for an old calvary standing in its midst with its figure of St James bearing his tau-cross. An incongruous-looking original portico rings the entrance to the church, carved with figures of the Old Men of the Apocalypse all seated in the familiar semi-circle above the door, like some surprised orchestra that has forgotten the tune. The rebuilt church of San Juan, so scrubbed and spick-and-span a piece of mediaevalry, is a place where (to misquote Dylan Thomas) one might expect that God would wipe his feet before entering. Indeed, the entire town reminded me of a film-set that the removal-men had forgotten to dismantle after the cameramen had departed. Only the sight of two long-horn cows led ever-so-slowly over the new bridge which has replaced the one built by Pierre le Pèlerin suggested this was a town with some sort of life of its own, and not just an architectural folly waiting to discover why it was here at all.

The two long-horns apart, the only sounds of life in Puertomarin were coming from the direction of the local Parador, which the Spanish tourist authorities have decided to build on the edge of the town, presumably in some obscure faith in Puertomarin as a spa of the future. The dining-room had been constructed as if to expect an entire congress of American ladies on their way to St James, though I found myself alone in it except for a distant gentleman whose teeth clicked. I had brought from the car my copies of Aymery Picaud and of Richard Ford to see what they chose to say about Galicia. Ford, so I read, maintained the area was seldom visited except by muleteers. Picaud was more forthcoming. The Galicians, he maintained, were closest to the French in their dress, but given to anger and double-dealing. Of the food, at that moment being placed in front of me by one of those Spanish girls so servile as to be positively arrogant, Picaud was less certain of himself and made me feel likewise: fine pastures, he avowed, ditto fruit, rye-bread (this wasn't), cider, milk, honey and enormous river-fish; on the other hand he was emphatic that the fish and meat in Galicia, indeed in all Spain, were bound to make all foreigners ill. Ah well. I tucked in, and the servile lady retreated with an air of silent malice.

The breeze of the afternoon tore at the clouds. A hum of bees rose among the heather and the white broom. Deep-roofed, stone farm-buildings squatted in the fields, and sickles had cut crescents in the rich hay. By the roadside, sheets were laid out to dry like markers for aircraft. A grey hen harrier marauded over the grass, wing-tips fanning the wind. A yellow wagtail looped across the road and settled on a rock, tail bobbing, and off again.

To the right of the road a track led to Villar de Doñas. A Baroque belfry by the field-side, among farm-buildings, disguised a much earlier church that squatted among stone walls. Here in this forgotten place a monastery once stood, and here the Knights of Santiago buried those of their company who had died fighting the Moors in the early years of the Reconquest. Passing under a carved Romanesque portico I entered a bare, dank nave, green with the damp of Galicia. The apse was painted and scratched into the walls were crosses of St John of Jerusalem. Along one wall were propped tombs engraved with the names of those who had died, bearing more crosses and scallop-shells upon them to identify the cause in which they had died. This abandoned barn with its few memorials was all that remained of a place consecrated to the heroes of St James to whom the Spanish church in all its later pomp and pride owed so much.

The Santiago road continues through towns with names that promise rather more than they offer, like Palas de Rey, and others supposed to be of Celtic origin, like Mellid and Arzúa, none of which urged me to do more than obey the speed limit and pass on, noting the tall camellias still in flower in June which spoke much for the Galician climate. (In England they bloom in March.) Traces of the old road broke surface in the fields here and there: a double line of stones between trees, or a track left to grass over where engineering had cut a straighter course, and a slender footbridge over the River Furelos (known at that point as the Rio Seco) close to the village of Libureiro. Not much else. A monotonous stretch growing more blustery and thicker with eucalyptus groves towards the approaching Atlantic. The smell and feel of a fresh climate. Different flowers along the hedgerows: striking blue lithospermum, small rock-roses, flowers cowering out of the gales, brightened by the grey light and by the rain. The windscreen wipers swept a blurred prospect of clouds and of low hills.

The mediaeval pilgrim walked to Santiago and back again. The richer ones did it on horseback. Those richer still took their household with them in caravan. Today they mostly do it by car, in my case, with a stretch of footslogging here and there to breathe and pause a little and let the mind catch up with the distances that sweep past so easily unnoticed. But most, or at least a very large number, now fly in by courtesy of Iberia who have provided an airport for their convenience—weather permitting—a few miles east of the city of Santiago on a low rise above the place where the former pilgrims paused and washed their tired limbs before the last climb to the hill of San Marcos, from where they would catch their first sight of the city of St James.

The stream is still there, flowing under the road at the village of Labacolla, and a tall calvary mounted on a green slope below a Baroque church marks the place where they laid down their packs and rested. A narrow track leads across a hay-field to the stream itself, no more than ten feet in width and tangled with alders. The unstable footbridge is new, otherwise I imagine the scene has changed little in a thousand years.

From Labacolla, it is said, parties of pilgrims, refreshed and washed, would race to the top of the last hill above the tiny village of San Marcos—a hill called Mons Gaudii or Monte Gaudi or Monte de Gozo—and the one who got there first was dubbed "king". Those who had done the journey in style would dismount at Labacolla and join them. The village of San Marcos is off the main road today, diminutive and crumbled, with raised granaries and circular hayricks and unbelievably ancient-looking ox-carts with solid wooden wheels wobbling through the mud of the village street. Not many changes here, for all the jet-planes circling in low from Madrid. At the far end of the village stands a plain little chapel among a grove of oaks. I left the car and picked my way through the gorse up the final slope. The sky was speckled with larks—toy kites on strings tugged by the wind and then let drop. A panorama of wooded hills began to unfold as I climbed, until there to the west below the setting sun rose three black spires. Santiago.

Monte Gaudi means Mount Joy, and its name also echoes the cry of the pilgrims as they reached this point where I stood now and set eyes for the first time on the city of St James: *Montjoie* (though there seems to be some confusion, on which I have been unable to throw any real light, as to whether the pilgrims were crying "Mount Joy" or "My Joy"—a confusion further confounded by the fact that this was also the cry uttered by the knights as they mounted for battle in the *Song of Roland* and by Charlemagne as he first caught sight of Rome, when he came to be crowned Emperor by the Pope).

I stumbled back down the hill, while the larks flew overhead, and tried to imagine something of the sense of elation a pilgrim would have felt at this moment in the Middle Ages. Impossible. Sadly so. A non-believer who was catching no more than a whiff—scented perhaps with a little sentimentality—of that joy. Yet happy, radiantly happy in a way that maybe no mediaeval pilgrim could have known, because I had not only the city of St James lying before me but the whole perspective of history, of *its* history, of the follies and lies and achievements, amazing bravery and persistence, which were woven together into the intricate pattern of this story to which I had devoted a slice of my life. Why had I done so? I did not in all honesty know, except that I was glad I had. I let the car slip gently down the western slope of Monte Gaudi, among the slab-stone walls that reminded me of Cornwall, among the eucalyptus-trees and apple-groves, past the white-washed houses with vines trained across the face of them, and past lines of ageless ladies in black, bent and squat under straw-hats upon which balanced giant wicker baskets laden with vegetables, and stuck through with an umbrella like a gigantic hat-pin: for the umbrella is the symbol of Galicia, it serves for sun or rain. And so I made my way towards that white-washed, rain-washed city of granite and dreams.

CHAPTER XI

—◆—

Santiago de Compostela

The city of Santiago de Compostela is a monument to a legend: a monument which life has crept up on, gradually, a little subdued by the rain.

Richard Ford found it a melancholy town in the 19th century, which it certainly is not today. To him the city was "damp, cold, full of arcades, fountains and scallop-shells . . . From the constant rain this holy city is irreverently called *El orinal de España.*" There he was right enough. Local inhabitants claim, with a frankness that would do credit to any Mancunian, that thirty fine days are all they are entitled to expect in a year; though they add, with an ingenious flash of pride, that the full loveliness of their city emerges only in the rain.

Here, too, they are to a degree right, though I hardly believed so on that first morning when I pulled back the curtains of my hotel window and gazed into a fine Scottish drizzle. But Santiago is a city constructed for the most part of granite—the walls, the streets, the market, the gutters—and granite which is dry under the sun's glare takes on a grimness and a deadness of texture. Once water flows upon it, on the other hand, all those myriads of crystalline granules of which granite is composed begin to sparkle like the night sky, and the massive flagstones with which the arcaded streets of Santiago are paved take on the sombre splendour of enormous dark jewels.

I strolled the streets that morning, having first bought an umbrella which jostled the thousands of other umbrellas manoeuvring their way at a midday pace up the Rua del Villar, side-stepping the cars in and out of the deep arcades over which lean the patrician mansions and former hostelries that make up this older district of the city. Scallop-shells were carved into the walls along the way in a pro-fusion which suggested that a child had got over-excited with a patty-pan. Dried palm-branches hung over wooden balconies. Trees of camellias burst scarlet over the walls of secluded gardens.

Ahead of me the cathedral diminished everything around it, so that it seemed at first to have elbowed its place arrogantly among the huddled houses, until I turned left to gain a view of the main entrance to find that it was myself who was diminished by one of the noblest squares a man ever set eyes on. This was the Plaza del Obradoiro. It makes upon the visitor the kind of impact he receives from encountering the Piazza San Marco in Venice for the first time: an impact created by the sheer unexpectedness and majesty of such a space. The Plaza del Obradoiro appears to have been conjured out of nowhere amid this compact city, an archi-tectured expanse of emptiness which is less like a mere space than a mighty building with the sky for a roof.

To the right of the Plaza del Obradoiro rises the west front of the cathedral itself, its most recent addition, rising and rising always by the longest possible route, in a balancing-trick of Baroque pinnacles, curlicues and broken arches, finally breaking into a pair of en-crusted bell-towers which are like flagmasts raised to the Church Triumphant. Indeed, seen across the square from the western side, the cathedral exudes a hat-in-the-air exuberance, as if it intended to announce to the world that here the Devil had finally lost the game and from now onwards this was a place fit for spiritual high-living. Then just as the purist in me was reflecting that here was perhaps a triumph of decoration over architecture, of fun over solemnity, I perceived that the entire structure was held in harmony by four-teen vertical rods of slender columns without which this whole jumble of fancy and artifice might look in danger of wobbling in the Atlantic wind and of crashing into the square below, just as the *Campanile* in Venice had once crashed into the Piazza San Marco. Hawks were flitting in and out of the convolutions of its stone, while the cathedral's gardeners were engaged in their annual task, high up, of hoeing the vegetation from the masonry, so that pink valerian and yellow ragwort feel like manna from heaven in the path of surprised visitors.

At that particular moment I wanted to save the cathedral for a later time and to wander on. The rain had ceased, as though to take breath. On the south side of the Plaza del Obradoiro stood the Romanesque college of San Jerónimo, hunched and retiring in the prospect of this opulent space before it. On the farther side rose the prison-like walls of the hospice erected at the command of King Ferdinand and Queen Isabella towards the end of the 15th century, to celebrate the capture of Granada from the Moors. Its original purpose was to house poor and sick pilgrims: its present rôle is to house wealthy Americans, for here, like the Hostal San Marcos to which I had treated myself in León, is one of the great hotels of Spain, converted from its former status as a pilgrims' hospice at the instigation of General Franco, with the aid of two thousand workmen, and formally opened by him for the Holy Year of 1954. And then, to complete the quartet of remarkable buildings which bound this square stood another masterpiece, this time a Classical building, broad in spread and simple in decoration, so that it acted as a foil to the frolic and fantasy of the cathedral's west front that faced it. This was formerly the Palacio de Rajoy and is now, more bluntly, the City Hall.

I made my way into the narrow alleys that edge along the cathedral walls on the far side just as the rain, having taken its breather, had begun to plummet on to the granite flagstones. Peering from under my umbrella I caught sight of a sign which read Museo Arte Sacro, and decided to seek shelter amid the holy art: and here, while the downpour endured, I kept company with a depressed congregation of wounded martyrs and tearful madonnas—most of them supplied with appropriate flesh-tints or blood-tints—and with countless other relics and bric-à-brac for my edification, none of which I estimated to be of an earlier date than the 18th century and most of it a good deal more recent than that. What, I pondered, had happened to the spirit of devotion during the long, soft, opulent years since Christianity had once fought for its very life, penned into this Dunkirk of north-western Spain? What had happened to soften hard faith into mere displays of piety, solemnity into sentimentality? Whatever it was had weakened the cast of faith from the obduracy of Santiago's granite to the gentility of soap—perfumed soap. I was reassured to discover amid such thoughts that the sky had grown clear again and I left the Museum of Holy Kitsch for the first and, I imagine, the last time.

Santiago has remained a small city. It contains forty churches, so they say, but it is still no larger than an English market town. It has a mere 60,000 inhabitants, which represents one church for every

1500 men, women and children, a rather high proportion of whom, it looked to me, made use of such a facility. But, as I say, it is a diminutive city. I walked back into the Plaza del Obradoiro past the walls of the Archbishop's Palace, crossed the square in front of the Hostal for millionaire pilgrims and took the narrow Calle de las Huertas which dips steeply from the level of the square down between a double row of granite and whitewashed cottages (many bearing scallop-shells engraved upon their lintels) that reminded me of Cornish fishing villages: indeed Santiago at that moment seemed scarcely larger than one of these, for within ten minutes I was walking among fields. The grass was dense and damp. A tethered donkey contemplated me with an air of resigned emptiness. Mongrel hens squatted in rows upon a fence. A farmer in a broad straw hat said good morning. The sun had come out, and he remarked on this fact as any Englishman might, and with even better reason for surprise.

I turned back from the fields, reclimbed the street into the city and crossed the square at a contented pace, to find myself in the Calle del Franco which was very evidently the corridor of outdoor social life in Santiago, then entered a plain, cool café for—and it seemed appropriate enough—a dish of scallops, *Coquilles St-Jacques* as I knew them. Before many minutes I was seated at a wooden table overlooking an enclosed garden of camellias, washing down my scallops with a white wine that had no name I could discover but was exactly the colour of lemon barley-water and carried upon it a fine head of froth. It tasted like cider. I took out my copy of Ford, as had become my habit when in the right mood, and read with pleasure that "residence in holy places has a tendency to materialise the spiritual sentiment . . ." And indeed, I thought as I disposed of my final scallop, why the hell not?

St James's Day in Santiago is celebrated on 25th July, and the years when that coincides with a Sunday are Holy Years. But Santiago is on a limb of Europe, on the way to nowhere except towards a windy sea, so that even on St James's Day the city attracts fewer visitors than do most of the great cities of Europe, and this comparative isolation has to a large extent protected it from the depredations that have befallen many of the cities that lie on the migration routes of tourism; though it has certainly not protected it from the kind of architectural expansion around the ring of the city which puts one in mind of some giant, possessed with a passion for children's Lego, who has not first grasped its constructional principles. My hotel rose out of just such an entanglement of concrete and steel, though mercifully my bedroom window looked westwards above the mess, over soft, shrouded hills splashed at this time of year with gorse and poppies.

It still feels isolated, Santiago, set on the rim of Europe and the goings-on of the world, goal though it may be of a journey that is still undertaken by thousands, even hundreds of thousands of visitors every year. And isolated it always was, even I suspect when it was the symbol and ensign-bearer of what was, after all, the most emotive cause in Christendom: the expulsion of the Infidel. Perhaps, to perceive this isolation one has to understand what happened to Europe after Roman authority crumbled, and power broke up into splinters of insubstantial authority, each of them far, too far, in distance from the heart of what remained of Roman control, Constantinople. These various powers were insubstantial precisely because for centuries there was nothing adequate to replace the order and discipline of the *Pax Romana*. Europe became de-urbanised, and this dispersed authority still further. What is more, such political stability as did survive was constantly under threat of attack from hostile races, whether they were the Moors from the south and the east, or the nomadic tribes of Barbarians from the north and from the Steppes of what is now Russia. There were the Arabs, the Normans, the Magyars, the Goths, the Huns: each of them representing quite different levels of civilisation—or lack of it—but each representing a continual threat to what had remained a *status quo* for centuries. In Europe the period from the Dark Ages to the early Middle Ages was no time to feel safe at home, and one of the results of this state of political and social instability was the establishment of isolated strongholds of order and—just as important—strongholds of culture. York was such a bastion; so was Winchester; so was Reims. And so, at a slightly later date, was Santiago de Compostela.

One of the contributions of Charlemagne to the course of history was his exercise of organised power towards creating a semblance at least of unification within the Christian Church, for which he was duly made Emperor by the Pope, whose authority over that Church Charlemagne and his Carolingian predecessors had done so much to establish. By about the year AD 800 there was such a thing as an Imperial Church under the Bishop of Rome, and the organisation of that empire was administered through the establishment of bishops responsible for their appropriate regions.

In north-west Spain the seat of that bishopric at the time of Charlemagne was at Iria Flavia, now Padrón, close to the mouth of the Ria Ulla; but within a hundred years the birth and burgeoning of the St James legend created a more vital centre of Christian faith in this far and insecure outpost of the Papal empire, inland to the north-east of Iria Flavia, and so the seat of that bishopric became transferred to Santiago. A little over two centuries later again, at the height of the popularity of the pilgrimage, Santiago was raised in status to an archbishopric, and the Pope responsible for conferring this dignity was Calixtus II, the very man fraudulently named as the author (or at least part-author) of Aymery Picaud's pilgrims' guide.

The growth and prosperity of Santiago really begins with its elevation to the status of archbishopric, and much of the initial credit for that prosperity must lie with its first archbishop, Diego Gelmirez, who held the position, first of bishop and subsequently archbishop, for thirty-nine years, and who began the reconstruction of the cathedral that had been wrecked by the Moors.

The description of Santiago given in the 12th-century pilgrims' guide is therefore of a city as it existed only a few decades after Gelmirez's time. Picaud recounts that it was a city with seven gates, the gate to the north-east being the one traditionally used by pilgrims: the Francígena Gate or Puerta del Camino. Theoretically, it is still possible to take up a position at the Puerta del Camino, though the gate and the walls it penetrated exist no longer, and anyone so doing stands in the direct line of traffic converging from five directions at the discretion of one policeman whose whistle often sounds more like a cry for help than an exercise of authority.

From the Francígena Gate pilgrims entered the city along a narrow street which was lined with hospices, arriving finally at the cathedral by the north door. Picaud's pilgrims' guide describes how a hospice for poor pilgrims—by which he meant the ninety-nine per cent not rich enough to travel on horseback, or literate enough to avail themselves of his guidebook—directly faced this north door of the cathedral and was separated from it by an open space in the

middle of which stood a fountain, he claims, without rival in the
world, shaped in the form of a cup and large enough to hold
fifteen men. From the centre of it rose a bronze column surmounted
by the figures of four lions spouting water. It was in this space
round the fountain, Picaud says, where pilgrims were "sold small
scallop-shells which are the insignia of St James".

Today the supposed relics of St James himself are contained in a
19th-century casket visible in a crypt to which visitors descend
behind the High Altar of the cathedral. But to every pilgrim since
the Middle Ages the climax of his immense journey, and a deeply
emotional moment, has been his encounter with the Capilla Mayor,
which is the statue of the apostle. It is 12th century or earlier
(possibly, say some, a later copy), and is raised high above the
altar so that it acts as the point of focus within the entire cathedral,
and the focus, too, of the pilgrim's spiritual experience in attending
service there.

The Capilla Mayor was heavily restored during the 17th century
(during the same period as the High Altar itself was constructed),
and it is now deeply encrusted with a sticky-looking paint which
contrives to give it an unpleasant sunburnt effect and totally to
disguise any antiquity it may possess or indeed any quality as a
work of art—which it may quite reasonably be argued is not the
point anyway. The Capilla Mayor is quite simply an icon, an object
of reverence, of astonishment and—quite supremely—of dramatic
impact. And this it certainly has. A cape of diamonds added in the
18th century contributes not a little to this effect. (The one of gold
he traditionally wore was removed by the French during the
Napoleonic wars.)

The pilgrim today is permitted to approach the Capilla Mayor by
means of some stairs which mount from the left and right to the
rear of the altar. These are invisible, for the most part, from the
body of the cathedral. One by one the faithful approach the painted
and adorned image of the saint from behind and are permitted to
embrace him and to place upon his head their hat—traditionally of
course the floppy pilgrim's hat with its scallop-shell affixed, though
few now wear it. The prospect of this touching ceremony seen
from in front of the High Altar is, to say the least, a little peculiar,
as every few seconds one pair of arms after another gently seizes
the apostle apparently from nowhere, while hats of different hues

and descriptions are placed upon the saintly head, only to vanish again and be replaced by another. I confess, it was with a certain self-consciousness that I took my place in the queue on that narrow staircase and in my turn offered the apostle my embrace to a clank of precious stones and more than a twinge of Anglo-Saxon embarrassment. The area around me dripped with gold, and I followed the faithful down the stairway to the body of the cathedral again with something of the sensation that I had been awarded the privilege of an introduction to foreign royalty and had found nothing whatever to say.

Richard Ford came to the rescue once more with a remark more cynical than I would have conceived, but one not altogether inappropriate under the circumstances, which was that—speaking of the Spaniard generally—"in the critical moment of need he loves to fold his arms, and clamours for supernatural assistance". I became aware that my needs at that precise moment were not at all critical, and that any clamours I may have uttered have never been for assistance of a supernatural kind. But then, says Richard Ford, "if . . . people can once believe that Santiago ever came to Spain at all, all the rest is plain sailing". I blessed him for his horrid good sense.

The cathedral of Santiago de Compostela today consists of layer upon layer of architecture encasing what is still, for the greater part, the spacious but simple pilgrim church conceived in the first place by Bishop Gelmirez; but this has expanded in growth through the centuries, like the rings of a tree-trunk, as money and pretensions poured in, as architectural styles altered and as the status of the place increased, until from the exterior there is now little to remind you of the church Picaud described in the 12th century. To obtain the feeling of what he saw you have to look around the stark and simple Romanesque nave, to wander round its typically spacious ambulatory to the side of and behind the monstrously ornate High Altar, and to explore the series of intimate apsidal chapels, some of which preserve their unadorned air of private devotion, while others have grown into Baroque toy-boxes, not only decorated with scallop-shells but apparently constructed of them as well.

Gelmirez's cathedral was begun between 1073 and 1078 (authorities disagree exactly when). It was finally consecrated in 1211.

Architecturally it was French, and it follows the pattern of pilgrim churches familiar in Conques, Tours, Limoges and Toulouse, though which particular church served as the primal influence has been another rich mine of dispute among *cognoscenti*. Kingsley Porter, the outstanding American scholar on the subject earlier in the 20th century, maintained that "Compostela was the model from which directly or indirectly was derived a majority of the great Romanesque churches of the 12th century in France", but Porter was inclined to be biased in this direction. At any rate, the plan of the cathedral was certainly never Spanish in origin.

Picaud offers a description of the cathedral he knew in some detail. It possessed, he says, a *tête* (which was the Chapelle du Saint Sauveur), a *couronne* (where you walked), a *corps* (the nave), *deux membres* (the twin transepts) and *autres petites têtes* (which were the apsidal chapels). In length, says Picaud, the cathedral was fifty-three times the height of a man, in width thirty-nine times and in height fourteen. This, basically, is the cathedral we see today from the inside, if we close our eyes to the pious furniture added during the centuries since.

Picaud's description is more valuable when he turns his attention to the exterior of the cathedral, since this is where more radical changes have taken place. He describes three sculptured doors, one at the north entrance, one at the west and a third to the south; but of these only one—the south door—remains, and that in a condition he might find it hard to recognise. It is now known as the Puerta de las Platerías (*plateros* being silversmiths). The door we now see is a badly-arranged jigsaw puzzle, or rather several jigsaws, the pieces of sculpture of which it is composed being pieced together, with a fair amount of crude guesswork, out of two and possibly three earlier carved doors, one of which, no doubt, was the door Picaud saw. He describes, for instance, a statue of St James which seems likely to be the one above the door, next to Christ, the figure of the apostle standing between two tree-trunks. The carving is similar to one that survives on the south façade of the pilgrim church of St-Sernin in Toulouse. John Beckwith has maintained, on this and other evidence, that the best artists working on the Puerta de las Platerías would have come from Aquitaine. What must be beyond dispute is that the finest carving surviving on this southern entrance is now set into the left-hand flanking wall: a figure of King David standing cross-legged and playing his harp with a remote and faintly disdainful expression, the folds of his tunic setting in motion a ripple of elegant curves that extends to above his ankles.

To see what the Santiago cathedral must have looked like in the 12th and 13th centuries one should really make a journey eastwards across the Galician mountains to the city of Lugo, for the cathedral here was modelled on that of Santiago in the 13th century, though on a smaller scale, and it has remained much as it was. In fact, many pilgrims chose this more northerly route to Santiago rather than endure the hazards of the highlands farther south.

Major alterations and additions to the cathedral at Santiago were begun during the 15th century and continued with more ambitious activity into the 16th, when the interior was tinkered with, the cloisters (very fine) were added, façades were radically transformed, more towers constructed, and the great pilgrim hospice mounted next-door. In the 17th century the Baroque style found favour with the cathedral architects, much of the exterior of the cathedral being coated with grandiose embellishments, now tinted with yellow lichen. The clock-tower (begun in the 14th century) was completed, too, and a cupola added in this period. Then, in the 18th century, ambitions reached their peak with, above all, the Obradoiro façade which dominates the entire appearance of the building today, as well as the square over which it presides. Gelmirez's plain church to the honour of St James had by this stage become a veritable palace for the glorification of the Church Triumphant: a monument fit to stand in rank with St Peter's in Rome.

But to return to the cathedral as Aymery Picaud knew it in the 12th century. The south door remains a muddled version of the one he describes. Of the other two doors described in his pilgrim's guide virtually nothing survives at all. The north door by which pilgrims entered the cathedral, having made their way from the Francígena Gate, has nothing of the original left except a bas-relief, depicting Adam and Eve chased from the Garden of Eden, a carving which has been reset into the wall. Otherwise, the entrance and the entire square on to which it opens, the Plaza de la Azabachería, was entirely and rather plainly redesigned during the 18th century, and in the place where mediaeval pilgrims purchased scallop-shells now stand stalls where tourists may buy their own scallop-shells in pink plastic or in the form of glass ashtrays, according to their fancy.

Picaud also describes a third door to the cathedral, a *porta occiden-tali*, or west door, which in his view surpassed in beauty the other two. This door can have survived only a few decades after his visit, since by the end of that same century (the 12th) the western entrance was already being totally redesigned by a man we know only by the name of Maestro Mateo, or Maître Mathieu, who was a Frenchman, as had been the other cathedral architects and sculptors before him.

The principal achievement of Maestro Mateo, and it survives complete to this day, was the creation of one of the outstanding sculptural ensembles in all Spain. This was the Portico de la Gloria, and an inscription beneath the lintel of the central arch of the Portico states, with a pride worthy of that of Gislebertus of Autun, that Señor Mateo was in charge of the work from its very foundations. We know from cathedral records that Mateo was at work there at least as early as 1168, and that he was still master-builder at Santiago almost half a century later, in 1217. The doors were hung in 1180, and it has been estimated that the monumental work of carving the figures on the Portico was completed in 1188, which means that Mateo's sculpture dates from fifty-eight years later than the west door in the (now destroyed) narthex at Cluny, and fifty-six later than that at Vézelay (which survives).

For Kingsley Porter the Portico de la Gloria was "the most over-whelming monument of mediaeval sculpture". It was the highlight of a golden age; and when he writes that Mateo's sculpture was the first work of Gothic sculpture in Europe, he may not be far from the truth. Like the carvings on the west door of Chartres, these monu-mental figures are what in scholarly terminology has come to be known as "proto-Gothic".

Under whatever label, the Portico de la Gloria is an astonishing achievement in sculpture and in architecture, the two being fused in such a manner that it is idle to attempt to separate them. The only disappointment from the point of view of the visitor, and of the photographer even more so, is that such a gigantic complex of sculpture lies not on the outside of the building itself (where admittedly it would look incongruous amid all the Baroque flam-boyance around it) but concealed within a narthex which is inade-quately lit, and from which it is impossible to step back far enough to enable one to appreciate it in the manner it deserves. One is compelled to admire it from oblique angles and in a curious dead light the quality of putty, except on those exceedingly rare occasions (and my visits have not coincided with one of them) when the outer doors are thrown open to the western sun and Mateo's masterpiece becomes bathed in the light of day.

The Portico de la Gloria is composed of three giant arches, each of them carved above, between and to the side. Dividing the central arch, which is the main entrance to the cathedral itself, is the traditional central pillar, except that in the position normally occupied by the Madonna sits St James himself, perched above an elaborately carved Tree of Jesse. By tradition, the pilgrim to Santiago completed his journey by placing his fingers between the twisted stems of the tree, and this is a custom still observed: I have watched many a toddler lifted by his father after Sunday Mass so that he might squeeze rubbery fingers into the folds of Mateo's stone, now worn smooth by generations of hands.

On the inside of this central column, and partly obscured by the gloom of the nave, squats another carved figure. He is the stone image of Maestro Mateo himself, humble enough in appearance, though one feels he can scarcely have been that in life, and this figure has been another object of respect and reverence among pilgrims. On leaving the cathedral they would lower their heads and touch the brow of the master-builder and sculptor, in order, so it is said, that they might themselves acquire some of the wisdom of the great man. The statue accordingly received the nickname of *O Santo dos Croques*, meaning the Saint of Skull-rappings.

Of Maestro Mateo's work on the Portico de la Gloria let it be said that it is of such richness and complexity that a week studying it daily would leave portions of it still unfamiliar and undiscovered. I still do not feel I know it well. I also have to confess that not all of it is to my taste. Areas of carving possess the sweetness of over-refinement, and this is partly due to the presence, unfamiliar to us today, of polychrome paint on the stone (the Parthenon was painted too, of course, and I often wonder what we would think of that), and partly because the new Gothic realism with which the figures of the apostles are represented is a trend towards mere life-likeness at the expense of true feeling. Why should I recoil because so many of the figures are laughing or smiling? It is not perhaps reasonable, but I know it is a reaction I have, and my mind turns from these figures of the apostles to the monumental solemnity of the carvings at

Moissac and Vézelay, and those at Santo Domingo de Silos, and I know that here I am in the presence of a statement about man which touches me far, far less. Something essential, something essentially serious, has been lost.

But enough of that. Here, as an ensemble, is a masterpiece. Christ is enthroned on high, with St James at his feet leaning on his tau-cross. The twenty-four Ancients of the Apocalypse are about to play once more their music we never hear, on instruments which include the *sinfonia* or *zanfoña* or hurdy-gurdy, that pilgrims' instrument *par excellence* on which the professional wandering players would recite the epic poems and wayfaring songs of the day: and, standing there, I thought once again of my (I think of it as *my*) Georges de la Tour "Blind Hurdy-Gurdy Player" in the museum at Nantes, and I wondered if that old reprobate drew from the instrument the same sound as these two ancients were about to produce, one of them turning the handle, the other plucking the strings.

Then on either side of Christ are the figures of St John on his eagle, St Luke on his bull, St Mark on a lion and St Matthew on his knees. And on the right-hand arch is a final reminder of that theme which had accompanied pilgrims all the way from Paris and Vézelay, Arles and Le Puy: the Torments of the Damned—and never have they looked more damned than here—with, nearby, other figures, who are enjoying the bliss of finding themselves on the other side of that barbed-wire fence, being conducted as if in a dream towards the Almighty by a squad of beautiful angels.

"Kings," says Richard Ford, "gave gold, and even paupers their mites" all in thanks to St James. In this way Santiago grew rich—the inn-keepers, the stall-owners, the merchants and, above all of course, the Church itself. The church of Santiago de Compostela grew immensely rich: one glance at those splendid, proud, magnificent towers of Babel that soar over the city provides ample demonstration of that. And then there was the thanks given by royalty who, due as they believed to St James, had got their kingdoms back. The generosity of kings towards the city of St James was prodigious: witness to the right of the cathedral that stern edifice with its handsome Renaissance entrance, the old Hospital Real, which King Ferdinand and Queen Isabella gave as their thanks; but it was also a generosity leavened with cunning, for it was the same pair of monarchs who seized the opportunity to extend that fraudulent corn-tax, the *Voto de Santiago*, to the rest of Spain now liberated from the Infidel. In the first chapter I describe in some detail that celebrated tax, supposedly instituted in the 9th century by order of King Ramiro I—though never enforced until the 12th century—in thanksgiving for the successful intervention of St James at the Battle of Clavijo, a battle which very likely never took place at all, and certainly not during the reign of King Ramiro I; neither was there ever the tiniest grain of real documentary evidence that Ramiro or any other monarch at the time imposed or even intended to impose such a tax.

However, the tax made Santiago rich and the Battle of Clavijo is duly honoured by a carving in the cathedral narthex by the hand of Maestro Mateo, and without such a tax we should, after all, have been deprived of one of the greatest ecclesiastical buildings of the world.

The *Voto de Santiago*, it must be admitted, was intended to succour the poor as well as enrich the church, and there can be no question but that pilgrims arriving at Santiago did receive from the authorities a degree of hospitality—provided they did not linger too long—which they could scarcely have found elsewhere. The Hospital Real was such an example.

There survives an account of this Hospital nearly two centuries after its foundation by Ferdinand and Isabella, made by a certain Luis de Molina in 1675:

> In the three large wards there are few days when there are under two hundred sick people, and the number is much larger in Jubilee year. Yet every patient is treated with as much care as if the hospital had been erected for his particular benefit. The hospital is one of the great things of the earth. Apart from its sumptuousness and the regal grandeur of its architecture it is a marvellous thing to feel its size, the multitudes of its officials, the diligence and zeal of its attendants, the cleanliness of its linen, the care taken about the cooking, the perfect order of the routine, the assiduity of the doctors. One may indeed regard it as a crowning glory of Christendom.

It is also written into the statutes of the Hospital Real that the place should have on its staff not only Spanish priests, but French,

Flemish and English also, so that pilgrims of foreign nationalities should be able to receive confession.

It is unlikely that English, French, Flemish or even Spanish priests are on the establishment of the place today; but in other respects Molina's account remains an accurate description of what has now become the Hostal de los Reyes Católicos. Cocktails of different nationalities may be more readily obtainable than confessions in four languages, but the multitudes of officials, the zeal of its attendants, its cooking, its orderliness and—I am sure—the cleanliness of its linen, remain assured features of one of the noblest hostelries of Europe. The fortress-like exterior of the building, with its tiny barred windows, deceives the eye. The potted rubber-plants and the liveried attendants who open your car door almost before it has drawn to a halt, are more reliable evidence of what to expect in the 1970s. Ferdinand and Isabella might not have disdained staying there themselves.

Inside, the aspect of the Hostal could scarcely offer a more surprising contrast with the severity of its appearance from the Plaza del Obradoiro. It is constructed round four symmetrical cloisters, or quadrangles, which are linked by somewhat chilly corridors in a manner reminiscent of an Oxford or Cambridge college. The quadrangles are named Matthew, Mark, Luke and John. Each is open in the centre and flanked by slender Renaissance columns of a delicacy unmatched in any part of Spain, except where the Moors left the mark of their exquisite geometrical sensibility. Each of the quadrangles is subtly different in design, but together they form an architectural harmony equal to that of a perfect classical quartet. The individual rooms lead off the four quadrangles, or off the interlinking corridors. Matthew, Mark, Luke and John, bless the bed that I lie on. I sampled an amazingly expensive Scotch and walked out into the square past the white-gloved salute of a liveried doorman.

It was the end of a journey. I drove on westwards towards the Atlantic to Padrón, where the body of St James is supposed to have arrived by sea, and where pilgrims came to gather scallop-shells. Then out towards Cape Finisterre, the farthest point west in Spain, along the shores of wooded bays that cut in and out of this mournful coast. The beaches were strewn with hulks of fishing-boats and with brightly-coloured marbles which I picked up aimlessly until my pockets were weighed down, and equally aimlessly I tossed them away again. I drove on into a thickening Atlantic mist, past fields splashed with foxgloves, past calvaries raised on spindly columns and heavy with lichen. Thanksgivings. Prayers to the sea. Then back over the low hills of eucalyptus to that stage-set of a city where tomorrow morning the gold and precious stones would once again glitter, and the huge dangling censer—known as the *Botafumeiro*—would begin its rhythmic pendulum motion wider and farther across the width of the cathedral to raise to its climax a play enacted here every week, every month, every year, every century, in the service of a legend.

That night there lingered the smell of incense in the rain, and the thump of a deep dead bell.

Selected Bibliography

Anderson, W., *Castles of Europe* (London, 1970)

Arnold-Foster, F., *Studies in Church Dedication* (London, 1899)

Barraclough, G. (ed.), *Eastern and Western Europe in the Middle Ages* (London, 1970)

Beckwith, J., *Early Mediaeval Art* (London, 1964)

Bloch, M., *Feudal Society* (Translation, London, 1961)

Bond, F., *Dedications and Patron Saints of English Churches* (London, 1914)

Bottineau, T., *Les chemins de Saint-Jacques* (Paris, 1964)

Boussard, J. M., *The Civilisation of Charlemagne* (Translation, London, 1968)

Brooke, C. N. L., *Europe in the Central Middle Ages* (London, 1964)

Brooke, C. N. L., *The 12th-Century Renaissance* (London, 1970)

Brooke, C. N. L., *The Structure of Mediaeval Society* (London, 1971)

Charpentier, L., *Les Jacques et le mystère de Compostelle* (Paris, 1971)

Chaucer, G., *The Canterbury Tales*

Cowdrey, H. E. J., *The Cluniacs and the Gregorian Reform* (Oxford, 1970)

Duby, G., *Rural Economy and Country Life in the Mediaeval West* (Translation, London, 1968)

Evans, J., *Life in Mediaeval France* (London, 1957)

Evans, J. (ed), *The Flowering of the Middle Ages* (London, 1966)

Evans, J., *Art in Mediaeval France* (Oxford, 1969)

Ford, R., *A Handbook for Travellers in Spain* (London, 1845 and subsequent editions)

Hall, D. J., *English Mediaeval Pilgrimage* (London, 1966)

Heath, S., *Pilgrim Life in the Middle Ages* (London, 1911)

Hell, V. and H., *The Great Pilgrimage of the Middle Ages* (Translation, London, 1966)

Hohler, C. "The Badge of St James" in *The Scallop* (London, 1957)

Huizinga, J., *The Waning of the Middle Ages* (Translation, London, 1924)

Huizinga, J., *Men and Ideas* (Translation, London, 1960)

Inglis, B., *A History of Medicine* (London, 1965)

à Kempis, T., *The Imitation of Jesus Christ* (Translation, Glasgow, 1822)

Kendrick, Sir T., *Saint James in Spain* (London, 1960)

Langland, W., *Piers Plowman*

La Orden Miracle, E., *Santiago en America y en Inglaterra y Escocia* (Madrid, 1970)

Levey, M., *Rococo to Revolution* (London, 1966)

Lomax, D., *Algunos peregrinos ingleses a Santiago en la Edad Media* (Estella, 1969)

McMahon, N., *The Story of the Hospitallers of St John* (London, 1958)

Mâle, E., *L'art religieux du XIIᵉ siècle en France* (Paris, 1922)

Mâle, E., *L'art religieux du XIIIᵉ siècle en France* (Paris, 1925)

Mâle, E., *Religious art from the 12th to the 18th century* (Translation, London, 1949)

Michener, J., *Iberia* (London, 1968)

Morris, J., *Spain* (London, 1970)

Oursel, R., *Les pèlerins du Moyen Age* (Paris, 1963)

Pernoud, R. M. J., *The Glory of the Mediaeval World* (Translation, London, 1950)

Pevsner, N., *An Outline of European Architecture* (London, 1948)

Pirenne, H., *Mediaeval Cities* (Translation, Princeton, 1925)

Pirenne, H., *Economic and Social History of Mediaeval Europe* (Translation, London, 1936)

Pirenne, H., *A History of Europe* (Translation, London, 1939)

Pirenne, H., *Mohammed and Charlemagne* (Translation, London, 1939)

Porter, A. K., *The Romanesque Sculpture of the Pilgrimage Roads* (Boston, 1923)

Rowling, M., *Everyday Life of Mediaeval Travellers* (London, 1971)

Secret, J., *Sur les chemins de Compostelle* (Paris, 1956)

Southern, R. W., *The Making of the Middle Ages* (Oxford, 1953)

Starkie, W., *The Road to Santiago* (London, 1957)

Taralon, J., *Treasures of the Churches of France* (Translation, London, 1966)

Trevor-Roper, H., *The Rise of Christian Europe* (London, 1966)

Tristram, E. W., *English Mediaeval Wall Painting: the 12th Century* (Oxford, 1944)

Tristram, E. W. (with Bardswell, M.), *English Mediaeval Wall Painting: the 13th Century* (Oxford, 1950)

Urrutibéhéty, C., *Voies d'accès en Navarre et carrefour des chemins de Saint-Jacques* (Bayonne, no date)

Vásquez de Parga, L. (with Lacarra, J. M. and Uría Riu, J.), *Las peregrinaciones a Santiago de Compostela* (Madrid, 1948–49)

Vielliard, J., *Le guide du pèlerin de Saint-Jacques en Compostelle*, translated from the 12th-century *Liber Sancti Jacobi*, Book V (Macon, 1938)

Zarnecki, G. *The Monastic Achievement* (London, 1972)

Zarnecki, G. (with Grivot, D.), *Gislebertus, Sculptor of Autun* (Paris, 1961)

Index

Index